Praise for Sallie Tisdale

A Buddhist woman who's written about porn. Do you really need another reason to read her?

Violation: Collected Essays

Sallie Tisdale's *Violation* is a writer's bible and a reader's best friend. Bold and wise, galvanizing and grounding, Tisdale's essays are propulsive and frightening in their poignance and content. This is the essay collection you'll want to have with you on that hypothetical desert island.

CHLOE CALDWELL, author of *Legs Get Led Astray* and *Women*

Sallie Tisdale possesses one of the most companionable and inquisitive voices in contemporary American nonfiction. She is guided by a restless, humane intelligence. And her range! Who else can write about Moray eels and obscene phone calls, about the harrowing work of firefighters and the dreamy effects of laughing gas, all the while unearthing the deeper meanings of the world around us? Mortality, desire, love, loss: these are Tisdale's underlying subjects, and in *Violation*, she brings them to life with bracing clarity and unfailing insight.

BERNARD COOPER, author of *The Bill From My Father*

Sallie Tisdale is the real thing, a writer who thinks like a philosopher, observes like a journalist, and sings on the page like a poet; in other words, the consummate and perfect essayist. She knocked my socks off when I first discovered her decades ago, and now, reading this collection, I realize I haven't found them since. *Violation* contains important work from an important writer. I'm so glad it's out in the world.

MEGHAN DAUM, author of *The Unspeakable: and Other Subjects of Discussion*

That Sallie Tisdale's a treasure comes as no secret to lovers of the essay, and yet this happy gathering that spans the decades is revelatory, a fascinating look at the epic wanderings of a life mapped by curiosity. Here we get elephants and houseflies, diets and fires, birth and the debris of death, all the mixed and messy vitality of family life. We travel far and we travel wide, but in the end we circle home to Tisdale herself, vulnerable and available, intimate and encouraging, our guide and our friend, her questioning presence lighting the way and celebrating it all, every little step in life's saga, one lovely sentence at a time.

CHARLES D'AMBROSIO, author of *Loitering: New and Collected Essays*

In essay, memoir, and literary journalism, Sallie Tisdale writes with fierce and finely tuned attention to what she calls "ordinary things, the journey of grime and wonder through the world." Abortion, elephants, female identity, family history, eating and dieting, her Buddhist view of living and dying, her work as an oncology nurse, the ethics of writing nonfiction – whatever her focus, she is never content with an easy resolution or anything less than the most nuanced, most honest, most finely crafted account she is capable of. Readers may not always agree with her, but they will know they've been in the company of an articulate intelligence thinking out loud in graceful and incisive prose.

JOHN DANIEL, author of *Rogue River Journal* and *Looking After*

I read Sallie Tisdale and within a few sentences, I am under her spell. It matters not whether she's writing about the tyranny of weight loss, the startling lives of blow flies, or what it's like to work in an oncology ward (she is a dedicated nurse as well as a brilliant writer): I'm all in, all the time. I will go anywhere she wants to take me. An alternate image – climbing into a submarine with Tisdale at the controls and diving down down down, into her singular sensibility, her genius for language, her love of our deeply imperfect world.

KAREN KARBO, author of *Julia Child Rules: Lessons on Savoring Life*

I've long admired Sallie Tisdale's essays, and this collection brandishes her impressive strengths: she's complicit without being woebegone, she's philosophical without being windy or airy, and she's empathetic without being hand-wringing.

DAVID SHIELDS, author of *Life Is Short – Art Is Shorter: In Praise of Brevity*

Women of the Way: Discovering 2500 Years of Buddhist Wisdom

[A] beautifully crafted volume. The universal wisdom and enlightened thinking preserved in this collection transcends gender.

BOOKLIST

A well-written, deeply moving collection of stories … Fanciful and eminently readable.

BUDDHADHARMA

With her frank and thoughtful writing style, Tisdale takes the reader on a philosophical adventure.

EAST WEST WOMAN

An enlivening and indispensable volume.

JANE HIRSHFIELD, author of *Women in Praise of the Sacred: 43 Centuries of Spiritual Poetry by Women*

A much-needed account of feminine teachers and leaders in Buddhism.

KANSAS CITY STAR

Tisdale's descriptive writing is especially imaginative.

PUBLISHERS WEEKLY

The Best Thing I Ever Tasted: The Secret of Food

Tisdale's forte lies in helping readers to see the big picture, in which she ties together history, folklore, personal anecdote, and sharp analysis to show that we truly are what we eat.

PUBLISHERS WEEKLY

[V]ery interesting and entertaining … Tisdale's coverage of food writers is very good.

LIBRARY JOURNAL

Tisdale is the Zen Buddhist Antichrist to her mother of the perpetual TV dinner.

KIRKUS REVIEWS

Sallie Tisdale takes subjects that might seem mundane or overdone and renders them unforgettable.

SAN FRANCISCO EXAMINER

She's an easy, chatty writer who never says anything the way you're expecting, which makes reading her a pleasure.

BOSTON GLOBE

This book reminds us to be mindful of every mouthful.

PHILADELPHIA INQUIRER

Talk Dirty to Me:
An Intimate Philosophy of Sex

Tisdale's provocative look at sexuality relates personal experiences alongside meditations on subjects such as pornography and prostitution.

PUBLISHERS WEEKLY

A beautiful book.

LIBRARY JOURNAL

Great intelligence, humor and curiosity ... whether or not you're taken aback by [Tisdale's] desires, you'll definitely exit her book with something to talk about.

GLAMOUR

These essays on sexuality, gender, and censorship offer the relief of a voice that is unmuffled by inhibitions.

MIRABELLA

Tisdale renders, with delectable eloquence, the sheer enormity of the sexual impulse.... These are conversations we need to be having, with as much of Tisdale's bracing honesty as we can muster.

SEATTLE WEEKLY

No doubt will raise both hackles and consciousness.

NEWSWEEK

Tisdale [has] managed to put her finger squarely on the hot button of public opinion.

THE BOSTON GLOBE

Stepping Westward: The Long Search for Home in the Pacific Northwest

An odd and lovely work.

KIRKUS REVIEWS

Tisdale has produced a loving, literate work ...

LIBRARY JOURNAL

[V]ividly written ...

PUBLISHERS WEEKLY

Ambitious, affectionate, sorrowful rhapsody ... Tisdale's voice is fluid and richly varied.

CHICAGO TRIBUNE

[Tisdale's] prose is music for the mind's ear.

SEATTLE TIMES

Conjures the Northwest in a rare and magical way ... This book will make you hit the road.

CRAIG LESLEY, author of *Burning Fence: A Western Memoir of Fatherhood*

Tisdale's portrait of her home territory is personal and ingenuous.

THE LOS ANGELES TIMES

Lot's Wife: Salt and the Human Condition

A rare book about a common subject.

RICHARD SELZER, author of *The Exact Location of the Soul*

Harvest Moon: Portrait of a Nursing Home

A rare combination of candor, compassion, and deft art. I recommend this book to anyone seriously intending to grow old.

JOSH GREENFIELD, author of *Homeward Bound: A Novella of Idle Speculation*

Library of Congress
Cataloging-in-Publication Data

Tisdale, Sallie.
[Essays. Selections]
Violation : collected essays /
by Sallie Tisdale.
pages cm
ISBN 978-0-9904370-8-6
(paperback)
I. Title.
PS3570.I717A6 2016
814'.54–DC23
2015029013

Hawthorne Books
& Literary Arts

9 2201 Northeast 23rd Avenue
8 3rd Floor
7 Portland, Oregon 97212
6 hawthornebooks.com
5 *Form:*
4 Adam McIsaac/Sibley House
3
2 Printed in China
   Set in Paperback

Violation

Collected Essays
Sallie Tisdale

*Dear friend,
"resigned to
reality"
so glad to
be walking
the path beside
you,
love, Sallie*

HAWTHORNE BOOKS & LITERARY ARTS
Portland, Oregon | MMXVI

Contents

VIOLATION

Introduction

WHEN I WAS SEVENTEEN AND A SOPHOMORE IN COLLEGE, I took any course that interested me. One semester, I signed up for Advanced Writing. (I had never taken a writing class, but I was a bit of a snob.) I bugged Dr. Ryberg constantly, haunting his office hours until he took pity, declared me his assistant, and set me to the filing. I gave him a lot of junk to read. Toward the end of the semester, I gave him a story with trembling hands. I was so proud of it; I thought it might win a few awards. He handed it back to me a few days later with entire pages crossed off in red ink. He had circled the last paragraph and written, "Start here."

The following spring, I ran into him in the college bookstore. I was dropping out, I told him. Going north to test my theories of love and goodness.

"You're a writer," he said. "You're already a better writer than me. What are you waiting for?"

I think I laughed. What an idea—that you could *be* a writer. But I wasn't ready; I was consuming life like a gourmand just let out of jail. I went north and joined a communal household and a co-op and tested, with some success, several theories of love and goodness. I was still signing up for every subject that looked promising. But after a few years, when I had a new baby and hardly any money and decided at the last moment not to move into another commune in the mountains, I thought that instead I could be a writer. I hocked my piano and bought a typewriter and joined a writing support group. The leader told us to study *Writer's Market*, so I sat in the reference room of the library and read about query letters and submission guidelines. I started writing essays about all kinds of things and sent them out more or less at random, with polite cover letters and self-addressed stamped envelopes.

Out they went and back they came. Sometimes there was a little note thanking me for my submission, but often not. I would type a fresh copy and send the story out again. The support group dissolved after a few months when the leader committed suicide. Others might have taken that as a sign, but I was young and ignorant and somehow immune to despair. I had decided to be a writer and so I wrote. I sent stories out, again and again. And then one didn't come back.

The essays in this book are a selection of work spanning almost thirty years. I have never lost my fascination with the essay, and the stories here range across the continuum of the form. You don't know what your voice sounds like until you speak. My writer's voice chose itself. I recognize it here, but I'm not in charge. I used to wish I was a comic writer or a novelist or an investigative reporter. I tried to be a poet for a while. What I am is an essayist.

Certain themes recur as well; why should this ever surprise us? Life is just following a trail around a mountain. The path loops back to the same view time and again. Sometimes we see all the way across the plain and sometimes we're lost in the woods, but the perspective is a little higher each time. So I return again and again to questions about the nature of the self, what it means to live in a body, why we are all lonely, how to use language to say what can't be said. These are questions of intimacy and separation, and the answers are ambiguous at best. Long before I knew how to describe it, I liked ambivalence. Certainty has always seemed a bit dishonest to me.

Being a writer of the long personal essay is a little like being the village blacksmith. It takes decades of training, and there may not be much demand. I think I'm a good writer, but not a very good author—that is, I'm rather introverted and uncomfortable with self-promotion. As the noise level rises, I retreat a little more. Writers are increasingly expected to be multimedia performers, chasing the zeitgeist and molding their work to fit. I remember hearing the word *midlist* for the first time, decades ago. My editor was gently explaining her modest expectations for my book, but my first thought was, *yes, that sounds about right.* The midlist is disappearing now, and I could spend a few more years fretting about it. But the cure is to write.

To write—which is to say, *solve the problem.* I sometimes imagine the barren stretches, false starts, and breakthroughs that I experience with almost every story are kin to what any scientist or inventor feels. The essay is the problem and I seek the solution: a structure, a start, an end, a phrase. A word.

My basement is filled with failures—boxes of unfinished drafts, scribbled outlines, entire books collapsed into chaos. Countless dead ends. But it is as important for writers to fail as it is for any inventor. A year of not succeeding is a year without editors or deadlines. No other voices intrude. There is, finally, nothing to fear. If you don't know what to do, and finally you don't know so completely that the entire world seems to be the question—well, then anything is possible. When we don't know the way, a thousand paths exist. All I have ever had to do to succeed as a writer was to fail, because not solving the problem means the solution lies ahead.

I write out of what really happened, a huge field in which to roam—but a bounded field nevertheless. I sometimes work with students who are struggling to write at all. I might ask them to draw a picture of their writer's block. One young woman covered a page in black and wrote across it, "I will be found wanting and thrown out of the universe." We are all imposters, never more so than when we try to tell the truth. To write the essay is to be haunted by our own lies. No story is the whole story. Everything we know is shadowed by what we've missed, forgotten, or been afraid to see. The title essay is my answer to a question that I have asked myself and been asked by others countless times: how do we know what is true? What is fair for me to say about others? What do I have the right to say, when I can never be sure about the truth?

I try to solve the problem.

Few things are worth writing down—that's why there are so many boxes in my basement. But there is only one way to find out what those things are. Now and then, I have imagined not writing. What a different shape my life would have had. How much time! Mine has been a very indie, mezzanine, remainder table, 367-followers-on-Spotify type of career. What if I wasn't writing or trying to write or avoiding writing all the time? What if I didn't have this witness on my shoulder? What if I just … *stopped.*

Instead, I fall asleep to language bouncing around my skull. Words pour through my life like drops of water, running together into a stream, becoming—

Start here.

Orphans

LAST CHRISTMAS EVE MY FATHER TOOK ME BY THE ELBOW and whispered: "Your grandmother died ten years ago today. Be nice to your mother." I had forgotten. He is a reticent and furtive man, but he remembers things. For years he would wait till a few days before Christmas and then hand me $20. "Go buy something pretty for your mother," he would instruct, gruffly, and turn away.

That evening while we watched television, all lined up beside each other and chatting desultorily, my mother spoke abruptly, in a new voice. "My mother died today," she said, wonderingly, as though she'd just been told. The television prattled on. She deflects expression and emotion by riposte and foil, deftly, and we exist in the cautiously defined spaces between. It is an inharmonious harmony, tense, with voices rarely raised.

She asked me what I remembered of my grandmother, and I told her of driving fifty miles out of our way on our last vacation just to see my grandmother's house, the house where my mother was raised.

"Was the ivy still on the chimney?" she asked, for since the house was sold she hasn't been back. The threads tangle while we talk, a tweedy web of shifting associations: my mother and her daughter, her mother and my grandmother, and around us father and husband, brother and children, their children, my children. This is her surprise for me, her secret: my mother yearns to be a daughter again.

My mother's mother was a forbidding woman, stern and

drawn, with an immaculate house and a tiny yipping dog that nipped at our heels from behind her calves. She would stand in the gleaming kitchen, hot in the summer morning sun, with a spatula raised as though to swat at the first sign of disobedience. It was a house of territories, borders, boundaries, permitted and forbidden places. I knew as an undeniable law that what I valued she often ignored; that she placed value where I couldn't see it. I searched for snails in the rose bed, hid dolls in the mail chute. She waxed the kitchen floor.

Once in fury at her I sat on the concrete steps and tore apart her favorite philodendron, leaf by leaf, scattering the green shreds like dung, like ruin. The old straight-backed woman cried, still and trembling in the doorway. It was an enormous crime. I sat in the curious silence of shamed regret, curling inward, surrounded by pieces of something I couldn't put back together again—and saw behind my grandmother my own mother's stricken face. She had somehow permitted this crime, had failed, and become subject to her own mother again, through me.

And so I always found it odd, watching from the doorway, that my dour grandmother and stoic mother spent hours talking over a single pot of coffee, relaxed, girlish. These scenes are elongated and mysterious, one of the forbidden places. I sprawled on the huge rag rug, following its oval track from the center outward, from the outside in, while they laughed and gossiped. At night my sister and I lay in the soft guest bed, fighting over territory, and heard more talk, muffled, more laughing, and now and then through the magpie voices my father's deep, short bursts of speech.

Now I have three children, and new appreciations. I call my mother, three hundred miles away, to talk about them, and she interrupts, anxious to return to her book, her television. She takes her cool pleasure in us from a comfortable distance, and our conversations are often short. She parries better than I can, and I forfeit. Hanging up in sudden discontent, I am all over them, passionate and physical, rubbing and wrestling and jouncing, whispering subliminal permissions, tiny pleas, in their downy ears.

I give up my common inhibitions, rules of conduct, when I hold my babies. It is a pleasure instinctive and heavy, and breathlessly free. Bit by bit time wedges us apart, forging separation, and amnesia. I love my parents because, after all, they are my parents, and my babies love me for the same good reason. We are bound in a loom of pulling away and pushing back, letting go and holding on. My children's task is to pull away and they do, they do, tugging furiously at the leash I strain to play out an inch at a time. We hold back, let go; I still tug. A friend, telling me of her mother's death, begins, "I remember when we were dying."

My mother was orphaned a decade ago, and she still shivers with loss, denied the requisite delights of regression. Nostalgia is its own reward, its own burden; it illuminates our imagined history. My grandmother lived in that house a long time after her husband died of cancer, long after she found out that she, too, had cancer. The house was sold, furniture parceled out. The tough woman in the kitchen became a weak bundle of pain, and I lifted her under her arms and swung her from the bed to the commode, commode to chair. She admitted no complaint. I could feel in her dried and sagging arms a most peculiar substance. I could feel, blushing, a twisted skin in the faces that watched us; my mother and her daughter, my sister and my mother's sister and my grandmother's granddaughters, all of us at once and together and almost wholly unaware of it: the clinging web that held us back and wouldn't let us go.

My mother and my glacial aunt tentatively asked me to quit school and stay with her. I refused. I held back, and my grandmother let go. When the furniture was divided, my mother kept her bed; it's where I sleep now when I visit them.

All my cross-grained, melancholy generations have gently collided with each other, as generations do, like bottles of milk rattling along, sliding up the track to jostle other bottles along. We wait our turn. My mother's father is dead, her mother is dead, my father's father and three stepfathers are dead. And between us my brother and sister and I have seven children jockeying for position by the fireplace, playing our old games. This Christmas my mother watches her grandchildren and her television from a hospital bed, where the tree used to go. She is dying of cancer, the same cancer that killed her mother.

Each year around my birthday the little ornamental cherry tree in front of her house bursts into bloom, luxuriant and top-heavy. I used to sit in its lap of low branches; now I pick blossoms off the top. The bubbling frog creek is a dry gully; the noisy park clean and quiet. I see strange faces in the streets, new shapes, house-peaks along empty hills. It is time to think things through, to follow the thread where it enters the knot until I find its exit. Time now to confess my tenuous hold on adulthood before I am orphaned in turn.

She has filled the drawers of my old dresser with her wedding albums and old baby pictures and clippings of my brother's high school football games, neatly scissored. She takes with her where she goes a voice I've heard from birth, a step, a chime, the smoky car. A door closes, irrevocably, on rooms cluttered in certain ways by her passage, on a dusty piano, sun-dried towels, and certain plays of light on certain trees. Chipped crystal stays, without her use, and the dark bedroom and high dark bed, without her smell. I begin a definition of love made fundamentally of the familiar. These things and these places, the way a shadow casts in August and seamstress hands and the cool wet smell of the grass in the early morning, are not things I've used much for years. I have been inattentive in my turn and made another family, holding hers in reserve, available. She is dying and sad and scared to die, and takes with her the remnants and desires of my life till now. She lets go and I hold back, watching her grow weak and frail, disconcertingly familiar as she disappears from sight.

She was never the mother I wanted her to be. We have never chattered over coffee, grown girlish together while my daughter watched. For a long time I tried to change her, reproachful, and failed, not seeing how she had tried to change me long ago. She won't change now; she is merely herself. So is my father, blustering and mad. He meticulously catalogs videotapes of old movies, John Wayne and Errol Flynn, their favorites, to watch alone half-asleep in the evenings after she dies. My silent brother and my shrill, half-panicked sister won't change, not much, and neither will I. We are the gifts we were given. I sit by her bed in sadness, an unspoken summing-up held, like so much else, back. These are the people I am accompanied by, my escorts. We dance attendance on each other, as families do, and little else. There is little else to do.

And I go home, wherever it is, and confront a son resentful of my tight rein. He demands a faster adulthood, receiving power in unexpected shifts and abrupt shufflings. I grab the leash and run the other way. He is hurt by my mother's coming extinction, blustering like my father, his grandfather, her husband. I grow dizzy in the sticky threads, resistance against the spin. He is letting go of me and I am holding back, for I know he has no idea, no possible idea of all the many surprises still in store.

Zyzzyva, Winter 1986–87

For more than thirty years I've been writing about the way family wraps around our lives. There is no escaping it, even when we escape—one way or another, we are made of it. This was one in a series of essays I wrote about the sticky threads woven around us by both parents and children—a web we create, long for, celebrate, and hate.

Fetus Dreams

WE DO ABORTIONS HERE; THAT IS ALL WE DO. THERE ARE weary, grim moments when I think I cannot bear another basin of bloody remains, utter another kind phrase of reassurance. So I leave the procedure room in the back and reach for a new chart. Soon I am talking to an eighteen-year-old woman pregnant for the fourth time. I push up her sleeve to check her blood pressure and find row upon row of needle marks, neat and parallel and discolored. She has been so hungry for her drug for so long that she has taken to using the loose skin of her upper arms; her elbows are already a permanent ruin of bruises. She is surprised to find herself nearly four months pregnant. I suspect she is often surprised, in a mild way, by the blows she is dealt. I prepare myself for another basin, another brief and chafing loss.

"How can you stand it?" Even the clients ask. They see the machine, the strange instruments, the blood, the final stroke that wipes away the promise of pregnancy. Sometimes I see that too: I watch a woman's swollen abdomen sink to softness in a few stuttering moments and my own belly flip-flops with sorrow. But all it takes for me to catch my breath is another interview, one more story that sounds so much like the last one. There is a numbing sameness lurking in this job: the same questions, the same answers, even the same trembling tone in the voices. The worst is the sameness of human failure, of inadequacy in the face of each day's dull demands.

In describing this work, I find it difficult to explain how much I enjoy it most of the time. We laugh a lot here, as friends and as professional peers. It's nice to be with women all day. I like the sudden, transient bonds I forge with some clients: moments when I am in my strength, remembering weakness, and a woman in weakness reaches out for my strength. What I offer is not power, but solidness, offered almost eagerly. Certain clients waken in me every tender urge I have—others make me wince and bite my tongue. Both challenge me to find a balance. It is a sweet brutality we practice here, a stark and loving dispassion.

I look at abortion as if I am standing on a cliff with a telescope, gazing at some great vista. I can sweep the horizon with both eyes, survey the scene in all its distance and size. Or I can put my eye to the lens and focus on the small details, suddenly so close. In abortion the absolute must always be tempered by the contextual, because both are real, both valid, both hard. How can we do this? How can we refuse? Each abortion is a measure of our failure to protect, to nourish our own. Each basin I empty is a promise— but a promise broken a long time ago.

I grew up on the great promise of birth control. Like many women my age, I took the pill as soon as I was sexually active. To risk pregnancy when it was so easy to avoid seemed stupid, and my contraceptive success, as it were, was part of the promise of social enlightenment. But birth control fails, far more frequently than laboratory trials predict. Many of our clients take the pill; its failure to protect them is a shocking realization. We have clients who have been sterilized, whose husbands have had vasectomies; each one is a statistical misfit, fine print come to life. The anger and shame of these women I hold in one hand, and the basin in the other. The distance between the two, the length I pace and try to measure, is the size of an abortion.

THE PROCEDURE IS disarmingly simple. Women are surprised, as though the mystery of conception, a dark and hidden genesis, requires an elaborate finale. In the first trimester of pregnancy, it's a mere few minutes of vacuuming, a neat tidying up. I give a woman a small yellow Valium, and when it has begun to relax her,

I lead her into the back, into bareness, the stirrups. The doctor reaches in her, opening the narrow tunnel to the uterus with a succession of slim, smooth bars of steel. He inserts a plastic tube and hooks it to a hose on the machine. The woman is framed against white paper that crackles as she moves, the light bright in her eyes. Then the machine rumbles low and loud in the small windowless room; the doctor moves the tube back and forth with an efficient rhythm, and the long rail of it fills with blood that spurts and stumbles along into a jar. He is usually finished in a few minutes. They are long minutes for the woman; her uterus frequently reacts to its abrupt emptying with a powerful, unceasing cramp, which cuts off the blood vessels and enfolds the irritated, bleeding tissue.

I am learning to recognize the shadows that cross the faces of the women I hold. While the doctor works between her spread legs, the paper drape hiding his intent expression, I stand beside the table. I hold the woman's hands in mine, resting them just below her ribs. I watch her eyes, finger her necklace, stroke her hair. I ask about her job, her family; in a haze she answers me; we chatter, faces close, eyes meeting and sliding apart.

I watch the shadows that creep up unnoticed and suddenly darken her face as she screws up her features and pushes a tear out each side to slide down her cheeks. I have learned to anticipate the quiver of chin, the rapid intake of breath, and the surprising sobs that rise soon after the machine starts to drum. I know this is when the cramp deepens, and the tears are partly the tears that follow pain—the sharp, childish crying when one bumps one's head on a cabinet door. But a well of woe seems to open beneath many women when they hear that thumping sound. The anticipation of the moment has finally come to fruit; the moment has arrived when the loss is no longer an imagined one. It has come true.

I am struck by the sameness and I am struck every day by the variety here—how this commonplace dilemma can so display the differences of women. A twenty-one-year-old woman, unemployed, uneducated, without family, in the fifth month of her fifth pregnancy. A forty-two-year-old mother of teenagers, shocked by her condition, refusing to tell her husband. A twenty-three-year-old mother of two having her seventh abortion, and many women in their thirties having their first. Some are stoic, some hysterical, a few giggle uncontrollably, many cry.

I talk to a sixteen-year-old uneducated girl who was raped. She has gonorrhea. She describes blinding headaches, attacks of breathlessness, nausea. "Sometimes I feel like two different people," she tells me with a calm smile, "and I talk to myself."

I pull out my plastic models. She listens patiently for a time, and then holds her hands wide in front of her stomach.

"When's the baby going to go up into my stomach?" she asks.

I blink. "What do you mean?"

"Well," she says, still smiling, "when women get so big, isn't the baby in your stomach? Doesn't it hatch out of an egg there?"

My first question in an interview is always the same. As I walk down the hall with the woman, as we get settled in chairs and I glance through her files, I am trying to gauge her, to get a sense of the words, and the tone, I should use. With some I joke, with others I chat, sometimes I fall into a brisk, businesslike patter. But I ask every woman, "Are you sure you want to have an abortion?" Most nod with grim knowing smiles. "Oh, yes," they sigh. Some seek forgiveness, offer excuses. Occasionally a woman will flinch and say, "Please don't use that word."

Later I describe the procedure to come, using care with my language. I don't say "pain" any more than I would say "baby." So many are afraid to ask how much it will hurt. "My sister told me—" I hear. "A friend of mine said—" and the dire expectations unravel. I prick the index finger of a woman for a drop of blood to test, and as the tiny lancet approaches the skin she averts her eyes, holding her trembling hand out to me and jumping at my touch.

It is when I am holding a plastic uterus in one hand, a suction tube in the other, moving them together in imitation of the scrubbing to come, that women ask the most secret question. I am speaking in a matter-of-fact voice about "the tissue" and "the contents" when the woman suddenly catches my eye and asks,

"How big is the baby now?" These words suggest a quiet need for a definition of the boundaries being drawn. It isn't so odd, after all, that she feels relief when I describe the growing bud's bulbous shape, its miniature nature. Again I gauge, and sometimes lie a little, weaseling around its infantile features until its clinging power slackens.

But when I look in the basin, among the curdlike blood clots, I see an elfin thorax, attenuated, its pencilline ribs all in parallel rows with tiny knobs of spine rounding upwards. A translucent arm and hand swim beside.

A sleepy-eyed girl, just fourteen, watched me with a slight and goofy smile all through her abortion. "Does it have little feet and little fingers and all?" she'd asked earlier. When the suction was over she sat up woozily at the end of the table and murmured, "Can I see it?" I shook my head firmly. "It's not allowed," I told her sternly, because I knew she didn't really want to see what was left. She accepted this statement of authority, and a shadow of confused relief crossed her plain, pale face.

PRIVATELY, EVEN GRUDGINGLY, my colleagues might admit the power of abortion to provoke emotion. But they seem to prefer the broad view and disdain the telescope. Abortion is a matter of choice, privacy, control. Its uncertainty lies in specific cases: retarded women and girls too young to give consent for surgery, women who are ill or hostile or psychotic. Such common dilemmas are met with both compassion and impatience: they slow things down. We are too busy to chew over ethics. One person might discuss certain concerns, behind closed doors, or describe a particularly disturbing dream. But generally there is to be no ambivalence.

Every day I take calls from women who are annoyed that we cannot see them, cannot do their abortion today, this morning, now. They argue the price, demand that we stay after hours to accommodate their job or class schedule. Abortion is so routine that one expects it to be like a manicure: quick, cheap, and painless.

Still, I've cultivated a certain disregard. It isn't negligence, but I don't always pay attention. I couldn't be here if I tried to judge each case on its merits; after all, we do over a hundred abortions a week. At some point each individual in this line of work draws a boundary and adheres to it. For one physician the boundary is a particular week of gestation; for another, it is a certain number of repeated abortions. But these boundaries can be fluid too: one physician overruled his own limit to abort a mature but severely malformed fetus. For me, the limit is allowing my clients to carry their own burden, shoulder the responsibility themselves. I shoulder the burden of trying not to judge them.

This city has several "crisis pregnancy centers" advertised in the Yellow Pages. They are small offices staffed by volunteers, and they offer free pregnancy testing, glossy photos of dead fetuses, and movies. I had a client recently whose mother is active in the anti-abortion movement. The young woman went to the local crisis center and was told that the doctor would make her touch her dismembered baby, that the pain would be the most horrible she could imagine, and that she might, after an abortion, never be able to have children. All lies. They called her at home and at work, over and over and over, but she had been wise enough to give a false name. She came to us a fugitive. We who do abortions are marked by some as impure. It's dirty work.

When a deliveryman comes to the sliding glass window by the reception desk and tilts a box toward me, I hesitate. I read the packing slip, assess the shape and weight of the box in light of its supposed contents. We request familiar faces. The doors are carefully locked; I have learned to half glance around at bags and boxes, looking for a telltale sign. I register with security when I arrive, and I am careful not to bang a door. We are all a little on edge here.

CONCERN ABOUT SIZE and shape seem to be natural, and so is the relief that follows. We make the powerful assumption that the fetus is different from us, and even when we admit the similarities, it is too simplistic to be seduced by form alone. But the form is enormously potent—humanoid, powerless, palm-sized, and pure, it evokes an almost fierce tenderness when viewed simply as what it appears to be. But appearance, and even potential, aren't enough. The fetus, in becoming itself, can ruin others; its utter dependence has a sinister side. When I am struck in the moment by the contents in the basin, I am careful to remember the context, to note the tearful teenager and the woman sighing with something more than relief. One kind of question, though, I find considerably trickier.

"Can you tell what it is?" I am asked, and this means gender. This question is asked by couples, not women alone. Always couples who would abort a girl and keep a boy. I have been asked about twins, and even if I could tell what race the father was.

An eighteen-year-old woman with three daughters brought her husband to the interview. He glared first at me, then at his wife, as he sank lower and lower in the chair, picking his teeth with a toothpick. He interrupted a conversation with his wife to ask if I could tell whether the baby would be a boy or a girl. I told him I could not.

"Good," he replied in a slow and strangely malevolent voice, "'cause if it was a boy I'd wring her neck."

In a literal sense, abortion exists because we are able to ask such questions, able to assign a value to the fetus that can shift with changing circumstances. If the human bond to a child were as primitive and unflinchingly narrow as that of other animals, there would be no abortion. There would be no abortion because there would be nothing more important than caring for the young and perpetuating the species, no reason for sex but to make babies. I sense this sometimes, this wordless organic duty, when I do ultrasounds.

We do ultrasound, a sound wave test that paints a faint, gray picture of the fetus, whenever we're uncertain of gestation. Age is measured by the width of the skull and confirmed by the length of the femur or thighbone; we speak of a pregnancy as being a certain "femur length" in weeks. The usual concern is whether a pregnancy is within the legal limit for an abortion. Women this far along have bellies that swell out round and tight like trim muscles. When they lie flat, the mound rises softly above the hips, pressing the umbilicus upward.

It takes practice to read an ultrasound picture, which is grainy and etched as though in strokes of charcoal. But suddenly a rapid rhythmic motion appears—the beating heart. Nearby is a soft oval, scratched with lines—the skull. The leg is harder to find, and then suddenly the fetus moves, bobbing in the surf. The skull turns away, an arm slides across the screen, the torso rolls. I know the weight of a baby's head on my shoulder, the whisper of lips on ears, the delicate curve of a fragile spine in my hand. I know how heavy and correct a newborn cradled feels. The creature I watch in secret requires nothing from me but to be left alone, and that is precisely what won't be done.

These inadvertently made beings are caught in a twisting web of motive and desire. They are at least inconvenient, sometimes quite literally dangerous in the womb, but most often they fall somewhere in between—consequences never quite believed in come to roost. Their virtue rises and falls outside their own nature: they become only what we make them. A fetus created by accident is the most absolute kind of surprise. Whether the blame lies in a failed IUD, a slipped condom, or a false impression of safety, that fetus is a thing whose creation has been actively worked against. Its existence is an error. I think this is why so few women, even late in a pregnancy, will consider giving a baby up for adoption. To do so means making the fetus real—imagining it as something whole and outside oneself. The decision to terminate a pregnancy is sometimes so difficult and confounding that it creates an enormous demand for immediate action. The decision is a rejection; the pregnancy has become something to be rid of, a condition to be ended. It is a burden, a weight, a thing separate.

Women have abortions because they are too old, and too young, too poor, and too rich, too stupid, and too smart. I see women who berate themselves with violent emotions for their first and only abortion, and others who return three times, five times, hauling two or three children, who cannot remember to take a pill or where they put the diaphragm. We talk glibly about choice. But the choice for what? I see all the broken promises in lives lived like a series of impromptu obstacles. There are the sweet, light promises of love and intimacy, the glittering promise of education and progress, the warm promise of safe families, long years of innocence and community. And there is the promise of freedom: freedom from failure, from faithlessness. Freedom from biology. The early feminist defense of abortion asked many questions, but the one I remember is this: is biology destiny? And the answer is yes, sometimes it is. Women who have the fewest choices of all exercise their right to abortion the most.

Oh, the ignorance. I take a woman to the back room and ask her to undress. A few minutes later I return and find her positioned discreetly behind a drape, still wearing underpants. "Do I have to take these off too?" she asks, a little shocked. Some swear they have not had sex, many do not know what a uterus is, how sperm and egg meet, how sex makes babies. Some late seekers do not believe themselves pregnant; they believe themselves impregnable. I was chastised when I began this job for referring to some clients as girls: it is a feminist heresy. They come so young, snapping gum, sockless and sneakered, and their shakily applied eyeliner smears when they cry. I call them girls with maternal benignity. I cannot imagine them as mothers.

THE DOCTOR SEATS himself between the woman's thighs and reaches into the dilated opening of a five-month pregnant uterus. Quickly he grabs and crushes the fetus in several places, and the room is filled with a low clatter and snap of forceps, the click of the tanaculum, and a pulling, sucking sound. The paper crinkles as the drugged and sleepy woman shifts, the nurse's low, honey-brown voice explains each step in delicate words.

I have fetus dreams, we all do here: dreams of abortions one after the other; of buckets of blood splashed on the walls;

trees full of crawling fetuses. I dreamed that two men grabbed me and began to drag me away. "Let's do an abortion," they said with a sickening leer, and I began to scream, plunged into a vision of sucking, scraping pain, of being spread and torn by impartial instruments that do only what they are bidden. I woke from this dream barely able to breathe and thought of kitchen tables and coat hangers, knitting needles striped with blood, and women all alone clutching a pillow in their teeth to keep the screams from piercing the apartment-house walls. Abortion is the narrowest edge between kindness and cruelty. Done as well as it can be, it is still violence—merciful violence, like putting a suffering animal to death.

Maggie, one of the nurses, received a call at midnight not long ago. It was a woman in her twentieth week of pregnancy; the necessarily gradual process of cervical dilation begun the day before had stimulated labor, as it sometimes does. Maggie and one of the doctors met the woman at the office in the night. Maggie helped her onto the table, and as she lay down the fetus was delivered into Maggie's hands. When Maggie told me about it the next day, she cupped her hands into a small bowl—"It was just like a little kitten," she said softly, wonderingly. "Everything was still attached."

At the end of the day I clean out the suction jars, pouring blood into the sink, splashing the sides with flecks of tissue. From the sink rises a rich and humid smell, hot, earthy, and moldering; it is the smell of something recently alive beginning to decay. I take care of the plastic tub on the floor, filled with pieces too big to be trusted to the trash. The law defines the contents of the bucket I hold protectively against my chest as tissue. Some would say my complicity in filling that bucket gives me no right to call it anything else. I slip the tissue gently into a bag and place it in the freezer, to be binned at another time. Abortion requires of me an entirely new set of assumptions. It requires a willingness to live with conflict, fearlessness, and grief. As I close the freezer door, I imagine a world where this won't be necessary, and then return to the world where it is.

Harper's, October 1987

I began my long relationship with Harper's by sending this essay in cold, "over the transom." It has since been reprinted in anthologies and textbooks many times, sometimes with a set of ham-handed study questions attached. That means I've corresponded with a lot of college students—and a few high school students—over the years. Many of them wonder whether I am "still pro-choice," and a few wonder if I have ever been pro-choice. The ambiguity—far more apparent to others than to me; I think this essay is indubitably pro-choice—is intended. I think the most appropriate response to problems as complex and nuanced as abortion must be complex and nuanced itself. But I have always been a stalwart supporter of reproductive rights and express this in time, money, and votes.

This story began my long conflict with my editors at Harper's over titles. It was originally published as "We Do Abortions Here."

The Only Harmless Great Thing

THE BEST TIME TO WATCH THE ELEPHANTS AT THE WASHING-ton Park Zoo is in the early hours of a sunny day, when their bulky bodies cast wide, dark shadows in the bright, transparent sunshine. The elephants are more energetic in the morning, more likely to wrestle in one of the wading pools or sing in a frequency that I can hear. (A variety of elephant calls are pitched too low for human ears.) The elephant barn, a complex of chambers and yards partly surrounded by a dry moat, is at the far end of the zoo, tucked along a curving terrace carved from a steep hill on the west side of Portland, Oregon. The largest of the yards, at the back of the complex, is separated by the moat from a small railroad track, travelled every half hour by the open-air zoo train, on its way to the Alaskan tundra and back to the bear grottoes; on the slope beyond the track is a thick stand of fir, vine maple, and alder, tangled with ivy and ferns, and hiding from the elephants' sight a neat Japanese garden, tiers of award-winning roses, and a cluster of distant skyscrapers. I like the crowds in the morning, too: most of the people pressed against the glass wall of the viewing room are young mothers with children in strollers; on a hillock above the moat, toddlers waddle beside a wood-and-wire fence, oblivious of the giants below.

These are Asian elephants, slightly smaller than their African cousins and, I think, more diffident. The Asian and the African elephant not only are separate species but belong to separate genera, and are the only surviving members of the order Proboscidea, which once covered much of the planet and may have included more than three hundred species. The genesis of the modern elephant is, in fact, a point of debate; its evolutionary tree is filled with dozens of branches that failed to bloom. On the basis of the sometimes obscure elements of taxonomy, the elephant's closest living relatives are the hyrax, a furry rodentlike animal; the rotund ocean-dwelling manatee and dugong; and the aardvark.

The Asian elephant has smaller ears than the African, one rather than two "fingers" on the tip of its trunk, a long narrow face under a giant domed skull of airy bone. The Asian has smaller tusks, if any; the popular image of the elephant—huge ears flung wide, long rails of ivory below the face—is of the African. But it is Asians we see as the centerpiece of circuses and in zoos. They are considered far easier to train—more amenable and less skittish. The Asian has been the elephant of domestic life all the years of recorded history and is sacred in many religions. It is still used as a work animal in India, Sri Lanka, Burma, and Thailand. According to trainers, the Asian is more willing to enter the intimate, emotionally complex relationship that domesticity requires. Pliny the Elder ascribed to the elephant the senses of modesty, shame, and delight, and in this herd—the most prolific herd of elephants in the Western Hemisphere, with twenty-four births in twenty-six years—I imagine a sense of style, too. Even in the spacious, sandy backyard, they move with a jungle delicacy.

It has taken me a while to learn to distinguish one elephant from another—by noting the pattern of pink freckling on their ears, the number of creases on the lower leg (a kind of fingerprint), and the angle and set of the ears, which are shaped like ginkgo leaves. Elephants rarely stand completely still; they pass among others, lean, touch, and blend into a single, soft contour. The trunk, which is both nose and upper lip (it is also the elephant's hand, with control fine enough to pick up a dime), never rests; it waves slowly, restlessly about. A few in the herd of eleven are easy for me to spot: Tunga, a bull, because he is the only one with tusks (they are banded in brass); Rosy, the oldest cow, who has a pleasing shape and the balance of an elder; Belle, a few years younger, who has the wrinkles. The elephants scratch themselves—foot to knee, head against pillar—and caress each other with their heads and trunks, and all this motion is oddly quiet. The elephant foot is encased in a fatty pad, and it is this wide cushion that makes elephants so silent and stealthy in the wild. They can pass undetected a short distance away from people, even at an easy lope. When standing, elephants swing their front legs one in front of the other in perfect time; sometimes two elephants will rock in rhythm, heads swaying in counterpoint to the beat.

I think it is a human trait to exaggerate difference—to imagine an odd thing as odder than it really is. I expected, when I first met elephants, to have exaggerated their size in my imagination. But elephants are so big, so much bigger than any other creature we meet on land, that I found the opposite to be true: I had actually reduced them in my mind, diminished their size and their difference. Up close, within reach, an elephant is a transcendent thing, entirely alien. Elephants resemble us in funny ways—they catch colds, get sunburns, babysit each other's children. Rosy and I even have the same body temperature. But I am really nothing like Rosy, and she is nothing like me; still, as I watch her and her kin pass by, my strongest feeling is one of society and relation.

At Washington Park, the elephants are guests, family, and royalty; they are by far the most popular animals on exhibit. One morning in early June, I watched as Sunshine, a five-year-old adolescent cow, bullied Chang Dee, the herd's only calf, into fetching a ball from the wading pool in the front yard; she shoved the bristly haired, short-trunked baby toward the edge of the water until he tumbled in. The mothers and cousins nearby ignored the children, and threw leaves of lettuce on their own and each other's backs, using each other as tables. In the backyard, Hugo, a bull, paced, and dusted himself with sand, and the people leaning on the fences sighed with pleasure. He was the Elephant, in myth an earthbound rain cloud, the beloved beast known variously as God's messenger, earth's egg, the carrier of the world. But Hugo is also a research animal, as they all are, and is subject to the keepers' law. Washington Park's elephants are participants in research aimed at protecting their species from extinction; through Hugo, Sunshine, and the others, certain essential mysteries are beginning to unravel.

The real key to recognizing elephants is personality. The keepers at Washington Park indulge in a cheerful and unapologetic anthropomorphism when discussing their charges, but this is a matter more of the conventions of language than of biological inaccuracy. All are quick to bristle at explanations of elephant behavior—such as the common assumption that Hugo dusts himself with sand in order to cool off. "We don't know why Hugo or any of them do what they do. How could we?" says Jay Haight, who has been a keeper at Washington Park for nine years. Each man brings his own degree of familiarity to each elephant, and it varies from a rude slap on the rump or a gentle stroke and whisper to a respectfully wide berth.

Between chores, the keepers tend to gather for a cigarette or a cup of coffee in the barn's central room, a huge, concrete-floored chamber with a cathedral ceiling split by skylights. This particular room, in spite of its size, isn't used by the elephants; its dominant feature is an enormous pile of timothy hay. Along one wall are a counter and a dusty, paper-strewn desk below a row of dusty cupboards; elephant cartoons are tacked on the cupboard doors. This room and the viewing room next to it are part of the original barn, which was completed in 1959. Behind a hydraulic door labeled with a red danger sign is a later addition: a hallway and several large rooms. One of these contains the crush, a contraption of hydraulic barred walls, which is used to confine the animals—painlessly, despite the name—for care. Asian bull elephants are subject to a recurrent phenomenon of unknown purpose called musth, which lasts anywhere from a few weeks to several months (longer in healthy, well-nourished elephants like these) and is marked by violent, unpredictable behavior. This and an inveterate need to dominate are what characterize the bull. The keepers will go into a room with cows, mingle with them, many times a day; they generally approach a bull only after he is settled in the crush. Few zoos have the equipment, the experience, or the will to care for even one full-sized bull; there are three at Washington Park, thanks largely to the crush. It is not a new idea: log or bamboo cages have been used in Burmese work camps for hundreds of years. Every elephant here goes in and out of the crush nearly every day—it also functions as a door to the backyard—and each is rewarded for the trip with a bunch of carrots or bananas or an armful of hay. The thick walls of wide-spaced bars slide both horizontally and at angles, shifting noisily, with simple controls, to match the animal's form. Here the periodic foot care is done, to prevent bacterial infections and overgrowth of toenails, and here medicine, vitamins, and other medical treatment are given. It is also in the crush that the trickiest part of reproduction research—sperm collection—takes place.

I have joined the keepers in the big hay room for conversation many times, and now and then one of them will go off to do an errand: move an animal or two or three from room to room or into one or another of the yards; pass out carrots. I've been startled to hear a sudden shout of "Bull coming through!" and see, through a crack in the hallway door, a trotting elephant, head high, trunk waving toward the scent of the hay as he heads up the hall.

One day last June, I visited the keepers to discuss elephant character. They had left open a door to a little side yard fringed with bamboo and fenced off from the backyard by a concrete wall. A group of cows in the backyard came to stare at us, leaning their great gray heads over the wall, their trunks weaving from side to side. The elephants will watch, sometimes for hours, the movements of the human beings nearby. Now and then, a bull will scoop up a pile of sand (and, occasionally, excrement) in the sinewy curl at the tip of his trunk and sling it at a keeper or a maintenance man. The damp sand flies out like a hail of buckshot and is aimed with an archer's skill.

"Rosy is better than money from home," said Roger Henneous, the head keeper. He is a short man with a graying, close-cropped beard and a gruff manner, and he has worked at the Washington Park Zoo for more than twenty years. "She used to be earth mother to all the calves, but now she's had a bellyful. There's no elephant you'd rather spend time with—you could trust your child with her. Now, Belle—she is so damned hardheaded. She won't bend and acknowledge that she's getting older and everybody else is getting better. So she proceeds to get her butt whipped up on with depressing regularity by the young cows moving up. She is not going gently into that good night. And Me-Tu, Rosy's daughter—that's Daughter Hog."

"Me-Tu lives to eat," Haight explained. "You could put four animals together and they would not eat as much as fast as she does." Jim Sanford, the zoo's third full-time elephant keeper, talked about his favorite, a young cow named Pet. "One of her trademarks is checking us out: 'How far can I go? How much does this guy know? Have the rules been changed?'" he told me. "It's one of the things you really like about her. I'd call it a sense of humor—she obviously gets pleasure out of seeing how much she can get away with. It slays her. I think the relationship between a human being and an elephant is based on mutual trust. They know what the rules are here. If one of us, particularly a new guy, chastises them for things that are okay with everybody else—well, they won't put up with it."

"Do they like you?" I asked.

Haight paused, considering. "Does it matter? I like *them*, but they piss me off a lot of the time. I know they're hearing me, and then suddenly it's 'I've never done this before! You can't be talking to *me*!'" He threw up his hands, mimicking elephant disbelief. "But you have to be the dominant animal. That's why the bulls come after us. If we weren't the dominant animal, they wouldn't care."

The herd's daily routine is complicated, with many comings and goings and tradings of place. Every task is punctuated with sound: the deep whoosh of an elephant's exhalation, the spray of a hose on concrete, the clang of massive hydraulic doors, the faint rustle of a scratching bull. There is sound, and there is smell—

a perfume of hay and manure, and, underneath, the musky, dry, sweet smell of the elephants themselves. The air in the barn is always warm, even in this high-ceilinged central room.

Elephant cows are irrepressibly social beasts. Washington Park has two separate family herds of mothers, daughters, and female cousins. (At the time of my visits last spring and summer, Chang Dee, the male calf, was still with his mother, Me-Tu. He has since gone to the Ringling Brothers and Barnum & Bailey Circus, and almost to the day his five-year-old half uncle, Rama, returned to the herd from a four-year sojourn at the Point Defiance Zoo, in Tacoma.) The groups rotate and are sometimes split into smaller groups throughout nine available areas, eating periodically in different places. (A single mature cow will consume ninety pounds of hay, three pounds of oats, forty-six pounds each of carrots and lettuce, a handful of vitamins, a quarter cup of salt, and fifty gallons of water every day.) The three mature bulls are always separate and solitary, but during mating a cow and bull are given a private room for several days or, sometimes, are allowed the use of one of the outside yards.

With each move to a new area, the animals must examine the evidence of the animals that have just left; it is in the first few moments in a yard or a room that the elephants seem to merge, recognizing and reassuring each other. To prevent boredom and to ensure cooperation, the cows and calves are trained to stand, to back up, to lie down, to hold still, and to tolerate leg chains, which are necessary during feeding to prevent the dominant animals from stealing food. Both Tunga and Hugo were once show animals—Hugo belonged to the Ringling Brothers circus—and can do such tricks as walking on a ball. Chang Dee, Hugo's firstborn, was the payment the zoo made to the circus in exchange for Hugo, and was thus trained to accept leg chains from babyhood. Sunshine (her real name is Sung Surin) was taught to lie down on command—a marvel of conditioned response. In the course of a week or two, a keeper would enter the barn while Sunshine was napping and rouse her just enough to feed her a banana. When she woke from her nap, Jim Sanford says, "it was with banana on her breath and the word down in her ears."

The keepers are full of such stories; they say, with a certain pride, that single-trial learning is normal in elephants. They tell long anecdotes—tales of one elephant determined to pull a door apart, another playing with an electrical heating panel, a third refusing to lift a leg for a chain—and they laugh at the elephants' cleverness and their own efforts to be a bit more clever. It is an affectionate one-upmanship; tomorrow, perhaps, the elephants will win another round.

"One day, Rog and I came back from a break, and there's Tamba, who had been with the herd in the backyard, all by herself over in the bamboo," Jay Haight recalled. At the time, Tamba, a seventeen-year-old cow born in Thailand, wasn't fully grown, and she had somehow managed to squeeze through a gap at one end of the wall between the two yards and was harvesting the bamboo, an elephant delight. "So she's really conspicuous, but as soon as she heard us coming she turned around and faced the other way, rock-still, holding her trunk in her mouth." Haight pretended to whistle, gazed at the ceiling. "'I'm not really here, don't mind me. It's just Mr. Squirrel.'" Another time, Tunga swung one of the elephants' playthings, a chained log, over the moat, climbed out along it as if he were on a balance beam, and fell in. It was not his first such mishap: an erstwhile performer, Tunga can balance on one leg, and he was once seen to "waltz," or spin on his hind legs, around the backyard until he tripped and tumbled into the moat.

Roger Henneous believes that the elephants are well aware of their keepers' expectations. "You ought to be here on a day when the routine is hopelessly screwed up and get a look at the expressions on their faces," he said. "If they had a watch, they'd be checking it. And asking you, 'Look, buddy, what's the problem? Have you forgotten everything we ever taught you?'"

"Come on and see the big guy," Jim Sanford said, and he led me down the hall, a narrow concrete alley lined with dusty pipes, to a room with a window about three feet wide and screened with heavy wire mesh. He was referring to Packy, the undisputed master of the herd. Packy, who stands more than ten feet high and weighs 13,320 pounds, is the largest known Asian elephant in the world. He is only twenty-six—young for an elephant—and he will continue to grow throughout his life.

When I peered through the window, the room at first seemed empty. Then, as in a dream, I saw a trunk float by, far above my head, and then I saw a leg—a tall pillar of dirty velvet—and another, another, another. He was moving past the window with a ponderous grace, outsized. I felt that he needed not a bigger room but a bigger planet. He turned when he picked up my strange new scent, his trunk weaving a hypnotic dance against the mesh, up and down. His tushes—the upper incisors, which in Tunga had grown to tusks—were rough points against the thick wire. Several years ago, a keeper was walking past Packy, who was in a barred room. The bull casually reached through the bars with his trunk, grabbed the keeper's arm, pulled him close, and crushed the limb against the bars with his skull, splintering the bone. Even with the heavy mesh protection, that sinuous trunk is disconcerting; Packy was looking me right in the eye, in a leisurely kind of way. Out of musth, he is usually a placid boy. But he is every inch the king of all the beasts.

There are between twenty-five thousand and forty thousand Asian elephants left in the world. Their gradual elimination in the wild is the result of a number of changes, most of them recent and a few subtle. The invention of the chain saw, for instance, made forest-clearing much easier and quicker work. But basically there is just not enough room in Southeast Asia for both elephants and people. The elephant's jungle habitat is being replaced by cropland, and many of the crops are delectable to the now homeless elephant. The elephant raids the millet and sugarcane, and is killed for his efforts, and kills in turn: in India, nearly a hundred and fifty people are killed by elephants every year. Wild elephants are found from India to Indonesia; most inhabit shrinking parks and preserves, in shrinking populations, separated from each other by human settlements as uncrossable as an ocean. Bulls, being more aggressive, are killed far more often than cows. Not only does this deplete the gene pool, but the cows' opportunities to breed grow fewer, and as the birthrate falls their mean age increases. Because elephants will feed on the youngest, most tender trees available, finding them the most appetizing, herds quickly denude small parks beyond the point of natural recovery. Several countries, notably Thailand and India, are attempting to conserve these insular environments and to confront the problems of the diminished gene pool and male-to-female ratio, but quite a few people in elephant biology wonder whether the wild elephant is past saving. (There are estimated to be a million elephants left in Africa; however, their numbers are also dropping.) Certainly its future, one way or another, resides in zoos.

The Washington Park Zoo is a century old. Its origin dates back to a pharmacist named Richard Knight, who found himself in Portland—then still something of a frontier city—with a brown bear and a grizzly on his hands. He gave them, with some relief, to the city, and thus began a zoo. In 1953, Austin Flegel, a Portlander who was working as an economic adviser in Thailand, was given a four-year-old female elephant as a gift, and sent her to Washington Park. She was housed in the zoo's dilapidated camel barn and—Portland being the city of roses—was immediately named Rosy. Rosy's advent caused the voters to approve a bond issue to build a new zoo—she led parades, attended store openings, and threw out the first ball at a Portland Beavers baseball game.

The zoo's director, Jack Marks, wanted to build the ultimate modern zoo, where the animals would live in natural settings and rarely require handling by their keepers. Together with the architects Abbott Lawrence and Ernest Tucker, Marks travelled the country in search of ideas, and Lawrence and Tucker eventually designed a large, open zoo with grottoes and moats in place of cages and bars. In September of 1956, before the new zoo was finished, another elephant arrived. A Portland engineer named Orville Hosmer had gone to Vietnam to help rebuild a village destroyed by a flood, and in gratitude the villagers gave him a female calf named Tuy Hoa (pronounced Tee Wah).

Rosy and Tuy Hoa moved into their spacious new quarters in November of 1959. The move from the camel barn had to be effected by truck, and neither of the animals was particularly willing to clamber aboard. They finally did so only with the guidance of a pair of more experienced elephants—Belle and a bull named Thonglaw, both of whom belonged to an animal importer named Morgan Berry, a friend of Jack Marks. Berry was destined to play an essential role in Portland's elephant future. He had imported four baby elephants (and a large number of other wild and exotic animals) some years before, and raised them in the basement of his house, in a residential neighborhood in Seattle. He later made a living with his own travelling elephant show and such odd jobs as helping to move Portland's elephants. By 1961, when Belle was nine and Thonglaw fourteen, Berry wanted a little break. He lent both, along with Pet, then six years old, to Washington Park for a few winter months, planning to retrieve them in the spring. Berry suspected that Belle was pregnant by Thonglaw, and he thought he knew the date of conception; he had, after all, stood right next to Belle while Thonglaw mounted her. But the conventional wisdom of the time held that both animals were too young to breed successfully, and Berry kept his suspicions to himself. No elephant had been born in the United States in the previous forty-four years; no elephant bred in captivity here had ever survived.

Elephant reproduction is rather simple and elegant, and resembles human reproduction in certain ways: elephants bear single babies; assist each other in labor, birth, and the rearing of the young; and live in family groups. The cows have two human-size breasts on the upper chest. Males reach sexual maturity at the age of nine or ten; females can conceive as young as six. A cow's most fertile years are from twenty-five to forty-five, after which she reaches menopause. The heavy, hidden matings of elephants have inspired fantastic and beautiful ideas; long treatises on the nature of love, lust, fidelity, and adultery among pachyderms; tales of poetry, yearning, and faith. Elephants were once said to have died from a broken heart; in fact, they do sometimes die suddenly, with no apparent cause, after separation from their loved ones. It is still widely believed that they mate only in privacy, or only under water, and in ancient times it was believed that male elephants fell in love with human women, particularly those who sold flowers or perfume. One such elephant courted a woman by laying apples on her bosom. J. H. Williams, in *Elephant Bill,* his 1950 memoir of twenty years in Burmese elephant camps, wrote:

> The mating of wild elephants is very private. The bull remains, as usual, outside the herd, and his lady love comes out where she knows she will find him.... They fall in love, and days, and even weeks, of courtship may take place.... When they have knocked off from the day's work, they will call each other and go off together into the jungle.

In a more comprehensive work, Richard Carrington's *Elephants,* the author states that the ancients believed that elephants copulated face to face: "This was regarded as additional proof of the animal's wisdom and intelligence.... They will indulge in innocent dalliance, much as young human couples in spring.... Dalliance turns to serious love play, the female using all her wiles to bring the male to the peak of his desire ... Anyone who has studied the way a female elephant encourages her lover by alternate advances and retreats, by provocative gestures of her body, and a teasing and erotic use of the trunk, will recognize her prowess as the Cleopatra of the animal world."

Some elephant keepers wondered if elephants *could* breed successfully in captivity; Morgan Berry told anyone who would listen that they would breed only in natural conditions. Elephant science was an esoteric and undeveloped field in the early 1960s. No one was certain of the length of the gestation period, and almost nothing was known of the estrous cycle, because cows show no overt signs of fertility. Wild bulls were thought to mate throughout the year, since elephant calves are born in all seasons; what may appear to be a season—a preponderance of births in a few months' time, for instance—can be tied to drought and famine, rather than to seasonal ovulation.

The only real experience with elephant reproduction came from the work camps of Southeast Asia, but the animals in such camps have never been systematically bred. Traditionally, they are released from their chains at night to wander the nearby forests and eat; the mahouts round them up each morning, having tracked each one by the sound of the bell around its neck. (After Jim Sanford returned from a trip to Thailand, he told me that the elephants sometimes used their trunks to stuff mud in the bells, which muffled the sound. "I wondered why they didn't just tear the bell off," he said. "Well, they get chastised for that. But stuffing mud in it isn't against the rules.") The cows mate at night with wild bulls, and the resulting calves are genetically sound and born to work. The working bulls are conditioned not to mate, according to Dr. Michael Schmidt, the Washington Park veterinarian. "Riders are afraid that if the bulls have total freedom of action and express sexual behavior, they will inevitably turn on the riders and kill them—which the bulls often do anyway," he told me. "The riders will do whatever they can to control that. A young bull who has an erection is beaten. So young bulls get the idea that being interested in cows is too painful, and their libido decreases to the point where they are just not interested in mating if there are people around."

In this country, bulls with erections are sometimes punished, but for a different reason. The mature bull elephant's penis, which weighs more than forty pounds, is long and flexible; this enables it to reach the female's cervix, at the end of a twisting, back-angled tube and well hidden from the world. The penis has tendons that allow it to make "searching" motions, from side to side and up and down, in the vaginal canal. I've watched Packy roaming around the yard with his penis fully extended and bumping against his hind legs as he seems to swagger for the viewing public. Such an unabashed offering by the male is deemed too great an embarrassment in most zoos and circuses. But the principal disincentive to elephant births in the United States is environmental. Many zoos keep only one or two elephants, and these are almost always cows; there have never been many mature bulls in this country. An unsocialized cow and a skeptical bull will be brought together as strangers, by keepers with no understanding of fertility; little wonder that the attempt has seldom been successful.

Beginning in January of 1962, when Belle's breast development made her pregnancy undeniable, a vigil was kept at Washington Park; no one knew when she might deliver, or how difficult the labor might be. It was a long wait. At 5:58 a.m. on April 14—a gestation, according to Morgan Berry's dates, of 635 days—Belle delivered a male calf in good health, after an hour of active labor. Mother clamped the umbilical cord with her trunk, and Thonglaw promptly ate his congratulatory cigar. The event was front-page news across the country. Less than twenty-four hours after the birth, Berry received an offer for Belle and her baby—$30,000 from the Brookfield Zoo, outside Chicago. The next day, Berry offered the two suddenly famous elephants to the city of Portland for $20,000, payable within a month. A citizens' committee was formed, and money began to trickle in: schoolchildren donated nickels; unions made donations from pension funds; charity car washes, bowling tournaments, square dances were held. The thriving baby, already accustomed to long lines of sightseers willing to wait hours for a two-minute view, was named Packy in a radio-station contest. Before the deadline had passed, Berry closed the deal and threw in Thonglaw and Pet for nothing. Thonglaw, during his extended winter vacation, had mated several times, and almost immediately the keepers realized that Rosy was pregnant; a few weeks later, they discovered that both Tuy Hoa and Pet were pregnant as well. Thonglaw's dynasty had begun.

WHEN MICHAEL SCHMIDT, fresh from the University of Minnesota, arrived at Washington Park in 1973 to serve as the veterinarian, there were eight elephants in residence: Rosy and her daughter, Me-Tu; Tuy Hoa and her daughter, Hanako; Thonglaw; Belle; Packy; and Pet. Both Pet and Hanako were pregnant. Thonglaw had sired ten calves; eight had survived, and all but Hanako and Me-Tu had been given or sold to zoos and circuses. Portland was elephant-happy. Packy had a birthday party every year, at which thousands of people cheered him on as he ate a forty-pound cake of whole wheat, carrots, and peanut butter. The zoo was developing an adoption program, encouraging businesses and groups to pay the cost of feeding a particular elephant for a year at a time.

"When I arrived, I had no special interest in elephants," Schmidt confessed to me one morning. We were in his office at the animal hospital, a flat-roofed inconspicuous building set in a draw filled with ferns and willow trees, behind the beaver and otter exhibits. "But you have to, here. This place was unique—the only place in the Western Hemisphere actually breeding elephants, and it had been the only place for years. We're still the only zoo with second-generation births. This was the biggest thing that this small zoo in the West was doing, and it was outdoing the Bronx Zoo and the San Diego Zoo and all the others in a very difficult task. So it wasn't a matter of whether or not to get involved—you'd *better* get involved."

Schmidt began teaching himself elephant medicine. He quickly discovered that Washington Park's success was something of an accident; no one really knew why Portland's elephants bred and other zoos' elephants did not. Schmidt began the first methodical testing of the elephants, making daily observations. He wanted to understand their reproduction and ultimately—by still undiscovered techniques of artificial insemination—increase it. One of the few things that were known about elephant reproduction by that time was the estrous cycle. In 1971, three biologists who had studied plantation elephants in Sri Lanka published a paper concluding that the elephant ovulates every twenty-two days. A second paper described a behavior seen in the bulls—an elaborate gesture in which the trunk is placed in a spot of urine and curled into the mouth. The authors called it urine testing, and suspected that the bull was checking cow urine for signs of fertility. Schmidt began seeing the gesture, too. "No one was paying any attention to this behavior," he told me. "I looked at it and thought, Well, that's certainly a way to tell if the bull is interested in a particular cow."

Schmidt thought that the attractant had to be a pheromone of some kind, and he invented the sniff test, making use of the elephant barn's hydraulic doors, which can be opened an inch at a time. The sniff test is a rather impolite but simple method of allowing a bull contact with a cow without endangering either cow or keeper. In a sniff test, Schmidt and the keepers place a bull on one side of a door opened wide enough for a trunk, and back a cow up to the opening on the other side. The cow holds still—usually with a placid patience but sometimes with a keeper's encouragement—while the bull checks her urine and urogenital secretions with his trunk. Schmidt keeps track of the length of time the bull seems interested. "We didn't know if the cows would get upset by being backed up to a bull, or what the bull would do, and so forth," he told me. "It turned out that young Packy was quite interested in breeding and in the cows, and very happy to check them. And the cows, once they'd figured out what we were doing—well, it was fine with them, no big deal. I started to make daily observations, which we have done, with only a handful of missed days, since the fall of '74." Schmidt was surprised by what he found: peaks of intense interest in a particular cow for a few days, followed by months of indifference. "And these were known breeding cows," he explained. "They'd all been pregnant and given birth, so they had estrous cycles. Something was fishy about the published estrous cycle. It sure couldn't be twenty-two days."

Schmidt's wife, Anne, who is a research biologist at the zoo, had done serum-hormone assays on the zoo's African lions, and had mapped the lion ovulatory cycle by noting changes in the levels of hormones in the blood. She suggested that the same might be done with the elephants, and Mike began drawing blood from the cows. He used a vein in the leg or the ear, laboriously bleeding each cow himself once a week, until Roger Henneous couldn't stand it any longer. "Roger said, 'I could do that.' I said, 'Okay, Roger, go ahead,' sure that he couldn't. But damned if he didn't get a vein the first time. After that, the keepers did it."

Over several months, Schmidt noticed patterns in the hormone levels, including a sixteen-week cycle of progesterone. The sniff-test results correlated with the progesterone cycle in a ratio "too good to be true," Schmidt told me. "The bull is interested in the cow at the nadir of progesterone—about a four-week period— and especially at the few days around ovulation. The cow ovulates, and the progesterone starts to climb. The estrous cycle turns out to be about sixteen weeks long—the longest of any mammal by far." The cow is willing to be bred for only a few days during her cycle: ovulation is a brief event, and the egg is viable for only about twelve hours. Schmidt tried mating three cows by cycle, placing each with a bull in a private room for several days of the magic period. All three became pregnant. "The pheromone was exactly, beautifully inverse to the progesterone," he said. "You never see anything that clear, ever. There were some jokes about it, actually, because it did look too good to be true. But we had enough data so that we didn't have to worry."

Schmidt is a careful man, never without a neat lab coat, and slow to offer a smile. But now he did. "At this time we were doing this work, the San Diego Zoo was using elephant urine to determine hormone levels," he continued. "One of its endocrinologists presented a paper on this work at a conference, in the course of which he said, 'Well, we all know that you can't get blood samples from elephants.' Now, that's true of okapis and hippos and rhinos, and I think it's great to develop urinary techniques for animals like that, because trying to get a weekly blood sample would be impossible. But elephants are domesticated animals as well as wild animals. The people in San Diego couldn't get blood samples from elephants, so they assumed that nobody could. But a veterinarian can do much more with elephants than with other animals. Elephants are intelligent; they have an arm and a hand, and being able to manipulate the environment accelerates the development of that intelligence. You can go into the cages with them. You can't do that with tigers, or polar bears, for example. You can't do that kind of work with a lot of species. You certainly can't get a bird to stand still and hold its wing up while you get a blood sample every week. You have to grab the bird, hold it down, it's struggling—whereas an elephant can be trained to stand there while you get a blood sample, and you give her an apple when you're done, and she thinks she's getting a bargain."

It is also Mike Schmidt's job to act as matchmaker to the elephants. One of his concerns is genetics; the herd at Washington Park represents a limited gene pool. Of the twenty-four calves born there, nineteen have survived. Two of the dead were the offspring of Packy and Hanako, who are brother and half sister, and one was the offspring of Thonglaw and his daughter Hanako. (The two other deaths were apparently due to random congenital defects.) Such close genetic pairings are no longer made, although Packy and his half sister Me-Tu have twice reproduced without any problems. Schmidt must consider not only the elephants' degree of relatedness but also the age and experience of both cow and bull, their relative size, whether the bull is in musth, and the personalities involved. Some cows have expressed strong opinions about certain bulls, and the bulls, while somewhat less discriminating, also have their preferences.

"When mating goes on, the cow has to cooperate," Schmidt said. "The bull has to be on good terms with that cow. We've seen enough cases where a bull doesn't like a specific cow, or cows won't stand for a certain bull, whereas they will stand nicely for another one. Elephants are capable of forming that kind of relationship. They tend to have the same sorts of problems that all complex, intelligent animals have—like the primates, and ourselves."

Schmidt allows the elephants whatever accommodations they need, which may mean a night alone in a yard for one pair and a private room for another. Tunga, having been brought up as a show animal, won't approach a cow in front of human beings. "Elephants—particularly the older animals—are not like cattle, where you have a female in heat and you bring in a bull and he jumps up and breeds her," Schmidt explained. "There's a chemistry between elephants. A really experienced bull doesn't like it when a cow doesn't act the way an experienced cow ought to—when her response is abnormal, to put it in scientific terms. The bull will often become immediately aggressive if the cow is behaving strangely. She may not *know* what to do. But a young bull doesn't care—a young, eager, excited bull will try to breed any cow he can. The difficulty the younger bulls have is that older cows can dominate them, because they're bigger or wiser. If the cow doesn't want to cooperate, a young bull doesn't have the equipment and the technique and the size to assert himself, whereas an older bull will sort the situation out in a hurry."

By November of 1974, Thonglaw had sired fifteen calves, of whom twelve survived. He would not submit to chains in order to undergo foot care, and had consequently suffered from foot problems for years. Schmidt resolved to do something about this, and after consulting Morgan Berry he decided to tranquilize the elephant—always a risky procedure. To everyone's dismay, Thonglaw died under sedation. (The crush was developed and built as a kind of memorial to Thonglaw, to spare future elephants the same risk.) Packy, then twelve, became the patriarch. He has since fathered seven calves.

"Packy makes it clear what he wants," Schmidt told me. "We'd be afraid to put Tamba in with Packy, because he seems to dislike her, and he's so much bigger than she is. She would tend to fight him a bit—to think that she shouldn't have to do what he wants. Tamba's sort of imprinted on people." Neither will Packy mate with Belle, his mother. "I think that he knows she's his mother," Schmidt said, "but I can't prove it."

I have never seen a pair of elephants mate—few people have—and I suspect that if I had the opportunity I would turn my back. I was shown a series of photographs of such an occasion, and I felt like a voyeur, a trespasser into private territory. In the photographs, the bull begins by laying his trunk across the cow, guiding her gently against a wall, stroking her until she assumes a spread-leg stance. It is too intimate, this soft control, the stolid acceptance by the female, and then the unexpectedly human posture. He plants himself behind her, upright and stately. It took me a moment to place that dignity; it is Ganesha, the elephant-headed Hindu god of wisdom. The bull stands erect and bows his head to his work with all the concentration of a man and all the power of a god.

TUESDAYS ARE BLOOD-SAMPLING days here. Early on a summer morning, before the zoo's gates opened and the crowds arrived, I watched while Jim Sanford and Jay Haight performed their deft art. They visited Hanako and Tamba first, in a room at the far end of the hall. The giant animals seemed genuinely glad to see them and immediately moved close to greet them. Haight carried an ankus, a tool that looks something like a boathook and is used to guide and control the elephant, and laid it lightly alongside Hanako's trunk, taking hold of her fleshy, triangular lower lip with his free hand. "She likes me to hold her," he told me. "It keeps her calm. She's not wrapped too tight."

Hanako stood still and patient for a moment, then began stroking Haight with her trunk, waved it in my direction—I was standing safely outside the hydraulic door, which was opened a foot or two—and finally swung it to her side, stroking Sanford's trousers. Sanford pulled out the fan of her thin-skinned ear, rippled with veins, and poked a small needle into the largest, a gentle line running like a riverbed from top to bottom. The needle lodged in place, and he held a vial to catch the steady drops. Hanako's trunk continued its undulations, from Haight to the unfamiliar air around me and on to Sanford. When the vial was full, Sanford pulled out the needle, stepped through the door, and took two bananas from a box.

"Tamba, get back, get back!" he shouted at the younger cow, who had rushed forward in her eagerness for fruit. He moved to

Hanako. "Trunk!" She swung the floppy member aside, and Sanford shoved the bananas in whole.

Tamba was restless. "She knows she's gonna get a stick and a treat," Sanford explained. "She's a happy camper. She's a doll." Tamba moved over to the door opening. She threw her trunk above her head like a lady flinging open a parasol; her mouth opened wide, presenting me with a giant pink cavity framed by two bright, intelligent eyes. Her tushes, short and dull, were at the front of a set of enormous molars, each nine inches long and weighing about four pounds. Her throat dropped away from me into blackness, the pale-pink tongue, as large as a loaf of bread, damp and vibrating with life. Sanford reached in and massaged her tongue, grabbing it with a firm hand and scratching its rough surface. Tamba seemed to sigh with pleasure at the touch. The men traded places, Haight moving to Tamba's ear while Sanford held her trunk. As they worked, they swore cheerfully, insulting each other and the animals, disparaging clothes, looks, and heredity with equal zest. Tamba wiggled her head, trying to watch, and Sanford, tall enough to meet her at the eye level, yelled in her ear, "Get your head down, or I'll get all over you like a cheap suit!"

Roger Henneous ducked in the door, carrying an electronic thermometer. Steadily, half bored, he took Tamba's skin temperature while Haight drew blood. Behind Henneous, Hanako bobbed gracefully. She rubbed her head against his back, the bulbous gray easily dwarfing the man in his brown uniform. Henneous ignored her, but I couldn't: I ventured too close to the door, and she was distracted by me, by my new smell, and came to press her trunk against me. It was a wet, bristly live thing, like the head of an anxious reptile, and she inhaled me in a rush of wind. By the time Haight stepped between us, scolding me for my reckless move, she had kissed tight to my shoe and was marching purposefully up my leg.

More cows were waiting in the viewing room, and the keepers rushed to finish before the zoo gates opened. This is the first place that people come, to see the elephants. Several feet inside the glass panel are widely spaced bars as thick as a man's arm; because Chang Dee was small enough to slip through the bars, four chains were strung between them. Sunshine held perfectly still while the keepers bled her ear. "She loves being treated like a grownup," Sanford said, and rewarded her with two bunches of blackened bananas. Chang Dee reached for the fruit with his under-sized trunk, and Sunshine marched away, bananas held high.

Elephants have many voices: they trumpet, rumble, squeal, growl, roar, snort. While Haight was patting Rosy under the "fore-arm," a high metallic whine began. "I gotta get some grease—she needs oiling," he said, laughingly, and only then did I realize that the whine was elephant speech. Rosy, Pet, Me-Tu, and Sunshine began to cry together, a shrill, stridulous, and very loud clamor rolling through the high-ceilinged room. It was an almost pain-ful yet beautiful noise, split by belly rumbles, birdlike eeks and squawks, and the ululating song of whales. The men paid no atten-tion and drew blood from Rosy's wrinkled ear, their voices raised above the din. Sanford scratched his back with the ankus and watched Chang Dee try, for the hundredth time, to climb over the chains strung between the bars. As suddenly as it had started, the squealing stopped. In the silence, Sanford began singing a Chuck Berry song to Sunshine, and the elephants joined in. There were wet exhalations, belches, growls and grunts, a repeating sonar blip, a keening whistle. The men passed out rewards, and Sanford gave Pet three bunches of bananas. Why three, I asked him, when the other cows got two?

"Because she's Pet," he answered with a grin. "They don't get any better than that."

IN ALL WORK with Asian elephants, there is one limit—the puz-zling circumstance of musth. Cow elephants, and bulls out of musth, can be dangerous; the casual motions of the keepers in stroking an unchained cow mask a constant caution. But musth bulls are deadly. Knowing this, one sees in a new light historical references to the use of elephants. In the Rome of Pliny's time, people would sit down to a banquet, and then a ceremonially dressed elephant, picking its way through the crowd, would come and take its place at the table. I'm sure it was an uncommon spectacle—the gargantuan guest swaying past the seated diners. But what a risk! I thought of the Romans when I found a photo of Morgan Berry and Thonglaw the other day. Berry stood in front of the bull, who was seated on the ground, his front feet dangling high and Berry's son, Kenneth, clinging to his back. All three seemed in a kind of repose, still for the camera, waiting to do the next trick.

Musth occurs in Asian males beginning around the age of ten, and recurs once or twice a year. (Whether or not musth occurs in African elephants is a subject of considerable debate.) It is both a physical and a behavioral phenomenon. The first sign is usually drainage from the temporal glands (once called "musth vents"), which are on either side of the skull. The glands swell and then drain continuously; the distinctive dark streaks along the sides of the face are cues for caution. The ancients believed that elephants had pearls in their skulls, because the fluid can have a crystalline appearance, like salty tears. It was variously thought to be an antidote for poison, an aphrodisiac, an antiseptic, a tonic to grow hair.

A musth bull also dribbles urine constantly, and ceases to bathe himself, leaving his legs streaked and dirty. His blood levels of testosterone become abnormally high—high enough, Mike Schmidt believes, to interfere with healthy sperm production. The most immediate symptom of musth, though, and one that keepers are often able to spot before the temporal glands begin to drain, is a change in behavior. The bull will first exhibit restlessness, then aggression; finally, in musth's full power, there is a drowsy, abstracted melancholy, full of motion. "As the intensity of musth increases, the elephant becomes more peevish and aggressive of temper," reports the Indian naturalist Ramesh Bedi in his book *Elephant: Lord of the Jungle*, continuing, "He resents everyone. Even those who were nearest him and on whom he depended annoy him." The elephant is "seized with frenzy and becomes ferocious," wrote Strabo. The *Encyclopædia of Islam* describes the elephant character this way: "Normally of a playful disposition, and in fact addicted to jokes, it is terribly vindictive and has the ability to choose the best moment to wreak its vengeance." The mahouts of Burma and Thailand tie their musth bulls near water and let them eat the ground bare; malnutrition eventually keeps the animals from sustaining musth. The mahouts of old had other remedies, such as feeding a bull in musth a pound of tobacco a day, or a coconut with opium hidden inside. Musth bulls are ur-elephants, restless with the need to orbit, pacing, swaying, swinging, searching, peering, ramming their heads against pillars and walls, their great sides heaving, tails swishing, trunks blowing—not in confusion but with a glittering concentration. They are psychotic.

In the wild, musth bulls range and fight; never still, they track their territory. In circuses and zoos, they must be isolated. Musth has condemned bull elephants—and, to a very large extent, elephant breeding—in this country. Dozens of young, healthy males have been executed, by gunshot, poison, and even hanging, and a few bulls are still executed each year for threatening or killing a keeper. Some of the dozens of bulls (and a few cows) that have been put to death in this country never hurt anyone; they simply frightened people too many times. They were guilty of making the obvious too glaring. Even at Washington Park, with the hydraulics, the crush, and the keepers' experience, musth means danger. A cow named Susie had the end of her tail bitten off by Tunga in musth. A few years ago, when both Hugo and Packy were in musth, Hugo stuck the end of his trunk into Packy's room. Packy—who is ordinarily, according to Roger Henneous, "an easily intimidated wimp"—immediately bit it off. For the next month, Hugo lived in the crush and was dosed with antibiotics, watered with a hose down his mouth, and fed. ("A bale of hay every day, by the handful," Jay Haight recalls. "There's a lot of handfuls in a bale of hay.") Hugo, lightly dubbed Master of Disaster, once made a nearly successful murderous assault on Haight, who was standing in an empty room next to Hugo's when the bull rammed the steel door between them with all his strength and barreled through it. "I jumped in time, or

I would have had two broken legs from the door," Haight told me. "I looked up and saw Hugo standing there with a ton of door on his head, still trying to harvest me." Yelling for help, Haight grabbed a pellet gun and fired it at Hugo's feet. ("Then he *really* got mad.") The stinging pellets made the bull retreat, and other keepers were able to distract him while Haight escaped. But no grudges are held against the demented. Recently, I watched Haight give Hugo a massage in the crush, grabbing fistfuls of the dusty gray skin, an inch thick in places, and crooning fond obscenities. Hugo's healed trunk, wormlike and deformed but still useful, scooped up carrots by the pound.

It is a zoo irony that musth lasts longer in a well-fed bull. "Our elephants are in superb physical condition," Mike Schmidt says. Their condition is so good, in fact, that Tunga once held musth for eight months. For all the potential danger, the keepers are clear on one point: if a human being is hurt by an elephant, it's the human being's fault. The bulls "can't help themselves," the keepers tell me; musth is a force beyond the bulls' reckoning.

After Morgan Berry turned Thonglaw, Belle, Pet, and Packy over to Washington Park, he moved to an eighty-acre farm near Woodland, Washington. In his sixties, living alone, he took with him ten elephants, seven of them bulls, and allowed them the freedom to roam much of the property. Berry's friend and fellow animal trainer Eloise Berchtold used Teak, one of Berry's bulls, in her traveling act. In 1978, she was in Toronto, due to perform, and all three of the bulls with her were showing signs of musth. Rather than cancel, she decided to work with Teak, who was normally a relaxed animal. Teak performed in front of several thousand people, and then, while he spun in a pirouette, Berchtold tripped and fell in front of him. Teak immediately turned and gored her with his tusks, pinning her to the ground. He stood guard over her body, refusing to move, and was finally shot by Canadian Mounties who had been called to the scene. Berry was grief-stricken. Berchtold had been his closest friend, and Teak a favorite. Thirteen months later, it was his turn.

No one witnessed his death. A neighbor, worried when Berry didn't phone—as he did regularly—visited the farm with Kenneth Berry, and in a meadow by the barn they found the battered, flattened body under a bull named Buddha. Buddha was a big animal, very good at tricks. He could stand on his head and a single foreleg. But he had a reputation for unpredictability and bad temper. That day, his temporal glands were draining. Perhaps (as some of Berry's friends believe) Berry had had a heart attack and the bull had tried to revive him; such things have happened. Kenneth Berry, who at the time was a primate keeper with the zoo in Seattle, was left with nearly a hundred thousand pounds' worth of elephants to babysit, feed, and find homes for. Finally, with real regret, he destroyed Buddha, after months of trying to place him somewhere and failing. Washington Park—the only facility likely to be able to handle Buddha—refused. Tunga, a far more even-tempered bull, was the zoo's legacy from Morgan Berry.

"Everyone wants to believe that he has the special secret to working with a musth bull," says Schmidt. "But you can be with elephants until the day they decide to go after you and kill you, and that's it. And when you go to Asia and look at the working elephants the mahouts will say, 'This one's killed four men, this one's killed two, this cow's killed three.' And you say, 'My God, what do you do?' Well, they put another guy on, and back to work they go. We used to think that the mahouts knew how to work with these animals and that if we could only learn their secrets everything would be all right. But it's a calculated risk. Our philosophy here is that you treat bulls pretty much the way you treat cows, except that you can go in with the cows and handle them, and you can't do that with the bulls. But the bulls here are at least able to go anywhere in the facility, at any time. No other zoo in the world is run this way."

THOUGH MUSTH HAS been recognized as long as human beings have been near Asian elephants, its biological purpose remains unknown. Some biologists have speculated that it constitutes a rut, or mating season, like the aggressive sexual period of the deer.

This notion has recently been given play by Cynthia Moss and her associate Joyce Poole, who study African elephants on a small preserve in Kenya. In Moss's book *Elephant Memories*, published in 1988, and in articles by Moss and Poole, the claim is made not only that musth is a rut but that a true musth occurs in African elephants, who also exhibit temporal gland secretion. Moss further states in her book that fertile females exhibit overt estrous behavior, including a particular gait. She also believes that musth bulls employ characteristic patterns of ear-waving and trunk gestures, and that they emit special sounds. She writes:

> Both my data and Joyce's on mating behavior indicate that females prefer mating with musth bulls and that they may actually exercise some choice in the matter.... I think it is worth considering that a female might come into estrus in response to a particular male being in musth, and in that case she may be exercising choice.

Mike Schmidt is impatient with these claims. "This is a problem in working with exotic animals in the field, and even in zoos," he told me. "For some reason, people think they can get away with a lesser test of the validity of what they're doing. If you have a theory stating that musth is rut, then you should have data that are in agreement with the theory—you should be able to demonstrate that all the bulls you are studying come into musth at the same time, because that's what a rut is. It's a seasonal thing. All the females will come into heat at that time, too." Seated behind his desk, thinning hair neatly combed, his lab coat freshly pressed, Schmidt seemed the picture of reason. On a cupboard door behind him hung a calendar tracking the estrous cycles of the cows ("Pet OV, Hanako OV")—a random overlay of sixteen-week periods. "We know that isn't true of Asians," he went on. "The females have independent cycles. They give birth all through the year—that's been observed in both species, in the wild. So musth is not a rut. It's primarily a phenomenon of aggression. When bulls are in the depths of musth, they're absolutely incapable of breeding. We see a decline in the quality of the sperm late in musth. Now, that is certainly contrary to rut. They physically cannot bring normal mating to successful completion. They're dopey, they're somnolent. They may develop an erection, but they're unable to control it."

The temporal-gland secretion itself is fairly complex, with twenty major components in a changing ratio. "The gland is a chemical-communication gland, and it may also function as a means of excreting testosterone," says Dr. Lois Rasmussen, a biochemist with a Ph.D. in neurochemistry who is working with the Washington Park elephants. "It may be multifunctional." Dr. Rasmussen is Lois on academic papers, and Betsey or Bets face to face. For the past eight years, she has been searching for the elephant sex pheromone, that odd thing that tells Packy or Tunga when Pet or Hanako is ovulating, the occult substance that Mike Schmidt measures in his sniff tests. Bets Rasmussen looks less like a biochemist than a high-school physical-education coach. Thin and wiry, with close-cropped sun-bleached hair, she is also an avid scuba diver and wildlife photographer, and her skin is tanned a nut brown from long spells under the equatorial sun. In addition to her pheromone work, she is deeply interested in musth, and has collected references to it from all periods of recorded history. Even a prehistoric cave drawing of a mammoth shows the dark streaks of temporal-gland secretion.

"It's important to note that there are two species of elephants, in separate genera," she told me one hot afternoon last August. We were sitting, shoulder to shoulder, in her tiny office at the Oregon Graduate Center, a private research institute outside Portland. The walls were covered with posters and photographs of elephants— elephants mating, elephants walking, fetal elephants, elephants in various stages of dissection. "In one of these species—the Asian—musth has been recognized for hundreds and hundreds of years. In the other species, there has been some recent evidence of a musth-like phenomenon. But you can't conclude that the two are the same, because the evidence is only starting to be gathered. You don't just take a term out of the dictionary and plug it in somewhere else." The first false assumption is that musth is a rut, she says, and the second is the application of that term to another species.

"Now, my experience is with Asians," she continued. "If these two states are the same thing, we should see the same behavior in both species, and we don't. If I take urine at certain times in the musth cycle, and make an extract, I get several reactions from the cows. There's an intense reaction at first—the cow checks the spot out. After that, there's an avoidance. Such data are not consistent with a cow's being attracted to a male, or signaling that she's getting ready to go into estrus. I remember watching Hugo in the viewing room when he was in very heavy musth. He was dribbling urine. We let him out and let the cows in, one by one. The first one in was Pet. Normally, she strolls around while she's waiting for the others to come in. This time, she stopped dead, and she seemed— well, it's anthropomorphizing, but she looked nervous, timid. She went around the room practically on tiptoe. Okay, in the early days of the attempts at breeding the elephants she was bred several times to Hugo when he was well into musth, and he tends not to breed then but to beat up the cows. He almost killed her one day. So she remembers the smell of that musth urine—which does smell horrible. Males avoid each other in musth. Cows avoid musth bulls, too. If cows are afraid of a musth bull, then how is musth a rut? It doesn't make sense. Musth is *not* a rut."

THE STUDY OF pheromones is a new one, as scientific studies go. The name wasn't invented until 1959, and then only after considerable argument. The roots of the word are Greek for "carry" and "excite"—a good term for the myriad roles of these substances. Pheromones are chemicals used for communication among individuals of a single species. They are secreted as liquids and usually received as volatiles, and they constitute a conversation of sorts. Slime molds, algae, and fungi all use pheromones. Social insects, such as ants and bees, may use a dozen or more pheromones in a typical day—one to raise an alarm, another to mark a trail or a particular plant, another to signal social status or group membership. Barnacles collect on rocks and boats by following pheromone signals. When a honeybee stings, it releases a chemical that alarms nearby honeybees.

Pheromones are also used in combination. Research on the Oriental fruit moth shows that not just one chemical but five must be present in a critical ratio in order to attract a male. There are releaser pheromones, which (like the honeybee sting) cause rapid behavioral responses, and primer pheromones, which affect physiology and trigger developmental changes; the most famous example of these is the pheromone that enables a queen bee to suppress ovarian development in worker bees. One of the most dramatic characteristics of pheromones is what the sociobiologist E. O. Wilson calls their "efficiency": they are among the most potent biologically active chemicals known, able to transmit complex information in tiny amounts over long distances for long periods. The Texas leaf-cutting ant, for instance, can point the way to food by leaving a trail some hundred yards long, which can be found and followed for months. The extreme dilution of the chemicals makes their identification exceedingly tedious for the researcher. The silkworm moth responds to only a few molecules of a certain chemical; hundreds of thousands of moths are needed to produce ten milligrams. Two hundred thousand fire ants must be sacrificed to collect a quarter of a milligram of a pheromone. Furthermore, many of the pheromones isolated so far have been new compounds.

Mammalian pheromones have proved much more difficult to identify than insect pheromones. Among mammals, pheromones have been clearly identified only in male pigs, in female marmosets and springboks, and in both male and female guinea pigs, hamsters, and mice—though it is thought that all mammals (with the possible exception of human beings) use them. In every species, it is the sex pheromones—with all they imply about behavior and free will, and the potential for use in husbandry—that are of the most interest. The typical exchange involves chemicals used by the female to attract the male; occasionally, the male will draw the female. Another insect example is that of an arrestant chemical found in certain mites and mosquitoes: it calls the male to an immature female and forces him to attend her until she is ready to mate. Pheromones exert a disturbing amount of control, fostering attraction, repulsion, a willingness to wait, to consort, to surrender. I was delighted when I first read of the male pig's pheromone: his salivary glands secrete a steroid related to testosterone, and when he spits in a sow's face she immediately takes up a spread-leg position, ripe for the taking. (This same steroid, it happens, is found in truffles.) But, being a mammal myself, the longer I considered the possibilities the more uncomfortable I became.

Much of what I know of pheromones I have learned from Bets Rasmussen. If she succeeds in isolating an elephant sex pheromone, it could be a turning point in the fight to restore and preserve the species. She talks of the possibility of chemical "fences" in the wild to attract elephants to preserves and hold them there, and of a stimulant to encourage breeding in zoos and facilitate sperm collection for artificial insemination. There is, too, she admits, the joy of solitary research: the voyage into the unknown and the delight of discovery. "Mammalian pheromones are just now being isolated," she explained. "Substances that were identified as pheromones in some of the early work have turned out to be impurities. Mammals are more complicated organisms than insects, and they have pheromones doing a variety of things. Even if you're thinking just sex pheromones, you have to separate the mating process into its components: attraction, pre-copulatory behavior, actual copulation. There may be more than one pheromone acting at each stage."

In 1976, Bets Rasmussen was raising two children while she did independent research on the interaction, in sharks and other primitive fish, of the brain and the cerebrospinal fluid. She lived in Pullman, Washington, where her husband, an atmospheric scientist, was teaching at Washington State University. In the lab one day, she met a biologist named Irven Buss, who was looking for an assistant.

"He said, 'You know, I've got this really interesting problem I'm working on. I've done a lot of work on elephant behavior and elephant reproduction. But I've always been interested in chemical communication.' This was a new term to me. So he started to tell me his ideas about temporal-gland secretion." She and Buss collaborated on the first analysis of the secretion. In 1979, the Rasmussens moved to Portland, where Bets's husband had an offer to work and teach at the Oregon Graduate Center. Bets received a faculty appointment without salary, giving her access to laboratories but no teaching duties. She was still principally occupied with fish, but as a last favor to Buss she visited the Washington Park Zoo and the elephants.

"The elephant keepers started to talk to me," she recalled, "and I said, 'You know, I'm really interested in this musth thing.' I got to like the elephant people, got to know them, and one day I met Dr. Schmidt." One of the first things Schmidt told her concerned the sniff tests and his suspicion that a pheromone was present in the urine. "I thought it was the most *fascinating* thing I'd ever heard in my whole life. Here was a problem that made everything I was doing with fish look like routine clinical chemistry."

She went to the chairman of the Chemistry Department at the Center, an organic chemist named G. Doyle Daves, and repeated what Schmidt had told her. Together, they began studying the urine of elephant cows in estrus, Daves doing the laboratory work of extracting compounds from the urine and Rasmussen the biological checks, recording the urine-testing reaction of the bulls to the laboratory samples. Their timing was based on Schmidt's blood data, and the keepers took responsibility for collecting the urine.

Urine collection changed the routine at the zoo in a permanent way. Whenever the designated cow of the day began to urinate, one of the keepers had to grab a bucket and race to catch the splattering stream. (There was no telling when this might occur. "Elephants can cross their legs till their eyeballs float," Roger Henneous says.) The keepers were lucky to collect twenty liters from a cow in her fertile period; Bets, admitting to a chronic fear of running out of elephant urine, still keeps gallons of it in her freezers at the Center.

A few months into the work of chemical extraction, Daves left the Center for Lehigh University, and Bets was alone, without funding. "I was absolutely devastated," she told me. "I was not trained as an organic chemist. I was a biochemist, which is very different. I had no choice—if I didn't do the lab work myself I'd have to drop the project." She began borrowing equipment and teaching herself to use it; she has since learned to repair it as well.

One of the central questions in pheromone research is that of transportation: how does the chemical signal move from, say, the female to the male, and how does the male perceive it? Most of the identified insect pheromones are dissipated on the wind in gaseous form. But mammals appear to have a more elaborate, intimate method. It is common, even daily, practice among mammal species for a male to check a female's secretion by sniffing and licking her urine, her genital mucus, and her saliva. Often a female will assist in the process by standing still, moving her tail, or even politely urinating a small amount nearby. The male accomplishes his testing in a very specific way, by a behavior known as flehmen. Classic flehmen is a grimace—an expression of bared teeth, curled upper lip, and open mouth. Both sexes of moose, giraffes, cattle, sheep, and goats, seeking information not only about fertility but also about status and identity, demonstrate classic flehmen. The curious expression, with its appearance of casual disdain, is thought to bring, by tongue and nostril movements, a bit of pheromone into the vomeronasal organ, a chemosensor present in almost every mammalian species and also in reptiles. (It is vestigial in human beings, with anatomical remnants visible in skull sections.) The vomeronasal organ is distinct from the olfactory system and is separately connected to the brain; in snakes, in fact, it is more highly developed than the sense of smell. (Eric Albone, a chemist at Bristol University, in England, thinks that tongue-flicking in snakes may be a kind of flehmen.) When a male flehmens a fertile female, he "tastes" her fertility with his vomeronasal organ. The taste stimulates him into mating; once the female has become pregnant, or has ceased to be fertile, she tastes different, and he will leave her alone.

It had been known for a long time that elephants had a vomeronasal organ, but little attention and less research had been devoted to it. When an elephant opens its mouth, pressing the trunk above the head and revealing its tunnel-like throat, two duct openings are visible in the roof of the mouth. Bets Rasmussen was able to get a good photograph of these pits when she noticed Packy out in the yard trying to pull down the rain gutter of the barn. She waited until he stretched his trunk to its limit, and then she snapped the picture; it was the first ever published of the duct openings.

The elephant's trunk, which is about eight feet long in a mature bull, has an astonishing number of uses. With its trunk, an elephant eats (hay, cigarette butts, a single ice cube, a half-dozen large carrots at once); sucks up water, as much as four liters at a time, and squirts it down its throat; digs, pulls up plants, or pulls down tree branches; fights; smells (an elephant can detect odors several miles away); bathes and dusts itself; caresses its kin. Elephants put their trunks in each other's mouths, and sometimes an elephant drapes its trunk over a tusk, as artlessly as a man drapes a suit coat over his arm. The elephant rubs its own eyes, scratches behind its ears, and snorkels while swimming. (They are strong swimmers.) Elephants also flehmen; this is what is happening when a bull checks a cow in a sniff test. But a clear understanding of the nature of the behavior was a long time in coming.

"Everyone knew that the males stuck their trunk tips in the female urine, but they didn't connect that behavior with the vomeronasal organ," Bets told me early one morning as we stood behind the fence overlooking the back elephant yard. This is her spot—a corner of dirt and scrub not far from a head-high pile of elephant manure, which was steaming in the spring fog. Here she has bioassayed over ten thousand samples of urine extractions, in every kind of weather, standing for hours at a time as a lone bull paces the sand. We were watching Tunga, who is normally a slow, rather dull animal. But today he was in the early stages of musth and restless; as soon as he spied us, he trotted over to the moat and stood opposite us, swaying from side to side, foot to foot. "That's one mad bull," Bets said, laughing. Tunga seemed to roll his head in indignation, and suddenly we were sprayed with wet sand, stinging and sharp.

Before Tunga was released into the yard, Bets had splashed six different samples along the newly washed concrete apron. One was a control—fresh urine from a cow who was not in estrus. The rest were new extractions. In the lab one day, she had shown me fifteen small flasks of liquid from the extraction process, each a different tint and with a different odor. She pulled the cork for No. 1, and I smelled a startlingly strong urine with a lingering, bitter reek. No. 15, the last in the line, was a very light coral color, with an aroma of cinnamon. Nos. 4, 5, and 6 were straw-colored and had the most surprising smell of all: elephants and hay. She laughed at my expression. "When I first smelled those, I was *sure* I'd found the pheromone," she said.

If a bull fails to respond to a particular sample, Bets doesn't know whether that means that the pheromone is not present or just that it is present in too small a quantity. On the other hand, if a bull responds with unusual vigor she has to steel herself against untoward optimism. "As you separate these compounds, you create novel substances," she told me. "The animal will often respond to them the first and second, and even the third, time you bioassay, simply because they *are* novel." Six years ago, she found a volatile long-chain hydrocarbon. It *felt*, she says, like a pheromone. It was a common chemical, available in quantity, and she bought a batch of it. "We got tremendous response. We had five or six flehmens in a row from the bull. We thought we had found the pheromone! We were all elated. The next day, there was a response, but it was less marked. The third day, there was virtually nothing. The fourth, no response. That's a pitfall in the work of others—they've only done their experiments a couple of times and then assumed they've found an active compound. So it was a valuable lesson."

Tunga paced the concrete apron, sniffing the air. Suddenly, his trunk straightened like an arrow; the single fingertip at the trunk's end flared, and he placed his nostrils flat against the wet surface. His jaw dropped open, and he held perfectly still for a moment, a sculpture of discovery and concentration. Then he deftly curled his trunk in upon itself, in a long and pretty oval, and pressed the tip against the two dark pits inside.

"Oh, that's a good one," Bets said. "I was a little worried about that sample." The extracts that pass the test are further purified in the lab and then sent to Dr. Terry Lee, a longtime colleague of Bets, who gauges their molecular weight using a mass spectrometer. Bets made a check on her clipboard, looking down only for an instant, and returned to watching Tunga. "I get so excited about this part of the work sometimes that I dream about it," she said. "I wake up and think, Gee, maybe tomorrow I'll get a flehmen on that particular peak." (She tends to refer to the samples as peaks, because this is how the various molecules show up in chromatographic analysis.) "The research wouldn't interest me half as much if I couldn't see the elephant do the flehmen."

Bets has become something of a connoisseur of flehmen, with an aesthetic appreciation of the different styles. Tunga, she told me, will shake his trunk to "clear his palate" between samples. The idea of elephant flehmen was for a long time unacceptable to many conservative biologists; they considered true flehmen a behavior limited to hoofed mammals, and possibly cats. Most mammalian species are now thought to exhibit some form of flehmen, but one reason it took so long for elephant flehmen to be recognized is the trunk. No other animal has one, so there are no analogies. Another reason is the speed of the gesture; while Tunga has a leisurely approach, Packy is fast—his trunk whips in and out of his mouth in a few seconds. Bets was immediately able to see the gesture for what it was because she was looking for a pheromone. She believed, because of the results of Schmidt's original sniff testing, that a pheromone had to be there. In turn, pheromone presence suggested flehmen, and so did a vomeronasal organ. In late 1981, after she became certain of the flehmen, and was able to obtain a series of photographs of the behavior, she submitted an article to *Science*. At first, she received what she refers to as a "scathing" review by the journal's referees. I was heavily criticized for having used only two bulls," she said. "I just drew on my knowledge of the literature and fought back." In July of 1982, the article was published, as a cover story, but the idea was not widely accepted for several years.

There is a constant interplay between olfaction—smelling the urine and, perhaps, the pheromone—and the perception based in the vomeronasal organ. (Eric Albone points out that we have no word for that perception.) But in the tiny concentrations used in the bioassays there is so little urine left that no noticeable odor remains. The perception is thought to be occurring entirely within the vomeronasal organ, long a mysterious place. In 1983, Bets had an opportunity to study one when Mike Schmidt made the difficult decision to euthanize Tuy Hoa, the Vietnamese gift of gratitude. Tuy Hoa had congenital skeletal problems and suffered from severe arthritic and foot pains. The zoo's only previous adult death had been Thonglaw's, and he had been buried, with enormous trouble, in an isolated spot on the grounds. ("The problem with a dead elephant is that you don't have the time for an autopsy which you might have with, say, a monkey," Schmidt told me. "You have ten thousand pounds of decaying flesh to deal with, and in a zoo any death is a very unpleasant situation, which everyone wants to get through as soon as possible." Tuy Hoa was "disarticulated" with chain saws and incinerated after an expeditious autopsy. Bets took Tuy Hoa's head and attempted to remove the vomeronasal organ, a cigar-shaped white tube about a foot long and tightly bound in the middle of the skull above the soft palate. She was only partly successful. A few years later, a circus elephant died suddenly in Portland, and again she managed to obtain the skull. She worked through the night in a cold-storage room, and in about eight hours had removed the vomeronasal organ almost intact. She began to prepare a paper with anatomical drawings.

This past summer, a colleague in Africa sent her the organ of a fetal African elephant, and she was able to work up comparisons. But questions remained. She was uncertain about how the organ connected to the nerves and glands, and exactly how it sat within the bone. Then there was another death in the Washington Park herd, when Susie apparently suffered a reaction to a routine drug.

"I'd just walked in the door from a trip," Bets recalled. "I was exhausted, and the phone rang. It was an opportunity I couldn't turn down, because there were probably five major questions I still had about the anatomy. With the circus elephant, my major objective had been to get as much of the organ out as quickly as I could, so that I could accurately determine the histology and cytology. Once I learned that Susie had been dead for four or five hours, I knew there was no point in looking for that. The thing to concentrate on was the anatomy. We can only speculate, on the basis of what we know from other animals, about what happens on the receptive side of the vomeronasal organ. You can't put a compound labeled with a fluorescein dye there and let the animal flehmen and then cut the skull apart to see how far up the vomeronasal organ the dye went. You can't do electrophysiological tests, so you can't know the response of the bipolar neurons inside the organ."

She could, however, map the anatomy. "I spent five days on Susie's skull, usually about eight hours a day," she said. "I went very, very slowly. The most fascinating thing is the enormous size of the sinuses. The elephant brain is back behind the ears, in line with the eyes, and all the stuff above that is sinus—incredibly honeycombed pockets. I dissected part of the skull with fine dissecting tools—the kind a neurosurgeon uses. In many places, I had to go through four inches of bone with a metal cutter. Then I would take photographs, and label the whole thing along the way."

She is not, however, immune to loss. The dissections were a strain. "I had to cut Tuy Hoa's trunk off. I'll never forget that. She had been dead three hours, but it felt as if I were killing her. With Susie, the eyes were there. Someone came and took the eyeballs out—I never could have done that. I would find it impossible to dissect Sunshine. I'd just say, 'Forget it.' But I guess if the guys are cutting them up for disposal, then I should be there getting the information, and I can't afford to be sentimental. If it was hard for me, it must have been *really* hard for Roger and Jay and Jim. I firmly believe in my own research. If I didn't believe in it, I would have quit about five years ago, because the last three or four years have been slow going. I can't believe I've been working so many years on this. That's one thing about working with elephants—you learn patience."

THE FECUNDITY OF the herd at the Washington Park Zoo masks the pressure on elephants in the wild, and captive breeding may be, as Mike Schmidt calls it, "the last hurrah" of Proboscidea. Schmidt continues to occupy himself with the ovulation cycle, but for several years he has taken his research in a particular direction—that of artificial insemination. The survival of the species can't be assured, he feels, by successful breeding in one herd, or even in several. The genetic pool is painfully small; he estimates that in the United States at this time there are 326 Asian cows and eighteen Asian bulls. And the Endangered Species Act has, since 1976, made the importation of Asian elephants virtually impossible.

"Artificial insemination is the best way to ensure the genetic variability of domestic elephants," he told me. "And it will also have implications for managing wild elephants. If you have a population of no more than five hundred elephants, they will sooner or later become extinct—though that sounds like a lot of elephants—because there's not enough genetic diversity. But if you take just six other animals every twenty years and inject them into that population it can go on forever. Where are you going to get those six unrelated animals? You're going to get them from your domesticated herds. But there are problems with A.I. in the case of elephants. If your timing is off, you've got a four-month wait. And elephant anatomy makes it difficult—you have to go four feet to get to the cervix. The route is circuitous—up, over, and down—and requires flexible fiber-optic tubing. Managing that and preserving the sperm adequately are going to take years and years of work."

Several months earlier, Schmidt had travelled to Thailand for a conference on elephant preservation and presented some of his research on artificial insemination. Another of his goals, he said, had been to persuade Asian elephant handlers to encourage their working bulls to breed. "I'm eager to collaborate with the Asians, because they have the numbers of animals," he told me. "Almost everything we've done, from the beginning, has been geared to practical application in the field. You could develop a terrific research method for inseminating elephants using stereomicroscopes and manipulation of embryos, or something, but so what? There might be only three places in the world that could do it. So how can we take the knowledge and turn it into a practical method to use on thousands of elephants? We can't save the Asian elephant single-handedly, even by building a monster zoo in America."

There is one profound problem to solve if artificial insemination does succeed, and that—once again—is musth. "Suppose A.I. is gloriously successful and you've got all these pregnant cows," Schmidt said. "Half the calves are going to be males. In ten years, most of them are going to be shot. It's not responsible to get into that situation—you have to have some way of dealing with surplus males. Some will be kept for breeding, but what are you going to do with the rest? Well, you can castrate them. They can be work elephants, they can be exhibit elephants. What about a little zoo in the Midwest with one elephant—an Asian cow that's never going to be bred? She should be in a social group, yet they've got room for only one elephant, and, in any case, they can't afford a group of cows. Well, they could have a neutered male instead—he's going to be a docile animal, easygoing, happy-go-lucky, imprinted on people. He doesn't need to be with other elephants, or to breed, to be happy."

The castration of elephants has until recently been a fatal proposition; the testes are lodged in a web of circulatory vessels near the kidneys, and mortality from the surgery used to approach 90 percent. In 1983, seeing the long-term need, Schmidt and several other veterinarians joined forces to solve the puzzle. The team has done six castrations so far, all on circus bulls facing execution as they matured and grew more dangerous. "We have yet to lose a bull," Schmidt told me. "We developed the surgical approach to the abdomen, and more understanding of the anatomy. And we know more about anesthesia now."

Schmidt is aware that some people consider all animal research exploitive. He is quick to point out that none of the elephant research at Washington Park contributes to human health; it is all for the benefit of the elephants themselves. "I think these animals' contributions will echo down the years," he said. "We always felt that way—that they were contributing to the preservation of their species. I tell them so—'Pet, you're making a contribution to your species.' She has more than paid her dues."

RECENTLY, I VISITED the elephant barn again, stopping first at the elephant museum next door, which opened in 1986 and is privately funded. It is a half-moon-shaped building filled with ceremonial helmets, paintings, and tusk rings—the trappings of the human relationship with all things elephantine. Its center-piece is the complete skeleton of a mastodon, on permanent loan from the Smithsonian Institution; it seemed unimposing here, so near the living thing. Then I walked over to watch the cows awhile, as they tossed hay about and rocked in place, their spongy feet compressing and springing back with every beat. Rama, back from the zoo in Tacoma only a few weeks and still nervous, was darting back and forth in a quarantine room, his trunk wild and fast. (Bets told me that when she splashed a sample of urine from Rosy, Rama's mother, on the freshly washed floor of the room he flehmened thirty-five times in a row.) Packy was in the crush, relaxed, downing carrots, seeming not to know—or care—that he couldn't walk out at will. Jay Haight took me right to the bull's gigantic, warm side. His trunk, as thick at its base as my torso and three times as long, snaked back to where I stood, questing for me. A wet print of his left forefoot had made a near-perfect circle on the concrete; Jay and I stood together inside it, with room to spare.

Roger Henneous was there, as he almost always is, his stained ranger's hat cocked back on his head, his feet spread wide on the damp, hay-covered floor. Behind him milled a wall of dusty gray. He talked about the research, and the keepers' efforts to help, no matter how great the inconvenience or the danger. A considerable amount of extra work is required of all the keepers, and much of it is dirty and difficult. "I have many times, over the years, found myself cussing and stomping my feet, wondering, Goddammit, why couldn't I have taken up rabbits?" he said, with a glint in his eye. "In the overall scheme of things, our efforts here may not make a nickel's worth of difference. Not in the big real world out there. But no other breeding program like this one exists. If we can't—or won't—do the work, who will? We have the facilities, and we have the animals. If Betsey isolates and identifies the pheromone, then, theoretically, it can be synthesized. If it can be synthesized, it could be used to lure wild elephants from inhabited areas—essentially trick them out of harm's way. It could save a lot of bulls in Asia from getting the lead pellet."

Down the hall, Belle has planted her face against the crack of a door. Behind her in the room is a trio of younger cows. The elephant guards the tree of life; the elephant worships the moon and stars. Elephants were once supposed to have had wings. Belle greets me with a grim stare, blocking me like a house matron uncertain whether I'm fit to be let in. I stand quietly for the inspection. Her trunk slides up, loose and confident, and rapidly slips under my collar, through my hair, down my sleeve, my pant leg. She's close, her trunk is enormous, the two huffing nostrils at the end strangely naked and pink, vacuuming in my smell, my volatiles, myself. All the while, she fixes her moist brown eye on mine. I remember—because I can't forget—photographs I've seen of butchered elephants. What was left of one bull knelt in apparent calm. The body, its head missing, was eerily still, as though waiting.

John Donne called the elephant "Nature's great masterpiece ... the only harmless great thing." As I submit to Belle's precise, intelligent examination, I remember that and the dead elephant's calm, and look straight back into her cautious and curious eye.

New Yorker, January 23, 1989

When I began writing an essay about a scientist's long search for a mysterious pheromone, I was given the keys to the kingdom: access to the elephant herd at what is now called the Oregon Zoo. The story felt like a gift—it was a great problem and it gave me a chance to go inside, to be close to animals I prize greatly.

I'm not particularly interested in the campaign to stop zoos from keeping elephants in captivity. I want them to be treated well, preferably in open spaces with the chance to socialize and wander in the most natural way. But we've been too busy killing wild elephants and destroying their habitat to stop keeping captive herds. That this animal could disappear from the Earth is a tragedy beyond words for me. Imagine a world without elephants: I can hardly think about it.

Burning For Daddy

EVERY WINTER NIGHT OF MY CHILDHOOD, MY FATHER built a fire. Each element of the evening's fire was treated with care—with the caress of the careful man. The wood, the wood box, the grate, the coal, black poker, and shovel: he touched these more often than he touched me. I would hold back, watching, and when the fire was lit plant myself before it and fall into a gentle dream. No idea was too strange or remote before the fire, no fantasy of shadow and light too bizarre.

But for all the long hours I spent before his fires, for all the honey-colored vapors that rose like smoke from that hearth, these aren't the fires of memory. They aren't my father's fires. When I remember fire, I remember houses burning, scorched and flooded with flame, and mills burning, towers of fire leaping through the night to the lumber nearby like so much kindling, and cars burning, stinking and black and waiting to blow. I loved those fires with a hot horror, always daring myself to step closer, feel their heat, touch.

My father is a fireman. My submission to fire is lamentably obvious. But there is more than love here, more than jealousy— more than Electra's unwilling need. It is a fundamental lure, a seduction of my roots and not my limbs. I am propelled toward fire, and the dual draw of fascination and fear, the urge to walk into and at the same time conquer fire, is like the twin poles of the hermaphrodite. I wanted to be a fireman before, and after, I wanted to be anything else.

Firemen are big, brawny, young, and smiling creatures. They sit in the fire hall with its high ceilings and cold concrete floors and dim corners, waiting, ready. Firemen have a perfume of readiness. They wash their shiny trucks and hang the long white hoses from rods to dangle and dry. And when the alarm rings, firemen turn into hurrying bodies that know where to step and what to do, each with a place and duty, without excess motion. Firemen wear heavy coats and big black boots and hard helmets. They can part crowds. They are calescent and virile like the fire, proud, reticent, and most content when moving; firemen have their own rules, and they break glass, make messes, climb heights, and drive big loud trucks very fast.

Forgive me; I am trying to show the breadth of this fable. I wanted to be a fireman so much that it didn't occur to me for a long time that they might not let me. Fires marked me; I got too close. The hearth fire was my first and best therapist, the fire-dreams were happy dreams of destruction and ruin. The andiron was the ground, the logs our house, and each black space between the logs a window filled with helpless people, my father and mother and siblings. The fire was the world and I was outside and above, listening to their calls for rescue from the darting blaze, and sometimes I would allow them to escape and sometimes not, never stirring from my meditative pose. If I felt uncharitable, I could watch the cinders crumble from the oak and cedar like bodies falling to the ground below and the fire turn to ashes while I, the firefighter, sat back safe and dear and cool.

At odd times—during dinner, late at night—the alarm would sound, and my father would leap up, knocking dogs and small children aside as he ran from the house. I grew up used to surprise. He was a bulky man, and his pounding steps were heavy and important in flight; I slipped aside when he passed by.

The fire department was volunteer, and every fireman something else as well. My father was a teacher. We had a private radio set in the house, and we heard alarms before the town at large did. It was part of the privilege of fire. Before the siren blew on the station two blocks away, the radio in the hallway sang its high-pitched plea. He was up and gone in seconds, a sentence chopped off in mid-word, a bite of food dropped to the plate. Squeal, halt, go: I was used to the series; it was part of our routine.

Then my mother would stop what she was doing and turn down the squeal and listen to the dispatcher on the radio. His voice, without face or name, was one of the most familiar voices in my home, crowned with static and interruptions. My mother knew my father's truck code and could follow his progress in a jumble of terse male voices, one-word questions, first names, numbers, and sometimes hasty questions and querulous shouts. She stood in the hallway with one hand on the volume and her head cocked to listen; she shushed us with a stern tension. She would not betray herself, though I knew and didn't care; in the harsh wilderness of childhood, my father's death in a fire would have been a great and terrible thing. It would have been an honor.

The town siren was a broad foghorn call that rose and fell in a long ululation, like the call of a bird. We could hear it anywhere in town, everyone could, and if I was away from our house I would run to the station. (I had to race the cars and pickups of other volunteer firemen, other teachers, and the butcher, the undertaker, an editor from the local newspaper, grinding out of parking lots and driveways all over town in a hail of pebbles.) If I was quick enough and lucky enough, I could stand to one side and watch the flat doors fly up, the trucks pull out one after the other covered with clinging men, and see my father driving by. He drove a short, stout pumper, and I waved and called to him high above my head. He never noticed I was there, not once; it was as though he ceased to be my father when he became a fireman. The whistle of the siren was the whistle of another life, and he would disappear around a corner, face pursed with concentration, and be gone.

Oh, for a fire at night in the winter, the cold nocturnal sky, the pairing of flame and ice. It stripped life bare. I shared a room with my sister, a corner room on the second floor with two windows looking in their turn on the intersection a house away. The fire station was around that comer and two blocks east, a tall white block barely visible through the barren trees. Only the distant squeal of the alarm downstairs woke us, that and the thud of his feet and the slam of the back door; before we could open the curtains and windows for a gulp of frigid air, we'd hear the whine of his pickup and the crunch of its tires on the crust of snow. The night was clear and brittle and raw, and the tocsin called my father to come out. Come out, come out to play, it sang, before my mother turned the sound off. He rushed to join the hot and hurried race to flames. We knelt at the windows under the proximate, twinkling stars, in light pajamas, shivering, and following the spin of lights on each truck—red, blue, red, blue, red—flashing across houses, cars, faces. We could follow the colored spin and figure out where the fire must be and how bad and wonder out loud if he'd come back.

There were times when he didn't return till morning. I would come downstairs and find him still missing, my mother sleepy-eyed and making toast, and then he would trudge in. Ashen and weary, my father, beat, his old flannel pajamas dusted with the soot that crept through the big buckles of his turnout coat, and smelling of damp, sour smoke.

I SHOULD BE a fire setter. I should be that peculiar kind of addict, hooked on stolen matches and the sudden conflagration in mother's underwear and father's shoes. There are plenty of them, many children, thieving flame and setting its anarchic soul free in unexpected places. But I lack that incendiary urge; my Electra is more subtle, the knotty recesses of my own desires cunning even to me.

"What we first learn about fire is that we must not touch it," Gaston Bachelard writes in his book *The Psychoanalysis of Fire*, in the course of explaining the Prometheus complex that the prohibition against fire creates. I talk about my father infrequently, always with hunger and anger; I build fires almost every winter night. But I've never built a wrong fire, and I worry over flammables like a mother hen. I'm scared of being burned and of all of fire's searing lesions. I class it with the other primitive, deadly joys: the sea deeps and flying—the runaway edge of control.

I fear one particular fire. My father was also an electrician, a tinkerer of small appliances. I am wary of outlets and wires of all kinds, which seem tiny and potent and unpredictable; the occult and silent river of electrical fire racing behind the walls can keep me awake nights. Electricity is just another flame, but flame refined. (In this way it is like alcohol: literally distilled.) Not long ago I put a pot of water to boil on my stove, and a little sloshed over; suddenly a roaring arc of electricity shot from beneath the pot and curved back upon itself. The kitchen air filled with the acrid smoke of burning insulation and the crackling, sputtering sound of short circuits, and I didn't have the slightest idea what to do. I wanted my father to put it out, and he was three hundred miles away. It seemed the most untenable betrayal, my stove lunging out at me in such a capricious way. It seemed *mean*; that arc of blue-white current burned down my adulthood.

Prometheus stole more than fire; he stole the *knowledge* of fire, the hard data of combustion. I wanted all my father's subtle art. I wanted the mystery of firewood and the burning, animated chain saw, the tree's long fall, the puzzle of splitting hardwood with a wedge and maul placed just so in the log's curving grain. I wanted to know the differences of quality in smoke, where to lay the ax on the steaming roof, how the kindling held up the heavy logs. What makes creosote ignite? How to know the best moment to flood a fire? What were the differences between oak and cedar, between asphalt and shake? And most of all I wanted to know how to go into the fire, what virtue was used when he set his face and pulled the rim of his helmet down and ran inside the burning house. It was arcane, obscure, and unaccountably male, this fire business. He built his fires piece by piece, lit each with a single match, and once the match was lit I was privileged to watch, hands holding chin and elbows propped on knees, in the posture Bachelard calls essential to the "physics of reverie" delivered by fire.

I build fires now. I like the satisfying scritch-scratch of the little broom clearing ash. I find it curious that I don't build very good fires; I'm hasty and I don't want to be taught. But at last, with poorly seasoned wood and too much paper, I make the fire go, and then the force it exerts is exactly the same. That's something about fire: all fire is the same, every ribbon of flame the same thing, whatever that thing may be. There is that fundamental quality, fire as an irreducible element at large; fire is fire is fire no matter what or when or where. The burning house is just the hearth freed. And the fire-trance stays the same, too. I still sit cross-legged and dreaming, watching the hovering flies of light that float before me in a cloud, as fireflies do.

How I wanted to be a fireman when I grew up. I wanted this for a long time. To become a volunteer fireman was expected of a certain type of man—the town's steady, able-bodied men, men we could depend on. As I write this I feel such a tender pity for that little, wide-eyed girl, a free-roaming tomboy wandering a little country town and friend to all the firemen. I really did expect them to save me a place.

Every spring we had a spring parade. I had friends lucky enough to ride horses, others only lucky enough to ride bikes. But I rode the pumper and my father drove slowly, running the lights and siren at every intersection and splitting our ears with the noise. We had firemen's children perched on the hoses neatly laid in pleated rows, bathed in sunlight, tossing candy to the spectators as though, at parade's end, we wouldn't have to get down and leave the truck alone again.

He would take me to the station. I saw forbidden things, firemen's lives.

On the first floor was the garage with its row of trucks. Everything shivered with attention, ripe for work: the grunt of a pumper, the old truck, antique and polished new. And the Snorkel. When I was very small, a building burned because it was too high for the trucks to reach a fire on its roof; within a year the town bought the Snorkel, a basher of a truck, long, white, sleek, with a folded hydraulic ladder. The ladder opened and lifted like a praying mantis rising from a twig, higher and higher.

Above the garage was the real station, a single room with a golden floor and a wall of windows spilling light. The dispatcher lived there, the unmarried volunteers could bunk there if they liked; along one wall was a row of beds. No excess there, no redundancy, only a cooler of soda, a refrigerator full of beer, a shiny bar, a card table, a television. I guess I held my father's hand while he chatted with one of the men. In the corner I saw a hole, a hole in the floor, and in the center of the hole the pole plunging down; I peeked over the edge and followed the light along the length of the shining silver pole diving to the floor below.

I remember one singular Fourth of July. It was pitch dark on the fairgrounds, in a dirt field far from the exhibition buildings and the midway. Far from anything. It was the middle of nothing and nowhere out there on a moonless night, strands of dry grass tickling my legs, bare below my shorts. There was no light at all but a flashlight in one man's hand, no sound but the murmurs of the men talking to one another in the dark, moving heavy boxes with mumbles and grunts, laughing very quietly with easy laughs. My father was a silhouette among many, tall and black against a near-black sky. Then I saw a sparkle and heard the fuse whisper up its length and strained to see the shape of it, the distance. And I heard the whump of the shell exploding and the high whistle of its flight; and when it blew, its empyreal flower filled the sky. They flung one rocket after another, two and four at once, boom! flash! One shell blew too low and showered us with sparks, no one scared but smiling at the glowworms wiggling through the night as though the night were earth and we the sky and they were rising with the rain.

ONLY RECENTLY HAVE I seen how much more occurred, hidden beneath the surface of his life. I presumed too much, the way all children do. It wasn't only lack of sleep that peeled my father's face bald in a fire's dousing. He hates fire. Hates burning mills; they last all night and the next day like balefires signaling a battle. He hated every falling beam that shot arrows of flame and the sheets of fire that curtain rooms. And bodies: I heard only snatches of stories, words drifting up the stairs in the middle of the night after a fire as he talked to my mother in the living room in the dark. Pieces of bodies stuck to bedsprings like steaks to a grill, and, once, the ruin of dynamite. When my mother died I asked about cremation, and he flung it away with a meaty hand and chose a solid, airtight coffin. He sees the stake in fire. He suffered the fear of going in.

I was visiting my father last year at Christmastime. There are always fires at Christmastime, mostly trees turning to torches and chimneys flaring like Roman candles. And sure enough, the alarm sounded early in the evening, the same bright squeal from the same radio, for a flue fire. There have been a thousand flue fires in his life. (Each one is different, he tells me.)

As it happened, this time it was our neighbor's flue, across the street, on Christmas Eve, and I put shoes on the kids and we dashed across to watch the circus, so fortunately near. The trucks maneuvered their length in the narrow street, bouncing over curbs and closing in, and before the trucks stopped the men were off and running, each with a job, snicking open panels, slipping levers, turning valves. We crept inside the lines and knelt beside the big wheels of the pumper, unnoticed. The world was a bustle of men with terse voices, the red and blue lights spinning round, the snaking hose erect with pressure. The men were hepped up, snappy with the brisk demands. And the house—the neighbor's house I'd seen so many times before had gone strange, a bud blooming fire, a ribbon of light, behind a dark window. Men went in, faces down.

My father doesn't go in anymore. He's gotten too old, and the rules have changed; young men arrive, old men watch and wait. He still drives truck. He lives for it, for the history and the books, his models, the stories, meetings, card games. But he's like a rooster plucked; I have a girlish song for Daddy, but I sing it too far away for him to hear.

I wanted to feel the hot dry cheeks of fever and roast with the rest of them. I wanted to go in, and I kept on wanting to long after my father and the others told me I couldn't be a fireman because I wasn't a man. I wanted to be the defender, to have the chance to do something inarguably good, pit myself against the blaze. I wanted it long after I grew up and became something else altogether, and I want it still.

"That which has been licked by fire has a different taste in the mouths of men," writes Bachelard. He means food, but when I read that I thought of men, firemen, and how men licked by fire have a different taste to me.

I live in a city now, and the firefighters aren't volunteers. They're college graduates in Fire Science, and a few are women, smaller than the men but just as tough, women who took the steps I wouldn't—or couldn't—take. Still, I imagine big, brawny men sitting at too-small desks in little rooms lit with fluorescent lights, earnestly taking notes. They hear lectures on the chemistry of burning insulation, exponential curves of heat expansion, the codes of blueprint. They make good notes in small handwriting on lined, white paper, the pens little in their solid hands.

Too much muscle and nerve in these men and women both, these firemen; they need alarms, demands, heavy loads to carry up steep stairs. They need fires; the school desks are trembling, puny things, where they listen to men like my father, weary with the work of it, describing the secrets of going in.

Harper's, January 1990

My father was a high school industrial arts teacher—wood shop, metal shop, welding, electronics. But when people ask me what my father did for a living, I almost always say, "He was a firefighter." Fire was one of the most powerful sirens of my childhood, representing a world of danger, power, mystery. I thought that getting close to fire would get me close to my distant and difficult father. It didn't work.

I disliked Harper's *title for this piece, which was "Bound Upon a Wheel of Fire."*

Gentleman Caller

OUR LIVES LIKE BOOKS, SPREAD FLAT WITH DOG-EARED disrespect. But the corners, turned down, torn, are signals of attention, too.

The phone rings. "Would you like to hear me come?" he whispers, and "Oh" is all I mumble in return. "It's you." He waits until the full, deep, dark of sleep to call; he waits to catch me with his hot surprise, to pull me from my moment into his, where things can't wait. I exhale dreams; he begins to speak.

"Do you know what I have in my hand?" Questions, I think, so many questions. "Would you like to touch it, too?" I'm constrained by dark, he knows this; I'm shivering in a chilly room, and he is—nearby, so near, whispering my name with sly, blue hopes. He knows my name; he calls me by my given name in odd, close times like these. So slow and whiskered; I can still smell the dark aroma of my sheets. I wonder what I had been dreaming, why my palm on the telephone is damp. What is love, I think, but listening?

At first I played the critic. I was cool and unimpressed. I was unmoved. He seemed so obvious, so knowing. Derivative. I could count the gimmicks, even when they worked, hear the ticking of deliberate device behind his words. I was not willing. I had heard it all before.

"I want to kiss your pussy," he says, all hissing consonants and short, dull vowels. Don't try so hard, I think. Don't let the reader hear your hurry; don't be a slave to slang. All those tricks of confidence (My name! Of all things!). All those sudden shifts of plot, dramatic entrances and exits. So it went, night after night, the sharp cry of the phone and my sleepy alarm, his repetitions. And me, the gentle critic, only half-impatient.

Practice: he got better. I began to appreciate his gift. He learned to wrap the story up, the short-short type so hard to master, boom boom boom, in, out, done all at once. I was impressed. Here was the tale: coarse, suggestive breath, the thin whisper of my name coupled to his dreams, the wish for peace, for hope, for something swollen coddled within his hand so bold and rude. "Would you like to touch it, too?"

I get my robe and pull up a chair and let him play it out word for word. Then there is only silence on the line. "Go on," I say. "Tell me more." He tries to tell me how it feels, to struggle with these devil words. I'm bored by that. We're all just waiting our turns, comparing stories. It's only his story I want. Stories in the full, deep, dark which come out hard or false—and sometimes work like magic, the words filter through the air above our skin, spun sugar hanging in the air like webs. Cry out into the world, cry out chapter and verse. All the good stories have been told; it isn't plot we worry over here, but voice. Dirty jokes and pleas for God are all the same. I sit; he calls to me for less, for this, for more.

"You want me in your mouth," he says. "You want me in your mouth." And there is a tiny query there, a catch and rise in the final word. Of course he's right, I do, I do, but my mouth is where he is. Right here in the dark between my teeth and tongue. He can only hear my breath tumbling down the wire. I take the telephone between my legs, rub the cool receiver along my thigh, let him hear the rustle of the downy hair. In the distance I can hear him moan, the build of word on word, scene on scene, that perfect, careful construction of the story to its climax.

He talks, I'm there, his flavorful, imaginary me, his reader, he with no one to sleep beside and so many words, and all he can do is pick up the phone and make his impolitic plea, to one reader after another, and another, all night long.

Zyzzyva, Fall 1991

I did receive a number of what you could call obscene calls for a while. At first, I was alarmed, but one evening I suddenly understood them as story itself—as an attempt to explain something that words can only partly say. It took all the fear away and made my caller human again, and I felt a surprising sympathy for his struggle to articulate.

The Weight

I DON'T KNOW HOW MUCH I WEIGH THESE DAYS, THOUGH I can make a good guess. For years I'd known that number, sometimes within a quarter pound, known how it changed from day to day and hour to hour. I want to weigh myself now; I lean toward the scale in the next room, imagine standing there, lining up the balance. But I don't do it. Going this long, starting to break the scale's spell—it's like waking up suddenly sober.

By the time I was sixteen years old I had reached my adult height of five feet six inches and weighed 164 pounds. I weighed 164 pounds before and after a healthy pregnancy. I assume I weigh about the same now; nothing significant seems to have happened to my body, this same old body I've had all these years. I usually wear a size 14, a common clothing size for American women. On bad days I think my body looks lumpy and misshapen. On my good days, which are more frequent lately, I think I look plush and strong; I think I look like a lot of women whose bodies and lives I admire.

I'm not sure when the word *fat* first sounded pejorative to me, or when I first applied it to myself. My grandmother was a petite woman, the only one in my family. She stole food from other people's plates, and hid the debris of her own meals so that no one would know how much she ate. My mother was a size 14, like me, all her adult life; we shared clothes. She fretted endlessly over food scales, calorie counters, and diet books. She didn't want to quit smoking because she was afraid she would gain weight, and she worried about her weight until she died of cancer five years ago. Dieting was always in my mother's way, always there in the conversations above my head, the dialogue of stocky women. But I was strong and healthy and didn't pay too much attention to my weight until I was grown.

It probably wouldn't have been possible for me to escape forever. It doesn't matter that whole human epochs have celebrated big men and women, because the brief period in which I live does not; since I was born, even the voluptuous calendar girl has gone. Today's models, the women whose pictures I see constantly, unavoidably, grow more minimal by the day. When I berate myself for not looking like—whomever I think I should look like that day, I don't really care that no one looks like that. I don't care that Michelle Pfeiffer doesn't look like the photographs I see of Michelle Pfeiffer. I want to look—think I should look—like the photographs. I want her little miracles: the makeup artists, photographers, and computer imagers who can add a mole, remove a scar, lift the breasts, widen the eyes, narrow the hips, flatten the curves. The final product is what I see, have seen my whole adult life. And I've seen this: even when big people become celebrities, their weight is constantly remarked upon and scrutinized; their successes seem always to be *in spite of* their weight. I thought my successes must be, too.

I feel myself expand and diminish from day to day, sometimes from hour to hour. If I tell someone my weight, I change in their eyes: I become bigger or smaller, better or worse, depending on what that number, my weight, means to them. I know many men and women, young and old, gay and straight, who look fine, whom I love to see and whose faces and forms I cherish, who despise themselves for their weight. For their ordinary, human bodies. They and I are simply bigger than we think we should be. We always talk about weight in terms of gains and losses, and don't wonder at the strangeness of the words. In trying always to lose weight, we've lost hope of simply being seen for ourselves.

My weight has never actually affected anything—it's never seemed to mean anything one way or the other to how I lived. Yet for the last ten years I've felt quite bad about it. After a time, the number on the scale became my totem, more important than my experience—it was layered, metaphorical, metaphysical, and it had bewitching power. I thought if I could change that number I could change my life.

In my mid-twenties I started secretly taking diet pills. They made me feel strange, half-crazed, vaguely nauseated. I lost about twenty-five pounds, dropped two sizes, and bought new clothes. I developed rituals and taboos around food, ate very little, and continued to lose weight. For a long time afterward I thought it only coincidental that with every passing week I also grew more depressed and irritable.

I could recite the details, but they're remarkable only for being so common. I lost more weight until I was rather thin, and then I gained it all back. It came back slowly, pound by pound, in spite of erratic and melancholy and sometimes frantic dieting, dieting I clung to even though being thin had changed nothing, had meant nothing to my life except that I was thin. Looking back I remember blinding moments of shame and lightning-bright moments of clearheadedness, which inevitably gave way to rage at the time I'd wasted—rage that eventually would become, once again, self-disgust and the urge to lose weight. So it went, until I weighed exactly what I'd weighed when I began.

I USED TO be attracted to the sharp angles of the chronic diet-er—the caffeine-wild, chain-smoking, skinny women I see some-times. I considered them a pinnacle not of beauty but of will. Even after I gained back my weight, I wanted to be like that, controlled and persevering, live that underfed life so unlike my own rather sensual and disorderly existence. I felt I should always be dieting, for the dieting of it; dieting had become a rule, a given, a constant. Every ordinary value is distorted in this lens. I felt guilty for not being completely absorbed in my diet, for getting distracted, for not caring enough all the time. The fat person's character flaw is a lack of narcissism. She's let herself go.

So I would begin again—and at first it would all seem so ... easy. Simple arithmetic. After all, 3,500 calories equal one pound of fat—so the books and articles by the thousands say. I would calculate how long it would take to achieve the magic number on the scale, to succeed, to win. All past failures were suppressed. If 3,500 calories equal one pound, all I needed to do was cut 3,500 calories out of my intake every week. The first few days of a new diet would be colored with a sense of control—organization and planning, power over the self. Then the basic futile misery took over.

I would weigh myself with foreboding, and my weight would determine how went the rest of my day, my week, my life. When 3,500 calories didn't equal one pound lost after all, I figured it was my body that was flawed, not the theory. One friend, who had tried for years to lose weight following prescribed diets, made what she called "an amazing discovery." The real secret to a diet, she said, was that you had to be willing to be hungry *all the time*. You had to eat even less than the diet allowed.

I believed that being thin would make me happy. Such a pernicious, enduring belief. I lost weight and wasn't happy and saw that elusive happiness disappear in a vanishing point, requiring more—more self-disgust, more of the misery of dieting. Knowing all that I know now about the biology and anthropology of weight, knowing that people naturally come in many shapes and sizes, knowing that diets are bad for me and won't make me thin—sometimes none of this matters. I look in the mirror and think: Who am I kidding? *I've got to do something about myself.* Only then will this vague discontent disappear. Then I'll be loved.

FOR AGES HUMANS believed that the body helped create the personality, from the humors of Galen to W. H. Sheldon's somatotypes. Sheldon distinguished between three templates—endomorph, mesomorph, and ectomorph—and combined them into hundreds of variations with physical, emotional, and psychological characteristics. When I read about weight now, I see the potent shift in the last few decades: the modern culture of dieting is based on the idea that the personality creates the body. Our size must be in some way voluntary, or else it wouldn't be subject to change. A lot of my misery over my weight wasn't about how I looked at all. I was miserable because I believed I was bad, not my body. I felt truly reduced then, reduced to being just a body and nothing more.

Fat is perceived as an act rather than a thing. It is anti-social, and curable through the application of social controls. Even the feminist revisions of dieting, so powerful in themselves, pick up the theme: the hungry, empty heart; the woman seeking release from sexual assault, or the man from the loss of the mother, through food and fat. Fat is now a symbol not of the personality but of the soul—the cluttered, neurotic, immature soul.

Fat people eat for "mere gratification," I read, as though no one else does. Their weight is intentioned, they simply eat "too much," their flesh is lazy flesh. Whenever I went on a diet, eating became cheating. One pretzel was cheating. Two apples instead of one was cheating—a large potato instead of a small, carrots instead of broccoli. It didn't matter which diet I was on; diets have failure built in, failure is in the definition. Every substitution—even carrots for broccoli—was a triumph of desire over will. When I dieted, I didn't feel pious just for sticking to the rules. I felt condemned for the act of eating itself, as though my hunger were never normal. My penance was to not eat at all.

My attitude toward food became quite corrupt. I came, in fact, to subconsciously believe food itself was corrupt. Diet books often distinguish between "real" and "unreal" hunger, so that *correct* eating is hollowed out, unemotional. A friend of mine who thinks of herself as a compulsive eater says she feels bad only when she eats for pleasure. "Why?" I ask and she says, "Because I'm eating food I don't need." A few years ago I might have admired that. Now I try to imagine a world where we eat only food we need, and it seems inhuman. I imagine a world devoid of holidays and wedding feasts, wakes and reunions, a unique shared joy. "What's wrong with eating a cookie because you like cookies?" I ask her, and she hasn't got an answer. These aren't rational beliefs any more than the unnecessary pleasure of ice cream is rational. Dieting presumes pleasure to be an insignificant, or at least malleable, human motive.

I felt no joy in being thin—it was just work, something I had to do. But when I began to gain back the weight, I felt despair. I started reading about the "recidivism" of dieting. I wondered if I had myself to blame not only for needing to diet in the first place but for dieting itself, the weight inevitably regained. I joined organized weight loss programs, spent a lot of money, listened to lectures I didn't believe on quack nutrition, ate awful, processed diet foods. I sat in groups and applauded people who'd lost a half pound, feeling smug because I'd lost a pound and a half. I felt ill much of the time, found exercise increasingly difficult, cried often. And I thought that if I could only lose a little weight, everything would be all right.

When I say to someone, "I'm fat," I hear, "Oh, no! You're not fat! You're just—" What? Plump? Big-boned? Rubenesque? I'm just not thin. That's crime enough. I began this story by stating my weight. I said it all at once, trying to forget it and take away its power, I said it to be done being scared. Doing so, saying it out loud like that, felt like confessing a mortal sin. I have to bite my tongue not to seek reassurance, not to defend myself, not to plead. I see an old friend for the first time in years, and she comments on how much my fourteen-year-old son looks like me—"except, of course, he's not chubby." "Look who's talking," I reply, through clenched teeth. This pettiness is never far away; concern with my weight evokes the smallest, meanest parts of me. I look at another woman passing on the street and think, "At least I'm not that fat."

Recently I was talking with a friend who is naturally slender about a mutual acquaintance who is quite large. To my surprise my friend reproached this woman because she had seen her eating a cookie at lunchtime. "How is she going to lose weight that way?" my friend wondered. When you are as fat as our acquaintance is, you are primarily, fundamentally, seen as fat. It is your essential characteristic. There are so many presumptions in my friend's casual, cruel remark. She assumes that this woman should diet all the time—and that she can. She pronounces whole categories of food to be denied her. She sees her unwillingness to behave in this externally prescribed way, even for a moment, as an act of rebellion. In his story "A Hunger Artist," Kafka writes that the guards of the fasting man were "usually butchers, strangely enough." Not so strange, I think.

I know that the world, even if it views me as overweight (and I'm not sure it really does), clearly makes a distinction between me and this very big woman. I would rather stand with her and not against her, see her for all she is besides fat. But I know our experiences aren't the same. My thin friend assumes my fat friend is unhappy because she is fat: therefore, if she loses weight she will be happy. My fat friend has a happy marriage and family and a good career, but insofar as her weight is a source of misery, I think she would be much happier if she could eat her cookie in peace, if people would shut up and leave her weight alone. But the world never lets up when you are her size; she cannot walk to the bank without risking insult. Her fat is seen as perverse bad manners. I have no doubt she would be rid of the fat if she could be. If my left-handedness invited the criticism her weight does, I would want to cut that hand off.

IN THESE LAST several years I seem to have had an infinite number of conversations about dieting. They are really all the same conversation—weight is lost, then weight is gained back. This repetition finally began to sink in. Why did everyone sooner or later have the same experience? (My friend who had learned to be hungry all the time gained back all the weight she had lost and more, just like the rest of us.) Was it really our bodies that were flawed? I began reading the biology of weight more carefully, reading the fine print in the endless studies. There is, in fact, a preponderance of evidence disputing our commonly held assumptions about weight.

The predominant biological myth of weight is that thin people live longer than fat people. The truth is far more complicated. (Some deaths of fat people attributed to heart disease seem actually to have been the result of radical dieting.) If health were our real concern, it would be dieting we questioned, not weight. The current ideal of thinness has never been held before, except as a religious ideal; the underfed body is the martyr's body. Even if people can lose weight, maintaining an artificially low weight for any period of time requires a kind of starvation. Lots of people are naturally thin, but for those who are not, dieting is an unnatural act; biology rebels. The metabolism of the hungry body can change inalterably, making it ever harder and harder to stay thin. I think chronic dieting made me gain weight—not only pounds, but fat. This equation seemed so strange at first that I couldn't believe it. But the weight I put back on after losing was much more stubborn than the original weight. I had lost it by taking diet pills and not eating much of anything at all for quite a long time. I haven't touched the pills again, but not eating much of anything no longer works.

When Oprah Winfrey first revealed her lost weight, I didn't envy her. I thought, She's in trouble now. I knew, I was certain, she would gain it back; I believed she was biologically destined to do so. The tabloid headlines blamed it on a cheeseburger or mashed potatoes; they screamed OPRAH PASSES 200 POUNDS, and I cringed at her misery and how the world wouldn't let up, wouldn't leave her alone, wouldn't let her be anything else. How dare the world do this to anyone? I thought, and then realized I did it to myself.

The "Ideal Weight" charts my mother used were at their lowest acceptable-weight ranges in the 1950s, when I was a child. They were based on sketchy and often inaccurate actuarial evidence, using, for the most part, data on northern Europeans and allowing for the most minimal differences in size for a population of less than half a billion people. I never fit those weight charts, I was always just outside the pale. As an adult, when I would join an organized diet program, I accepted their version of my Weight Goal as gospel, knowing it would be virtually impossible to reach. But reach I tried; that's what one does with gospel. Only in the last few years have the weight tables begun to climb back into the world of the average human. The newest ones distinguish by gender, frame, and age. And suddenly I'm not off the charts anymore. I have a place.

A man who is attracted to fat women says, "I actually have less specific physical criteria than most men. I'm attracted to women who weigh 170 or 270 or 370. Most men are only attracted to women who weigh between 100 and 135. So who's got more of a fetish?" We look at fat as a problem of the fat person. Rarely do the tables get turned, rarely do we imagine that it might be the viewer, not the viewed, who is limited. What the hell is wrong with them, anyway? Do they believe everything they see on television?

My friend Phil, who is chronically and almost painfully thin, admitted that in his search for a partner he finds himself prejudiced against fat women. He seemed genuinely bewildered by this. I didn't jump to reassure him that such prejudice is hard to resist. What I did was bite my tongue at my urge to be reassured by him, to be told that I, at least, wasn't fat. That over the centuries humans have been inclined to prefer extra flesh rather than the other way around seems unimportant. All we see now tells us otherwise. Why does my kindhearted friend criticize another woman for eating a cookie when she would never dream of commenting in such a way on another person's race or sexual orientation or disability? Deprivation is the dystopian ideal.

My mother called her endless diets "reducing plans." Reduction, the diminution of women, is the opposite of feminism, as Kim Chernin points out in *The Obsession*. Smallness is what feminism strives against, the smallness that women confront everywhere. All of women's spaces are smaller than those of men, often inadequate, without privacy. Furniture designers distinguish between a man's and a woman's chair, because women don't spread out like men. (A sprawling woman means only one thing.)

Even our voices are kept down. By embracing dieting I was rejecting a lot I held dear, and the emotional dissonance that created just seemed like one more necessary evil.

A fashion magazine recently celebrated the return of the "well-fed" body; a particular model was said to be "the archetype of the new womanly woman ... stately, powerful." She is a size 8. The images of women presented to us, images claiming so maliciously to be the images of women's whole lives, are not merely social fictions. They are absolute fictions; they can't exist. How would it feel, I began to wonder, to cultivate my own real womanliness rather than despise it? Because it was my fleshy curves I wanted to be rid of, after all. I dreamed of having a boy's body, smooth, hipless, lean. A body rapt with possibility, a receptive body suspended before the storms of maturity. A dear friend of mine, nursing her second child, weeps at her newly voluptuous body. She loves her children and hates her own motherliness, wanting to be unripened again, to be a bud and not a flower.

RECENTLY I'VE STARTED shopping occasionally at stores for "large women," where the smallest size is a 14. In department stores the size 12 and 14 and 16 clothes are kept in a ghetto called the Women's Department. (And who would want that, to be the size of a woman? We all dream of being "juniors" instead.) In the specialty stores the clerks are usually big women and the customers are big, too, big like a lot of women in my life—friends, my sister, my mother and aunts. Not long ago I bought a pair of jeans at Lane Bryant and then walked through the mall to the Gap, with its shelves of generic clothing. I flicked through the clearance rack and suddenly remembered the Lane Bryant shopping bag in my hand and its enormous weight, the sheer heaviness of that brand name shouting to the world. The shout is that I've let myself go. I still feel like crying out sometimes: can't I feel satisfied? But I am not supposed to be satisfied, not allowed to be satisfied. My discontent fuels the market; I need to be afraid in order to fully participate.

American culture, which has produced our dieting mania, does more than reward privation and acquisition at the same time: it actually associates them with each other. Read the ads: the virtuous runner's reward is a new pair of $180 running shoes. The fat person is thought to be impulsive, indulgent, but insufficiently or incorrectly greedy, greedy for the wrong thing. The fat person lacks ambition. The young executive is complimented for being "hungry"; he is "starved for success." We are teased with what we will have if we are willing to have not for a time. A dieting friend avoiding the food on my table, says, "I'm just dying for a bite of that."

Dieters are the perfect consumers: they never get enough. The dieter wistfully imagines food without substance, food that is not food, that begs the definition of food, because food is the problem. Even the ways *we don't eat* are based in class. The middle class don't eat in support groups. The poor can't afford not to eat at all. The rich hire someone to not eat with them in private. Dieting is an emblem of capitalism. It has a venal heart.

THE POSSIBILITY OF living another way, living without dieting, began to take root in my mind a few years ago, and finally my second trip through Weight Watchers ended dieting for me. This last time I just couldn't stand the details, the same kind of details I'd seen and despised in other programs, on other diets: the scent of resignation, the weighing-in by the quarter pound, the before and after photographs of group leaders prominently displayed. Jean Nidetch, the founder of Weight Watchers, says, "Most fat people need to be hurt badly before they do something about themselves." She mocks every aspect of our need for food, of a person's sense of entitlement to food, of daring to *eat what we want*. Weight Watchers refuses to release its own weight charts except to say they make no distinction for frame size; neither has the organization ever released statistics on how many people who lose weight on the program eventually gain it back. I hated the endlessness of it, the turning of food into portions and exchanges, everything measured out, permitted, denied. I hated the very idea of "maintenance."

Finally I realized I didn't just hate the diet. I was sick of the way I acted on a diet, the way I whined, my niggardly, penny-pinching behavior. What I liked in myself seemed to shrivel and disappear when I dieted. Slowly, slowly I saw these things. I saw that my pain was cut from whole cloth, imaginary, my own invention. I saw how much time I'd spent on something ephemeral, something that simply wasn't important, didn't matter. I saw that the real point of dieting is dieting—to not be done with it, ever.

I looked in the mirror and saw a woman, with flesh, curves, muscles, a few stretch marks, the beginnings of wrinkles, with strength and softness in equal measure. My body is the one part of me that is always, undeniably, here. To like myself means to be, literally, shameless, to be wanton in the pleasures of being inside a body. I feel loose this way, a little abandoned, a little danger-ous. That first feeling of liking my body—not being resigned to it or despairing of change, but actually liking it—was tentative and guilty and frightening. It was alarming, because it was the way I'd felt as a child, before the world had interfered. Because surely I was wrong; I knew, I'd known for so long, that my body wasn't all right this way. I was afraid even to act as though I were all right: I was afraid that by doing so I'd be acting a fool.

For a time I was thin. I remember—and what I remember is nothing special—strain, a kind of hollowness, the same troubles and fears, and no magic. So I imagine losing weight again. If the world applauded, would this comfort me? Or would it only com-promise whatever approval the world gives me now? What else will be required of me besides thinness? What will happen to me if I get sick, or lose the use of a limb, or, God forbid, grow old?

By fussing endlessly over my body, I've ceased to inhabit it. I'm trying to reverse this equation now, to trust my body and enter it again with a whole heart. I know more now than I used to about what constitutes happy and unhappy, what the depths and textures of contentment are like. By letting go of dieting, I free up mental and emotional room, I have more space, I can move. The pursuit of another, elusive body, the body someone else says

I should have, is a terrible distraction, a sidetracking that might have lasted my whole life long. By letting myself go, I go places.

Each of us in this culture, this twisted, inchoate culture, has to choose between battles: one battle is against the cultural ideal, and the other is against ourselves. I've chosen to stop fighting myself. Maybe I'm tilting at windmills; the cultural ideal is ever-changing, out of my control. It's not a cerebral journey, except insofar as I have to remind myself to stop counting, to stop thinking in terms of numbers. I know, even now that I've quit dieting and eat what I want, how many calories I take in every day. If I eat as I please, I eat a lot one day and very little the next; I skip meals and snack at odd times. My nourishment is good—as far as nutrition is concerned, I'm in much better shape than when I was dieting. I know that the small losses and gains in my weight over a period of time aren't simply related to the number of calories I eat. Someone asked me not long ago how I could possibly know my calorie intake if I'm not dieting (the implication being, perhaps, that I'm dieting secretly). I know because calorie counts and grams of fat and fiber are embedded in me. I have to work to not think of them, and I have to learn to not think of them in order to really live without fear.

When I look, really look, at the people I see every day on the street, I see a jungle of bodies, a community of women and men growing every which way like lush plants, growing tall and short and slender and round, hairy and hairless, dark and pale and soft and hard and glorious. Do I look around at the multitudes and think all these people—all these people who are like me and not like me, who are various and different—are not loved or lovable? Lately, everyone's body interests me, every body is desirable in some way. I see how muscles and skin shift with movement; I sense a cornucopia of flesh in the world. In the midst of it I am a little capacious and unruly.

I repeat with Walt Whitman, "I dote on myself ... there is that lot of me, and all so luscious." I'm eating better, exercising more, feeling fine—and then I catch myself thinking, Maybe I'll lose some weight. But my mood changes or my attention is caught by something else, something deeper, more lingering. Then I can catch a glimpse of myself by accident and think only: that's me. My face, my hips, my hands. Myself.

Harper's, March 1993

This is another Harper's *essay that has been reprinted many times, and another title fight. This was published as "A Weight That Women Carry." I'm not sure why* Harper's *editors like these long-winded titles. To me this story is about reducing the self, the venality of deliberate hunger, the cultural imperative to be small. I wish the title didn't focus on women; men struggle with weight as well, in different ways. This is our cultural issue. Thinking about dieting and hunger in this way eventually led me to write the book* The Best Thing I Ever Tasted, *which is about why Americans are the best fed and least satisfied people on the planet.*

I've gained weight since this was written.

The Happiest Place On Earth

I'M JUST BACK FROM MY THIRD TRIP TO DISNEYLAND. I
visited for the first time at thirteen, courtesy of a grandmother.
From that weekend I remember little more than descending into
Monsanto's Adventure Thru Inner Space ride, and glancing up to
find a giant eye staring at me through a telescope. I rode that ride
again and again. Inner Space was subsumed into the new and
recurring futures of Tomorrowland, and I vanished into adolescence. Except for a single day twelve years ago, I never returned,
yet Disneyland always has a familiar, avuncular feel. Disneyland
seems obvious, yes, but more than that, inevitable.

Recently I had a windfall, and I looked at my nine-year-old
daughter who has a poster of Mickey Mouse on her bedroom door,
and I made secret plans. I told her only a few days before we left,
a few days to pack and anticipate the details and call Grandma to
exclaim about it with a certain wild silliness. Then we flew to Los
Angeles, rented a car, drove across town to the hotel, and took
the hotel shuttle to Disneyland all in a few hours on a hot Friday
in August. The hotel, which I'd picked out of a Column A-B-or-C
list at the travel agent, was nearly new, one of many look-alike
mountains of rooms thrown up by investors in the crowded, noisy
blocks around Disneyland. The wallpaper was beginning to peel,
rugs bunched up in the corners. The shower was broken, a light
bulb burned out, the door to the balcony stuck shut. Room service
plates lay outside a half-dozen doors in the long, empty corridor,
the sticky yellow cheese of leftover nachos drying to a rubbery

sheen. But from our big corner windows we could see the rumpled gray Matterhorn, and the shuttle waited below.

Every day, beginning around seven o'clock in the morning, cars trickle into the Disneyland parking lot, which is bigger than Disneyland itself. Only in the United States of America is there ever a parking lot as big as Disneyland's under a sky as bright and dirty as the sky in Los Angeles. (Excuse me, *Anaheim*, as my friends in Los Angeles are quick to remind me.) The streams of cars give way to parking lot shuttles for people who don't want to walk from their cars to the gates, pass the hotel shuttles, and become streams of people, on foot, in strollers, in wheelchairs, small creeks of people converging into rivulets and then rivers, all heading toward the spillway of the narrow gates, where they pile up like a torrent of white water and shove themselves through. We left the shuttle, entered the stream, squeezed through the gates. Coming and going, the signs call Disneyland "The Happiest Place on Earth." And there, right there, right inside, is Winnie the Pooh larger than life, bending clumsily down to pat a child, his Pooh grin never wavering. The thing that works about Disneyland is that it works. We submit. We're glad to be here.

I HAD BOUGHT the trip as a Disney Package, airfare and rental car and hotel and Disney Passports all rolled into one big credit-card charge. Part of the package is something called the Magic Morning, an outdoor breakfast in Disneyland early in the morning, before the park officially opens, attended by a half-dozen characters. The characters appear without warning, all over the park, cartoon characters come to life, who dash or pad or stomp or dance around depending on their species, and never speak lest the illusion be shattered. Whenever they appear, they draw families with strollers and diaper bags and camcorders, happy kids, and sometimes shy, tearful, frightened kids pressed forward by eager parents. Captain Hook, who stands several inches taller than me and whose hat casts long shadows around him, is greeted by a respectful distance wherever he goes. Snow White, petite, slender, smiling, is happily stroked by toddlers. My nine-year-old, cheerfully growing up as slowly as she can, still believes in Santa Claus and only this summer learned about the Tooth Fairy. She is frightened by clowns. Does she know? I wondered, each time she held her autograph book up to a silent mask. Should I tell her? That morning, at the breakfast, we saw Aladdin, the Genie, Snow White, Eeyore, Pluto, and Tigger. "Tigger!" she screamed, and raced for a hug, smiled for the camera, asked for an autograph. Late that day, she said, "I bet they get hot in those costumes."

As far as I was concerned, the point of Magic Morning wasn't the characters or the sticky, sweet breakfast, but the park's emptiness. Perhaps a few hundred people shared Tomorrowland and the Matterhorn with us at 7:30 on a crystalline, rosy morning, and they all but disappeared in the silent open spaces. The bustling, noisy herd of the day before was gone as though it had never been. But the emptiness was strange, more dreamy than the rides themselves, and disconcerting.

There is a fine psychology built into Disneyland's long lines, which are well hidden and bend continually back upon themselves and around corners and through doorways. You have no idea, really, how long a line is until you are unavoidably part of it; the gasp of understanding when you finally see what a forty-five-minute wait with a child means is held back until you can't change your mind. "If you aren't the sort of person willing to invest an hour of agony for two minutes of joy," says my Disneyland guide, "you probably shouldn't have had children in the first place."

More importantly, the waiting draws you slowly down into each ride's particular shifting world, working bit by bit on one's natural disbelief. Each major ride and each "land" has its own employee costumes and myriad other cues transcribing the borders of the imagined world; each creates, with varying degrees of success, a conditioned response to sights barely seen and sounds barely heard, subtly and casually dropped into the background as though they had no importance, no effect. There is first the willingness to accede to fantasy, and then, without warning, the body's own unwilled and astonishing ability to suspend its own knowledge of reality. So the foyer of Star Tours, an intergalactic travel agency, is rather dull and as bland as a Greyhound bus depot, and the slow descent into Space Mountain takes you into a coolly decorated, impersonal space station designed for maximum bureaucratic efficiency on a cosmic scale. The Matterhorn has a buoyant alpine bouquet, and you are handled by strapping young Nordic men in lederhosen, and Thunder Mountain, a Wild West roller coaster, feels hot, arid, and lawless. Splash Mountain is all Brer Rabbit and Zippity-Doo-Dah, and its lines curl slowly along with the tranquil repose of Valium.

On Magic Morning, there were no lines anywhere. We climbed over the fence to leap on the Matterhorn, jogged gleefully up into Star Tours without pausing to listen to C-3PO's complaints, and sat in an empty shuttle for our trip. The assembly-line shiver, the sense of being part of some enormous piece of carefully timed machinery, was gone. My daughter talked me into Space Mountain. One enters first by climbing, up moving sidewalks and then ramps, and then far down a switchback walkway. The ride slowly pulls you up into darkness and then throws you brutally into space like a slingshot. One feels obligated to scream. We screamed with vigor, alone in our car, and after two minutes slid into the space station, where no one was waiting. We had only to stay seated a moment to ride again, and again.

When Magic Morning ended and the entire park was about to open for real at eight o'clock, we stood with about fifty other Disney Package customers at the edge between Tomorrowland and Main Street, waiting for the security guard's signal. When he looked at his watch and waved us on it was like a Mother's Day stroller dash, the beginning, for many families, of a long day force-feeding high-stimulation fun to small children who preferred to linger at the fountains and watch pigeons, but would not be allowed to do so. Their parents were too willing to be rude on behalf of them, too hungry to see and do, photograph and experience, to fill up, to fill out.

By the afternoon I couldn't stand the place any longer. The crowds are amazing, enormous, they're Hong Kong at rush hour, Tokyo subways, a pan-Manhattan Labor Day sale. Families and camp groups come dressed the same way, moving like schools of fish through the churning rivers of people; Junior and Grandpa and all the cousins dressed in bright green t-shirts and red shorts for easy spotting in the throng. On a busy day, when more than fifteen thousand cars fill the parking lot and one hotel shuttle after the other disgorges its passengers every half hour, and the monorail fills up at the enormous Disneyland Hotel with more guests for the park again and again, there may be fifty or sixty thousand people inside at the same time. And they're all in line, or rushing to the end of one.

Then, near the 60-MINUTE WAIT FROM HERE sign, I watched a Space Mountain employee patiently try to explain to a large family why the ride has a height requirement, why the very tiny girl with bows in her hair, holding Daddy's hand and standing mutely near the moving sidewalk, could not be allowed to go on the scariest ride in the park. They wanted to argue. I wanted to go. So we tramped back to Main Street, through the gates to get our invisible, indelible hand stamps, back through the parking lot to wait for the shuttle, back to the empty hotel hallways, the water stained wallpaper, the silent view of the shadeless parking lot crawling with cars.

My friend Harry, who lives in Beverly Hills, refused to come see me in Anaheim. He never goes to Anaheim, he tells me, loftily. And I won't go to him. I'm exhausted, beaten into submission, dozing by the pool, gathering strength for another onslaught. My daughter seems as happy to bob in the pale blue water as she was to ride Space Mountain. "No one ever comes here to go to Disneyland and does *anything* else," he tells me, but he's wrong. Our package included One Other Attraction, we could have gone to Knott's Berry Farm or Universal Studios, and lots of people are doing that around us, packing up the kids into the rental car and driving all over hell and back for another parking lot, more long lines, big crowds, more sensation. We used ours for a third day in Disneyland.

WHEN DISNEYLAND OPENED in 1955 a complicated intellectual debate began—about Disneyland as a work of art, as a cultural artifact, a piece of architecture, a symbol of capitalism. It was, above all, taken seriously. The debate seemed to end, without conclusion, decades ago, and now Disneyland is treated as a lark. (Except, that is, as a market force, where Disneyland is taken very seriously indeed.) Most people I know treat a trip to Disneyland as an indulgence just for the kids, a kind of mental slumming. Disneyland is low-class fun, lower-class no matter what it costs. Disneyland is common. One definition of common, of course, is whatever satisfies the masses. But in fact Disneyland is uncommon to a fault, it's unique, unrepeatable. The park and everything in it is well made, never tawdry or thin in any way; its textures are always complex and layered. And Disneyland is awfully good at what it does.

Everywhere, an incredible attention to detail. Everything unsightly, disturbing, or mindful of ordinary life is hidden from sight. Thirty tons of trash are collected every *day* in Disneyland, twelve million pounds a year, the detritus of four million hamburgers and more than a million gallons of soda pop, and rarely is there a single straw wrapper on the ground, never does a trash can overflow or a distant glimpse of a garbage truck mar the view. It has always been thus, always a miracle of anal-retentive inspection, compulsive control, unceasing surveillance. The park was built on the bones of orange groves in a year and a day by workers using only hand tools, workers who are always smiling in the photographs. In fact, they went on strike several times during that year, the park wasn't actually finished when it opened, and the opening day was an unmitigated disaster. But in the Disney tradition, people have forgotten all that now.

The intense orderliness of Disneyland, its extremes of cleanliness and unflagging courtesy, its Teutonic precision and appalling vision, and especially the way it deliberately shuts out the niggling problems of reality and gives us an illusion of goodness are all deliberate. Walt Disney was a hard-drinking, pill-popping, anti-union, Communist-baiting, bad-tempered man, an obsessive, depressive, control freak. He gave names to the House Un-American Activities Committee and proudly informed for the FBI. Disney was stingy, mildly anti-Semitic, and feared death so badly he investigated cryonics. But Disney was never cynical. He was amazingly uncynical, in fact. Disneyland is the world he wanted to live in, and as soon as he could build it, he did.

Disney's world is one of impulse without risk, childish spontaneity devoid of danger. All is cued and manipulated, telegraphed and choreographed, manufactured, manicured. Disneyland offers freedom from decision in the guise of endless choice, freedom from confusion, from having to do anything we don't want to do. (Except wait in line, which makes the fun more virtuous.) Even the grand fireworks are introduced over the park-wide public-address system by an unseen Big Brother with a primetime commercial voice, soothing and boosterish, their explosions accompanied by patriotic music to be sure we all understand the point. Disneyland is an exceptionally smart place, a conception of wide-ranging intelligence that allows visitors to be as stupid as they could possibly be and still breathe.

And more. Disneyland is a dream that flitters with genius and then turns into the repeating shrieks of nightmare without warning. (One friend of mine compares it to a particularly bad episode of *The Prisoner*.) In every Disney film there's a moment when the cheerful music turns sour or threatening, when the Sorcerer's Apprentice realizes he can't stop the water coming, when Dumbo's mother screams in grief, chained in the dark. In every film the giggles of psilocybin eventually give way to the mania of speed. Disneyland is Pleasure Island from *Pinocchio*, the island of endless fun that ruins you if you stay a moment too long. As Richard Shickel wrote, it's a dream without any of the dark, dangerous elements that are the essential characteristics of real dreams. There is no incongruity, no unpredictability. No sex, no violence, except the childish sex of an animatronic pirate and the bloodless violence of cartoons. As a dream, Disneyland isn't much good for therapy. It's more a daydream than anything else, closer to Marie Antoinette than Carl Jung.

I can't imagine working here, spending every day in this amalgam of the excruciating and the sublime. After we watched the 3-D Michael Jackson movie, *Captain EO*, the young man in charge said to the crowd, "Thank you for coming," and "Have a nice day," and then murmured into the microphone. "*I'm* going to stay and see the show again. And again and again and again." I listened to "It's a Small World" for fifteen minutes while waiting in line and tried to imagine listening to it on tinkly speakers *all day long*. We were caught in the Electrical Parade mob and literally couldn't get out, at one point I couldn't even stand up from where I'd sat down, there was no room and no one would give an inch, and I was under-neath one of the enormous speakers hanging discretely from a tree, blaring the tinny parade music over and over, and I tried to imagine being Mickey Mouse on the lead float, dancing and smiling and dancing to that music until one day I just snapped and pulled an automatic weapon out of Mickey's pocket and went boom. Bye-bye, Donald Duck. Bye-bye, Pooh.

I'M SEDUCED AGAIN. I buy iced tea on a sunny morning and sit on an ironwork bench in the Main Street Square, and the sudden, intense pleasure I feel isn't just because Main Street is, literally, a scale model; it's not just that the bricks and lamps and shingles are all five-eighths normal size and the second story doors and windows are deliberately foreshortened that gives me a powerful sense of peace. There is something curiously, fundamentally, safe here. There is a woman on the bench opposite me, slowly rocking a stroller with her foot. Here comes the little fire engine, right on time. Here is the ice cream parlor, the magic shop, the candy store. There is Goofy in the distance, nodding and smiling and nodding and smiling. That night, at twilight, as we swung slowly in the tram above the park, a great splash of crows swooped into the tall eucalyptus trees around us, across a clear, abalone sky, and I couldn't imagine wanting to be anywhere else.

I'm seduced, too, by the genuine pleasure around me, the cheerful diversity of all I see. I explain how to use the pay-token lockers to a Mexican family who speak only Spanish. We ride the lovely whirling teacups with a Japanese nuclear family and a trio of green-haired tattooed teenagers all having the same wonderful time spinning in the morning light. I see time and again how many pubescent girls ride the Storybrook Land boats without a shred of wistfulness. I see a woman in a Christian Fellowship t-shirt standing next to a handsome young man in a "Nobody Knows I'm a Lesbian" t-shirt. I see two little old ladies flying into the Peter Pan ride alone; that night two little old men elbow me out of the way for seats at the parade. Time and again, I hear conversations around me in the long lines—reminiscences of Disneyland ten, twenty, thirty years ago, sparkling images carried on into adulthood and cherished always, to be passed to one's own children later, today, now.

Over the years, a tradition of private graduation and prom night parties has developed at Disneyland. What could be safer for teenagers wanting a good time? Now, I'm told, any group can rent the park in its off-hours. "*Any* group?" I ask, disbelieving, still digesting Walt Disney's peculiar political beliefs. "I can't think who we'd turn away," I'm told, and I don't press the matter with suggestions. So Disneyland hosts Scout troop celebrations and church parties and business outings. Twenty years ago my friend Nancy got herself kicked out of Disneyland for dancing with a girl, but now there's an unofficial Gay and Lesbian Night in the park every year.

Disneyland is separate-but-equal opportunity, it's parallelism, a globe along which the lines of latitude never meet. Disneyland is a just world, an evenhanded declaration that we are all the same, except that we're different, and isn't difference wonderful? Wonderful in this democratic utopia of happy segregation. While Mickey Mouse's House is filled with books and games and machinery,

Minnie Mouse's House next door is filled only with the paraphernalia of beauty and her lists of things to do for Mickey Mouse. In the Main Street Electrical Parade, which happens two times every evening, all the women are blondes, all of them, dozens of them, with the unavoidable exception of Snow White and the perhaps not conscious redheadedness of Cinderella's Wicked Stepsisters.

It's a Small World, supposedly the quintessential celebration of diversity, has virtually no Indians, only a cheerful little maiden next to a cheerful little cowboy. So we went to the ride's own official toy store next door, and found that it has no *It's a Small World* dolls. The store, like the ride, is "sponsored" by Mattel, as though Disneyland were some church-run charity largesse, and sells only Disney character dolls, a few other action figures, and Barbies. Lots of Barbies, Jamaican Barbie and Eskimo Barbie and Japanese Barbie, lined up on the shelf next to Army Barbie and Army Ken.

Only employees with vaguely Persian features work at Aladdin's cafe, only pert white teenage girls work at Storybook Land. There is never a black Cinderella and never a blonde Princess Jasmine. The fact that small children who love these characters wouldn't care if Cinderella was black isn't important. Neither is the fact that the enduring characters like Mickey Mouse aren't even human. These carefully drawn dividing lines are part of the precision, the vision, the idea—the ideal.

AS I HANG in an open car on a slim cable above the park, as the Matterhorn bobsled begins its clackety climb, as we shoot down into the dark humidity of the Pirates of the Caribbean, I imagine disaster. I see its possibility in every bolt and cotter pin. There is regular disaster planning, but rarely any kind of disaster here, and those are small, individual, human-sized ones. Occasional heart attacks whisked quickly away by ambulance, purse-snatchings, epileptic fits, sprained ankles. There have been only a few well-publicized deaths, like that of a woman who stood up on the Matterhorn and fell. In the mid-1980s an employee took a shortcut through the Carousel of Progress and, in a monumentally ironic moment, was crushed by the machinery like Charlie Chaplin in the assembly line. Murders, suicides, fires seem not to exist inside the walls. Even Los Angeles's almost-yearly earthquakes have never damaged Disneyland. Now and then a ride stalls. When Splash Mountain first opened it broke down at least once a week, requiring the smiling, cheerful employees to walk passengers out through the emergency exits, hidden inside giant bumblebee hives and behind fat talking bears.

If Los Angeles is anarchy, then Disneyland is fascism. And like Los Angeles, Disneyland seems an impossible, post-apocalyptic place at times. Suddenly I see the enormous potential for political action here. But again, hardly any such thing ever happens. The most memorable event was in 1970, when a band of Yippies took over Tom Sawyer Island and raised the Communist flag over the fort. As we ride through the Small World ("It's a small world, *after* all! It's a *small* world, *after* all!") I imagine Native Americans climbing out of the boats to stand in defiance inside the mechanical doll displays. ("It's a world of laughter, a world of tears!") I imagine drag queens lining up with the auctioned women in Pirates of the Caribbean, Black Panthers joining the headhunters on the Jungle Cruise. I have visions of sabotage, terrorism, the unspeakable heresies possible here. I imagine vandalizing Tinkerbell's harness. Something truly big and daring. Yet the most dramatic thing I saw was a series of out of order signs taped to trees. Finally, I call the Disneyland publicity department and ask about terrorism. The P.R. man I talk to seems surprised at the idea. "That's not why people come to Disneyland," he says.

AND THEN I find myself sliding effortlessly, and in fact involuntarily, unwillingly, back into bliss, riding the steam train around the park. I am breathless at the elaborate fireworks. I get misty-eyed listening to a robot of Abe Lincoln talk about healing. We eat lunch at the Blue Bayou, a pseudo-Cajun restaurant perched inside the Pirates of the Caribbean, under a moonlit, starry New Orleans sky, cooled by light breezes, listening to the locusts. My daughter meets Mickey Mouse for the first time.

Outside the park is a messy, blurred world. Inside one finds only clear boundaries and distinct expectations. This vision, this hope, that such a world as this could be is promulgated so well and so deeply that for moments—sterling, distinct moments, Magic Moments—our very lives seem safe and free. A true generosity fills the heart, we are joined in a community without threat. We wait our turn. We smile at the child who waits restlessly beside us.

My brother remembers, with a surprising intensity, his first visit to Disneyland at the age of twelve. He had all the world in his hands that day, and he spent all its hours on Tom Sawyer Island, chasing other whooping, wild twelve-year-olds through a fantasy of pure girl- and boyhood. When he told me this, I thought about how different twelve-year-olds are these days. But perhaps, for a time on Tom Sawyer Island, even now they're all the same.

Kids' Stuff, Left Bank #6, 1993

Left Bank was a terrific small press in Portland. This was written for a collection called Kids' Stuff. *I took the opportunity to express my ambivalence about Disneyland. It's a place I still find hard to resist, even knowing as much as I know now, which is far too much.*

Meat

I WENT TO THE BUTCHER'S SEVERAL TIMES A WEEK AS a child. Meat was always in my life. The butcher shop was just down the street from our house, past the old, squat Carnegie Library, the Elks Club, the Groceteria, the bakery, and the big stucco fire department with its long driveway. I loved the Meat Market best; it was orderly, with the hushed front room encased in windows. The floor was golden oak, shiny and clean, facing a horseshoe of white metal display cases curving away like the fabric of space. The air held the scent of clean skin.

I would lay my hot cheeks against the cool glass and gaze at the meat inside: flaccid steaks, roasts, and sausages in neat rows like tile or shingles laid atop each other in patterns of soft red, pink, and maroon. I knew the textures—they were my textures. I liked to examine the down on my legs, the way the irises of my eyes opened and closed when I turned the light above the bathroom mirror off and on, the intricate maze of my belly button. I pulled scabs off and chewed them, and licked the ooze that followed. The rump roast in the glass case made a delicate curve, the curve of my own pliable buttocks. Me, but not me.

I was an inscrutable child, I think; a puzzle to my mother, who had had a girl's youth of starch and oxfords. I threw off the nice things she wrapped around me. My feet are still hard and rough, jerkied from the dry days spent wandering my little town, dashing over the softened asphalt in summer, wrapped in hardy boots in the cold.

On panting summer days the basement beckoned, crowded and lifeless, the air cool, musty, and dim after the glazed sunlight. No one would find me there, if anyone cared to look. Most of the small basement was filled with a freezer, which my mother, one in a long line of carefully organized women, kept always filled as a hedge against catastrophe. (Distantly, my mother's voice at the top of the stairs: "Shut the freezer!"—trailing off into words I didn't bother to hear.) Its heavy white lid seemed to lift from the stiff latch with relief, and swing up so that a waft of the freezer's queer fog blew in my face. My taut, tanned skin could breathe in the damp. There was often a whole side of beef in the freezer at a time, broken up among the TV dinners and the quarts of bean soup and the ice cream. Each cut was wrapped in white freezer paper and labeled with a red wax crayon in strange abbreviations: "FLK STK 4 #" and "P CHOPS - 6." The irregular, heavy packets sat in the cold trough like a haphazard pile of white rocks littered with food.

The ancient grass skirt my father had brought home from the war hung on one wall, its clackety tendrils yellow with age. He kept a safe there, too, tucked inside a rough cavity torn by hammers from the cement foundation. Here were the dusty boxes of Christmas tree lights, the empty jam jars, a bike frame, a trunk, the lethal table saw I was never to touch. My silences were sometimes the silence of the lost, the wandering, but they could be deliberate and ungiving, too. I would lean on a post beside the freezer and fade half away from the world gazing at my father's old toy train, wrecked against a tiny hillside.

THERE WAS NEVER a meal without meat; every afternoon the house filled with the scents of frying oil and roasting flesh. The long dining table leaned toward my father's end, anticipating the heavy cuts on the platter beside him—the pot roast, the round roast beef, the piles of rust-colored chops dripping juice. He carved. At Thanksgiving he leaned over the enormous turkey to get a good purchase, the double blades of the electric carving knife slicing in a noisy blur. When he lost his temper at the table, voices suddenly raised, a hand out to swat, to knock aside a complaining child, he forgot the knife sometimes, holding it out in front like a Samurai as he bellowed at us three children. On quiet nights we squabbled for drumsticks, thick hamburger patties, the fatty end of the roast. I always had the chicken's back with its fat, heart-shaped tail that my grandmother called the pope's nose, and when we were done our plates were littered with the rags of bones.

My father was a volunteer fireman; it was his one great victory. Like all the firemen, he had a closed-circuit radio with its own codes and shrill calls, so we could follow the progress and crises of each fire from a distance. The town had a siren for everyone else, and its long whooing call was as sweet as the coo of a dove to me. Every few weeks, the alarm would sound during dinner, and he would move so fast, so instinctively, that time seemed to stand still: the knife or fork or bite of food falls to the table, his chair scrapes back along the floor, we children scoot close to the table out of his way as he thunders past, "Goddammit!" trailing him out the back door, the door slams, and seconds later his pickup roars out of the driveway. My mother listens to the radio, we go get our books, because when my dad is gone my mother lets us read at the table. Afterward, she takes us to the Richmaid for ice cream.

Buying meat was like this every time: I am with my mother, an efficient, plain woman with the smell of academics around her. She much preferred reading to cooking, but she cooked every day. The butcher, Mr. Bryan, is my father's best friend. He stands behind the counter, a tall jolly man with a hard round stomach covered in a white apron streaked with blood. He has saved his best meat for my mother, kept it apart for her inspection: a pot roast, a particular steak, perhaps giblets saved for her special dressing, the hard nubbins of chicken hearts and kidneys, the tiny livers purple-red like gems in his palm.

Now and then Mr. Bryan went to the back of the store and brought my mother something really special: a whole beef heart, balanced like a waxy pyramid on his hands, or a cow's tongue, one of my favorite things. Sometimes I would come into the kitchen in the middle of the morning and find a tongue set out waiting for the pot, an enormous apostrophe of flesh covered in pale papillae. Tongue takes forever to cook, boiling for many hours on the stove, and it filled the kitchen with a tender mist and steamed the windows gray. When it was done, my mother sliced the tongue as soft as angel cake into thin, delicious strips unlike anything else, melting, perfumed. When all the rest of the world wouldn't bend, flesh would bend. That was what flesh was.

Mr. Bryan spreads his hands full of meat on stiff wax paper out to my mother, as though making an offering, and at her nod lays the flesh upon the scale. Together, with hardly a word, they watch the red needle pass, the delicate cross-hatch of numbers, roll up, linger, stop; he murmurs the price, which goes into a monthly account book, and wraps the meat in careful white bundles, along with a pile of bones for our dog.

I wait, and smell the blood rising from the sawdust spread across the floor behind the counter.

"I've got something for you." Mr. Bryan has a little bottle-brush mustache, a Hitler mustache, coarse and black. He leans over the counter and holds out his two huge hands in fists, his hairy hands and big round sausage fingers hiding a surprise. His arms are like my father's arms, thick and powerful and tanned dark brown, his hands are my father's hands, workmen's hands, and he waggles them in front of me like a magician.

Abracadabra! I grab for the wiener he has hidden: "Which finger do you want?" he laughs with a big Santa Claus belly laugh, the sausage balanced in his knuckles. I laugh politely, too, and finally grab it and retire silently to a corner. The sphincter on each end is like my old aunt's mouth I am sometimes forced to kiss, a dark center with radioles of pinched wrinkles. Inch by inch, beginning here, I peel the shiny pink skin off with my teeth. I eat the spongy mulch slowly, sucking its sweet and salty juices like a popsicle, transfixed by the window, watching the steady, slow passage of people outside in the glare.

SOMETIMES I WOULD do little errands with my father. He was a weary man, infinitely restless. He always went through back doors, never the front, and so I learned to walk in like I belonged everywhere: the hardware store where I could plunge my arms up to the elbow in bins of nails, letting the sharp edges bite a little, and the sporting goods store where I could study the rows of staring animal heads that circled the room, and the Elks Club, and the lumber yard. Then he'd have another snort, and get back in his old pickup and drive two blocks to the next brief chat, the next chore.

My father liked foods no one else in the family ate. He made his own rich soups, his own jerky. He liked the gifts of game my grandfather would bestow at times, the big cuts of purplish venison, the whole ducks with their peculiar, wild taste. He liked tripe, fresh jalapeno peppers, horseradish, Limburger and feta cheese, Rocky Mountain oysters: foods strong and biting, with a certain presence, foods unmistakably here. I was the only one who'd share his little treats with him, and this strange intimacy bound us across the table when nothing else held us near. The two of us sitting alone at the big dining table with a pot of steamed clams between us and little bowls of melted butter, shucking the sweet tidbits out with a clatter of forks. For him I ate what only he would eat, the far corners of flesh: pickled pigs feet, elk, brains, sweetmeats. I was proud to eat these things. It made me less a daughter, and more a son.

With my father it was this: he parks his truck in the alley and we enter the Meat Market through the unmarked alley door. The floor in the back of the market is gritty with fine yellow sawdust, streaked with blood; it grips my shoes like flypaper and piles up along the walls in little drifts. On the tables, the big block tables too heavy to move, knives and saws, pikes and hooks striped with blood. A slab of beef hangs in the hall, ready to be sliced into the day's steaks, and while the men talk over my head I sidle up close beside it, sniffing its fragrance, stroking its soft, waxy fat. I don't listen to the men because I know they won't say anything important.

At the very back of the Meat Market is the walk-in freezer,

behind a huge shiny door with a silver handle as big as a car jack. One of the assistant butchers steps past me and opens it, and a breath of moist air escapes like a faint snow, almost maternal. Inside in the dim light I can see the rows of beef sides, pierced by huge hooks, the ribs bumpy and the fat dangling. There are yellow chickens hung like underwear on a line, and whole gutted pigs with giant snouts.

I know what this means now, these dead by the hundreds and thousands that haunted my days. I saw the carcasses, the knives, I licked the blood off my fingertips. But then I was very young. The world was solid, the world was what it was, and nothing more. It had no ghosts, no God. No dead pigs and trussed chickens, just the meat my mother cooked for supper while my father ducked out back for a quick drink before we ate. I watch the man walk among these objects hanging in the frigid air, brushing them gently with his shoulder so they sway a little in the breeze of his passing, and I wait for the quiet conversation of the smiling men to end, and hope Mr. Bryan will give me a wiener.

MR. BRYAN, OF course, was a fireman, like all my father's friends, and his kids were fire brats like me and sat beside me on the fussy rows of hose when we rode the trucks in the parades. The fire department turned a hundred years old the day before I was born, and by then my father had been fighting fires for years.

Now and then I was taken to the fire department on one of my father's little errands, entered its high ceilings and its echoes and wandered among the stately, patient trucks. I could peek underneath them, and examine the long rows of turnout clothes, stiff rubberized overalls and Wellington boots smelling of oil and smoke. I loved fires and their pure destruction, I loved the prescribed movements of ritual and chaos that were the same every time. For years I wanted to be either a nun or a fireman, and the fact that I was neither a Catholic nor a man didn't bother me. I just trailed after the firemen whenever I could. I often could—I was very free to come and go, and willing to walk miles if need be to find the circled trucks and milling men, to come in close beside the whirling lights and listen to the urgent, murmured voices and the dashing spray of foamy water, hissing down into the heat.

In late August, when the afternoons were close with heat, the fire department had a barbecue for the families. Mr. Bryan provided the meat and the huge steaming barbecue grill with its electric spit. We all gathered in the farthest corner of the big city park near my home, where the shade was thick and cool, and you could hear the thwack of tennis balls from the nearby courts. The men stood around in small clumps, holding beers, laughing, basting the huge joint of beef. The spit turned heavily with a fluctuating whir, and the juice dribbled off the blackened flesh and landed spitting in the coals.

It was forbidden to drink in the park, but the firemen did it; even some of the firemen's wives, like Mrs. Bryan, whom I always thought a little notorious and outspoken. My mother just smoked, one cigarette after the other, leaning forward over a picnic table to make a point to one of her friends, another fireman's wife. I climbed a nearby pine tree and spread myself around the trunk, hidden in its needles, and practiced saying out loud the unsavory insults I learned from my peers. They were mostly flesh words, skin-and-bone words, animal words: Chicken shit. Wienie. Horse's ass. And later, the rest of the flesh, all that was sliced off at the butcher's when we weren't looking: Prick. Pussy. Cunt.

When Mr. Bryan pronounced the beef ready, with his deep and hearty chortle, I quickly slid out of the tree and lined up to eat. I held out my plate for a gentle slab of rare meat cut very thin, the pink juices draining through the thin paper plate onto my hand. I added sweet baked beans, potato salad, garlicky French bread, and chocolate cake, and begged my mother for one more soda, just one more. The smoke swirled around and around my head.

After the picnic we drove up to the huge municipal swimming pool; ours alone for the afternoon. One useless white-nosed lifeguard stayed behind. The crowd of full-bellied men in swimming trunks would have knocked each other aside for the chance to rescue someone; it would make the day complete. I lay baking in the sun and imagined drowning, dropping into the water, lost; I am saved by firemen, raised up sputtering from the water by a host of hard, stout hands that pull me up and out and into the cathedral of sun in one motion.

The lifeguard with his poker face scans the crowd, ignoring the flirting girls. The air is filled with the bright sounds of splashing water, the muscular double bounce of the diving board, hollering boys, sing-song children's cries. The firemen even drink beer on the swimming pool deck, a sin so great and marvelous I fall backward into the water with joy. My brother scrambles to the top of the high dive and blasts off into a cannon ball, tucked and spinning, hitting the hard blue water with a wanton splash.

I wash the sticky pitch and sauce away without a thought. The sweat is gone, the juices gone, dried up by the sun and rinsed away by the chlorine scent of the pool. We stay while the flat empty sky turns from chalk blue to ivory to black, our little voices carried off like vapor, until the men and women lean back to watch the stars appear, and I rest my own sleek head in the breast of water, and sink away.

YOU WILL THINK me disingenuous if I tell you now that I didn't know what meat was. I couldn't know, the shift from cow to beef is a shift so monumental and sudden that it's hard to conceive. Perhaps small children cannot know this even when they are witnesses, and I was never a witness. I have never seen an animal slaughtered for meat. And if you had leaned over me when I was four or five or six, and suggested I eat an animal, I might have struck out with shock. I loved animals more, and more easily, than I loved my parents. I held my old dog, a dour, mongrel Lab, for hours in my room sometimes, telling him what I couldn't tell; I was weak with him because he kept that secret. I loved horses, goats, deer, and the cattle chewing stupidly by the backroad fences; in my bedroom I kept lizards, snakes, chameleons, and a rat, and that was all my mother allowed. And it was my mother who one day told me where meat came from, as though it were the most natural thing.

I was about seven when I asked, that age when one begins to see the depth of betrayal in the world, that one can't really count on things after all. And my mother answered, yes, the chicken we ate for dinner was the same as the chickens down the street I would cluck at through the fence, the ones with the thick white feathers that filled the breeze. That the peeled skin of the wieners Mr. Bryan gave me were loops of intestine washed clean, and their pulp a ground mash of bodies and bones. That the unbelievable objects had a name, a face, a history, the sweet and salty taste was the taste of blood, the same as my blood. It came all at once, like a blow, that pickled pigs feet was not a colorful metaphor but the very thing, that I had eaten a pig's foot, and much more.

I lived on bare noodles and butter sandwiches for a long time after that. I wouldn't allow her to spoon the sausage-flavored spaghetti sauce onto my plate. A few years later, it seemed less important, the resistance too hard. Perhaps I had had other surprises; it's hard to remember whole sections of those years. I've gone years without eating meat as an adult, and years when I was too tired not to eat whatever I found in front of me. And lots of times when I craved flesh, when I broiled and roasted, made scratch gravy and giblet dressing like my mother's or sat at my long dining table with a pot of steamed clams clattering against my fork, times when I longed for the irreducible flavors of meat, to be full of meat. And I will even now find myself knocked flat sometimes when I see meat in front of me and realize what I'm doing. It is a heart-felt knowledge—that word, like all those other words for sudden understanding—it is visceral, gut-level, organic. I hold the steak with a fork and begin to cut a slice and my stomach turns upside down; it feels as if I'm cutting my own flesh off and that I'll choke to death upon it, like a prisoner fed his own treacherous, boiled, tongue.

One shock after another. Breasts and hips and hair, more of the pleasures and debts of flesh. I began to bleed several days a month, and when I sat to pee the smell rose up yeasty and rich. I found furtive darting touches: I found lips, saliva, tongues, sweat, fingers. My dog decayed from the inside out, and stank and stumbled and licked the mysterious lumps under his fur. I traced his ribs so near the surface the day before he died. Then my mother yellowed and thickened and wept and died and my father's big arms hung loose and his black hair turned gray. He took his snorts out back in the garage. I knelt between the knees of a boy a little older than myself, and took his penis in my mouth, and smiled not with pleasure or appetite, but with triumph, behind the curtain of my swaying hair. I moved out to the fleshy edges of things, and finally I grew wings like angel wings, and I flew away.

The word butcher comes—a long way down the years—from the word buck. He-goat. They are set aside, butchers, into their own unions, their own neighborhoods, their own bars, set aside. I don't know if it means anything that besides Mr. Bryan, my father's closest friend was the undertaker; it may not mean anything more than the limits of a small town. But I think of the Butcher's Mass, their special blessing, and the *shehitah* of the Jews. The *shohet*, the slaughterer, who must be pious and above reproach, must be as swift and painless as he can be in the killing, murmuring a benediction near the animal's ear and following with a graceful stroke across the throat. I think of Mr. Bryan's cleaver.

The Meat Market burned down on a hot day under a blank blue sky. It was apocalypse. It was a great fire.

I stood at the end of the alley and watched the flames spurt out the back door in gouty bursts. I heard a shriek of metal inside, and guessed the white metal cooler had turned red and ignited its own frost. The smoke billowed out the back door in a cottony black cloud, and I clapped my hands. Men in turnouts and boots rushed past and paid me no attention, and I could see my father paying out the hose from the pumper with great speed.

The meat burned; the water washed it clean. I learned later that Mr. Bryan had inherited the Meat Market from his father, and he'd secretly hated it all those years, going home at night with the stink of blood on his hands and hair. He is still jolly and thick-fin-gered, and he still comes by to see my father, who is tired and gruff and without cheer. They have been retired from fires, too old to go into the heat and pull things out. For myself, I know you can't be cleansed until you know how dirty you really are. I still live far away, still seek salvation from my many sins.

Antioch Review, Summer 1994

My father was a firefighter—have I mentioned that? And his best friend was the butcher. One day I remembered how those things connected and how flesh is one of the problems every thoughtful child eventually must solve.

The Basement

GRANDMA STELLE IS A VERY SMALL WOMAN, WITH LAVEN-
*der hair curled around her little wrinkled face like sunset clouds. She
smells of face powder and cigarettes, and waves the smoke away from
her with a lacquered cigarette holder. I have to sit next to Grandma at
the annual family birthday dinner, the one with all my gray-haired
aunts and uncles. I don't know why she wants me there; she usually
ignores me, but this time she suggests it.*

*The birthday dinner is held in the banquet room of a country
steak house around a long rectangular table. The room is cold and
echoes a little under the high beams of the ceiling. The walls are rough
wood, decorated with horseshoes, checkered curtains, and mountain
scenes in elaborate brass-colored frames. Sputtering white candles in
nubbly red glasses sit on the plastic red-white checked tablecloth. The
waitress, smelling of sweat, brushes against me with her ruffled apron
and calls me hon. I play at making rivers of gravy on my mashed potatoes and kicking my brother under the table, caught up in the fragments of noise around me. We are eating fried chicken, and Grandma
loves fried chicken.*

*She picks up a drumstick in her fingers, manicured red nails
extended out away from the sticky juice, and nibbles delicately
through the crispy skin. Bite by bite she eats the dark meat, dribbling
a little oily puddle onto her plate. With steady, tiny nips and pecks, her
dentures clicking quietly, she turns the drumstick like a cob of corn
until it's clean. She looks away from me, brings her napkin up to dab*

at her red lips, smiles at someone I can't see, and in one hidden motion
slips the bone onto my plate. And reaches for another piece.

WE ARE GOING to Grandma's house, as we often do, Mom, Dad,
my brother, my sister, and me. It's a long drive, but I don't mind
the car. I'm used to beauty on this drive, a splendid, moving beauty.
First the volcanic plain, undulant with empty hills. By daylight
they run for miles, without a single sharp edge in them. In moon-
light their bare skins look like the hides of rhinoceroses, rough
and warm. Lonely rock walls climb the hills and disappear without reason, and here and there I see a scatter of white beehives
and the polka-dots of sheep. Then lush carpets of pine and fir, full
and dark, with spiky teeth of enormous granite towers rising out
of the trees, like dragon lands in unmapped places. In the middle
is the mountain, immense and solitary, covered in snow, visible
from every turn. I know stories about this mountain, how some
people think superior beings live inside—tall, slender people in
white robes who play extravagant, alien bells. Sometimes I see
strange clouds around the peak.

    We drive to Grandma's house, through the plain, past the
forests, up into the steep hills near the mountain, rolling down the
highway in our tired station wagon, past the sheep, the beehives,
the mountain, past the dark ribbon of the river, shallow, fast, and
cold, and past the railroad and the trains.

    Grandma's house is perched halfway up a long, steep hill;
the whole bright town steps block by block up a slope, facing the
mountain. The houses are built on levels, first floors turning into
attics, front porches hanging off in space, bedrooms opening
into yards—a crooked cartoon town with fountains on every corner, making a ceaseless murmur, bubbling out water that looks
like silver and tastes the way silver should taste. Mountain water,
come all the way down and up again. Sometimes there is grass and
roses, and sometimes there is snow, great heaps of snow shoved
up against the houses, above the windowsills, packing them in.
Always there is light.

Dad pulls off the highway into town and drives along the wide street until he comes to a small church made of darkened wood planks and embroidered with wisteria vines. At the church, he turns up, straight up, and I spin around in my seat to stare out the back window at what we are leaving behind, the receding church below, the lines of railroad tracks beside the winding river, the toothbrush silhouettes of trees beside the cockeyed houses, until we reach the top and turn the corner on Grandma's street, and park.

Before we arrive Grandma lays down plastic runners on the carpet, marking the children's required path, and covers the huge sofa and armchairs with crinkly plastic sheets. We march in single file like soldiers, through the living room, down a short hall, and into the shiny kitchen, where suddenly we are two stories high. Out the kitchen door are two flights of wooden stairs down to the sloping flower garden. Flying straight out from the tiny porch like a flying buttress over the sea is a long double clothesline on a pulley. The spotless, pale kitchen is split by sun, the light unencumbered by trees; below Grandma's house is the slope of the town—the backyard neighbor's house, and his neighbor below that, falling off into the sky, the forest, the plain, and far away, looking on, the white mountain. Whenever I think I've left it behind it is there again, closer than before, a cold luxury of light.

"Go on down to the basement, now," someone says, and we go, and stay.

THE LONG FLIGHT of wooden basement stairs descends to the center of a clean cement floor. The main room is lit by a bare bulb with a silver pull chain that shakes the bulb, making the shadows flicker for a long time after someone turns it on. In dimness we come slowly down the stairs, gooseflesh on our arms, into the spotlight. The movement of the bulb illuminates our faces in new, strange ways; our faces become anyone's faces, all faces, no longer familiar. We step off the last of the wooden stairs and someone in the kitchen notices we've left the basement door open and closes it, and the square of sun disappears.

From visit to visit, day to day, nothing changes. We explore, wearing t-shirts and sneakers, shorts in the summer and jeans in the winter, never warm enough. The walls are hidden by piles of boxes, cupboards, dressers, bureaus and trunks, a wicker pram, a big highboy decorated with faded paintings of geese and ducks, a dusty steel safe, and heavy things lost in shadow, submerging me. Grandma saves everything; she keeps it here, keeps the house, keeps it all.

I am more than two years younger than Bruce. Bruce and I are sturdy, competent children, and look so much alike, with our brown hair and green eyes, that we sometimes pass for twins. Bruce is scared of ants, and girls, in that order, something he only tells me. But he's brave, too; I admire his bravery; he takes my father's blows without tears. I know how much he hates Pop Warner football, too, but he never mentions quitting; we know that's not an option. Susan, barely a year younger than me, isn't brave at all. She's squeamish, chubby, pale, and black-haired—she's the one left out, the baby. At home, Bruce and I often tease Susan, with bugs and gory stories, or simply ditch her when we've had enough. In the basement at Grandma's house the three of us form a band. We wander through the dim, cold rooms, round and round. "Don't touch anything," Grandma calls down from the kitchen, a little alarmed at our distant sounds, and we promise we won't, and she closes the door again.

We try again and again to open the safe, flipping the dial through endless combinations, and pry unsuccessfully at the locks on the trunks. We trace the painted ducks with our fingers. Bruce, being brave, looks in the darkest corners and under the stairs, where we long ago hid the only toy we have here, a battered red scooter that belonged to my father when he was a boy. At the end of the stairs are two small rooms with a tiny bathroom between them, smelling of rust. Grandma calls them the guest rooms. Each has a musty twin bed with a chenille bedspread that feels damp under my hands. There are bookshelves in the rooms, old paperbacks and hardback novels with cover paintings of masted sailing ships blown by storm and gunmen atop rearing horses. On top of the bookshelf sits a pair of tiny bronze shoes with stiff, metallic laces tied in bows.

I go upstairs to ask my mother about them, and find her in the kitchen making coffee. She says they are my father's baby shoes. Upstairs, the mantelpieces are covered with porcelain animals and rococo clocks, vases and picture frames, paperweights and china dolls. I follow my mother through the living room into the front bedroom, where Grandma is searching for something in her strange trousseau. The bedrooms are full of hampers, big jewelry boxes, cupboards, valises and hatboxes, piles of blankets, mountains of ironed and folded linen, closets stuffed with clothing, and a chiffonier, each drawer filled with nightgowns and bathrobes. In the den is a rolltop desk covered with files, a wardrobe filled with several sets of china packed in quilted covers, shelves packed with dark, bound books. In the main bedroom and both bathrooms, the long vanity tables are covered with lace runners and doilies, big pink boxes of powder, vials of cologne, hand lotion, hair spray, and creams. Nothing is ever threadbare or worn, and nothing is ever new. Nothing changes.

Grandma's small bent body barely clears the pile of blankets beside the bed. She has red lips and yellow teeth, and her hands are swollen and thick; her fingers look like chicken bones, clutching a cigarette.

She turns and sees me standing there in the doorway, watching, and sighs, white smoke dribbling out of her nose. Her intense dark eyes are like the shiny eyes of teddy bears, which I hate. My stuffed animals have soft cloth eyes and long lashes. She stares at me a moment and says, "Go on down to the basement, now." My mother doesn't say a word, only looks at me and I go.

Downstairs, I sit on the bedspread a long time, holding the weight of the tiny shoes in my hands. How could a baby wear such heavy shoes? I wonder. They've made my father a weary man. He has trouble waking up in the morning, and often mother has to coax him out of bed, and he sleeps in his chair in the late afternoon before dinner, and he sleeps again after dinner, laid out flat on the sofa like a corpse while we sit in the front of him on the rug, watching television.

We are all quiet at once. The airless clutter slowly fills with sound—the lack of sound, the sound of someone making no noise, someone holding very still, subterranean, buried. I jump up and grab the scooter.

Round and round and round we ride, counting the laps, the short oval laps, counting one, two. "That's four!"

round and round

Upstairs, the grown-ups are in the den. My grandmother is at the center, prim, elegant, smoking with a restrained grace. My grandfather leans back in his dark brown leather armchair, holding a glass of whiskey on ice. My father sits in the smaller chair. He is my grandmother's only child, her destiny, her hope. He lives in a house his father built, next door to the house where he was raised. His hand shakes a little as he reaches for his drink. My mother sits nearby—nervous, homely, laughing at every little joke.

She is fond of a photograph from her college days—a dozen anonymous young people on the grass, one blond and one brunette cheerleader leaning on the football captain's arm in the center of the picture, and my mother alone in her patch grinning, pleased to be so close. I know, because she told me when I asked, that she proposed to my father herself, tired of waiting, and when he refused she left him, but then there was the war, two years of worry and a few cryptic letters, and when he came back he was different, he was ready. In the wedding picture she looks happy, really happy, standing upright and proud in a fashionable dress, and he looks thin and dark and serious. A year later, Bruce was born, and in a photo taken shortly afterward, Dad holds my newborn brother in the crook of one big hand, and a can of beer in the other. He is already getting fat.

Upstairs they're playing cards, they're drinking highballs and smoking cigarettes, one after the other, so that the small den fills with a high thin blue haze, and under the sound of murmuring laughter is the clatter of ice and the mumble of the television.

"That's eight!"

round and round

And the scooter flies out from under my sister. My brother and I are sitting on the bottom step keeping score. The scooter goes one way and my little sister the other on the hard, cold, cement floor. She scrapes her knee and it starts to bleed and of course she cries, she always cries; she's weak but we don't torment her. Here we help.

Later, when my son is born, he is the first grandchild, the first great-grandchild. When he is a week old, my parents drive hundreds of miles to bring Grandma to visit. Grandma sits propped by pillows in an armchair and I hand my infant to her so Dad can take pictures. After a few minutes, he begins to wake and whimper—the mewling puppy sound of hungry babies—and I reach for him. But Grandma pulls back, guarding him, staring. She says, "Boys don't cry," and again, singsong, "Boys don't cry," staring me down.

It doesn't occur to me to go up the steps and ask for a Band-Aid. My mother would be glad to help, I know, but I also know my mother has her hands full here and I prefer to improvise with toilet paper and a piece of cloth we find until my sister quiets down.

LUNCH IS MELTED cheese sandwiches on white bread, served on paper plates at the kitchen table. Afterward, I ask my mother if I can take a magazine with me to read. She gives me the Saturday Evening Post, and I sit on the bottom basement step a while and meditate on the pictures of astronauts and royalty.

At home, my brother and I go to the movies every Saturday, walking alone down the street to the theater for the matinee. In every scary movie there is a basement scene, a moment when some doomed fool creeps cautiously down those stairs. I don't like scary movies, but it's not because of Grandma's basement. Even in the long-forgotten fruit cellar, hidden behind a heavy door, I'm not afraid; I've quit feeling afraid and feel other things instead. The thick plank shelves are cobwebbed and musty, covered with cloudy Mason jars. When I pick one up, odd shapes move heavily in the thick syrup, like captured elves. These are the basement's bones, the hidden things, put away. They are so dead they can't even be ghosts.

I vaguely knew things. I'd heard my mom say that the tall, bald man I called my grandfather wasn't really that at all, that my real grandfather had been dead a long time. Grandma married and was widowed, and then remarried and was widowed again, and remarried once more, all before I was born. When this third husband died, Grandma sold their house and moved in next door to my parents, back into the house where my father was raised, where his real father killed himself. She brought all her things with her, a museum for the detritus of marriage. She filled the house next door, and she filled the walls and ceiling of the double garage in between, and she put some in the attic and some in my parents' little half basement, and some in the basement below her, a wretched coal bin hole, where the high soft bed from the basement bedroom moldered into a rat's nest of cotton dust.

A long time later, I have a daughter and take her to visit Grandma. She sits, as she sits every day, on the big sofa, smoking endlessly, a can of beer discreetly propped beside her, the barely chewed remains of the meal-on-wheels on the end table. She wears no makeup and her stained, faded housedress has cigarette burns in it. She leans forward to my daughter and says, "Give me a kiss now." My daughter presses back against my thighs, silent. Grandma leans a little closer. "If you give me a kiss, I'll give you twenty dollars." I turn and leave, carrying my daughter on my hip, passing a tinted photograph of my brother at her age, smiling.

AT THE END *of the day, when it's time to go home, we children are called up from the basement at last, and we wearily climb the stairs and file like prisoners of war out to the car. Except me. I'm not going home this time; I'm checking out of here. I hide, and watch my father climb into the driver's seat and my mother lean in to shush my sister and pat my brother's arm. She doesn't notice that I'm gone, no one notices but Bruce. He presses his face against the window, mouth open. When he was very small, Grandma came to him, leaning forward with those knobby hands, and wrapped his face in plastic like the sofa, and he's spent all these years screaming for air, clawing at the mask. His screaming makes no sound. My mother climbs into the passenger seat and rolls down the window and Grandma and Grandpa stand on the stoop and wave goodbye—"Bye!"—and Mom waves goodbye—"Bye now!"—and Dad pulls away. He drives to the end of the block and turns the corner, and I know they're heading straight down the hills into the earth, down the long, long street that ends in a dark, silent church, round and round along the twisting roads to home.*

Out the kitchen door, to the porch, and sky. I climb up on the railing way above the garden, and loop my hands over the clothesline, and push away. Out I swing over the sunny green yard, swaying in the high blue sky, out above the steep hills.

round and round

I dangle a moment, hearing the scurry of my grandmother's return, watching the mountain a few miles away, watching me. I hear a distant peal, deep and long. I'm a rocket, I'm a bird, I take wing. I'm snapping free, like my mother's clean white cotton sheets in the sweet cool breeze. My grandmother grabs the pulley and, squeak by squeak, tries to reel me in, but it's too late, I'm gone.

Home: American Writers Remember Rooms of Their Own
(Pantheon, 1995)

I could not write this story. It was for a terrific anthology called Home, *in which each essay described the author's memories of a particular room. I asked for the workshop, but someone had gotten there first, and so I asked for the garage, but it was taken, and finally I settled on the basement.*

The World Made Whole and Full of Flesh

SUMMER IS COMING ON AS I WATCH—BEARING CRICKETS, dust, carnal iris flags. The baby maple we'd given up for dead shows sudden leaves, limp on thin branches. Spring grass shimmers in the light and from my seat on the shaded porch I can see the big spiders in its unkempt length run from shadow to sun, sun to shadow. A car raises the dirt on the road a few hundred yards distant. People always take that corner too fast, and get a scare; they have to slow all at once and pull hard on the wheel. Sometimes I can see a pale face go by, concentrating, listening to the brakes tighten and hold with a long, thin cry.

I reach for my papers, shifting in the wooden chair, and hear its hammer feet scrape sharply across the porch. I do very little on these still, hot days; I read, but not well, whatever is at hand, and the neatly printed words rise up like vapor and are gone, into air so hot and blue it seems a windowpane of solid light. The telephone rings and I get up and go in the dim house to answer. The musty, unused room smells of acrid wood smoke and field dust; the faded carpet around the stove is littered with pale yellow chips. I tell the caller that Paul is in the fields. I can see him there, small and far away, through the old warped window glass. He is getting ready to· plant the summer wheat, bending and lifting, streaked with dirt. After I hang up, I look around the room and think I'll clean the house, pick some flowers for the table, but I don't. I find it hard to work here, to change a single thing in this big strange house, to make sounds into words, words into all that isn't spoken. Even in the evening, when David or Alan or Lee come to call or we leave for town—even when we talk for hours, words seem less important than the spaces between them. Words take apart time, and time is all I have here. The silence here is pendant and strong, draped over the days, and suddenly it's more than I can bear. I reach for the radio and listen through the static to the meaningless news.

There are only the two of us in this big old house, and sometimes only Paul. I only visit—and many people visit Paul. When I come, the house is always the same, as though no one was ever here, as though no one but Paul had lived here in the hundred years the fine old farmhouse has been standing. Paul pays scant attention to its details—to its big beams and tongue-and-groove siding and sunny rooms. He attends to the dirt instead. Most of the rooms haven't been used in years, and when I'm here I spend my afternoons on the porch, in the shade between Paul's fields and the empty rooms that don't belong to me, don't belong to anyone. Outside, the distant twitter of two birds, nothing more.

This day returns every summer. It's back with me now, as I write this, trying to ignore the city—the wordless noise of cars, the wordless world's cries. On this day I am seventeen and getting lost, lost as though I'll never find my way back home again; lost in love with Paul, who is twice my age. I'm falling with the same despair with which I might fall off a cliff after a single misstep, tumbling eternally down. I don't say a word about it, not a word to anyone. These are secrets—the delight, the mismatch, the hopelessness. These are secrets everybody knows but me, I think. Paul knows, today, long before I find out, that days like this don't last. He knows that nothing lasts.

A pair of hummingbirds appears every day, outside one of the bedrooms no one uses, the one with nothing in it but a bed broken in two as though by an ax. The birds climb and dive around the eaves, slipping through the tracery of cherry trees. Every day I watch them spiral together in a double helix, in a spring dance. I watch the gnats bouncing and the spiders running; I can follow their tiny shadows in the grass. A faint rustle slowly fills the air, so slowly it takes me a long time to notice—a flutter in the world's roots.

All day long I speak to no one but the occasional caller, who only wants Paul. Many people want Paul, and sometimes he goes off at night with an apologetic smile, goes off to the rest of his life. "You can stay here if you want," he has said to me more than once, but I leave. Shook awake, I only mumble, "No."

But this is truly summer. Paul is planting summer wheat, and winter dreams are laid bare and clean in wet shadows, to sprout along the earth's long curving beam. A veil stirs with the breeze of the day's ordered passage—and behind it, shapes I can't make out. My mouth is dusty from the field dirt that drifts in the air and settles on every surface, all over my skin.

The sink still holds the morning dishes, dripping with maple syrup. The sun falls across the floor, I am watching the water splash in the sink, and the silence is gone. I hear murmurs in the damp earth below. The breeze is turning to wind and it fills with sighs and sloughing words too low to understand, the whisper of fruit ripened past its glory, tearing the skin, adding to the world's insistent roar. I stand in the kitchen alone, holding the glass, shot with light.

The day wears on. I watch Paul. There is a rope tied between my waist and Paul's; I feel the tug when he bends and lifts, I feel the pull when he walks away. He crosses the field to the far end, to that big stump he puzzles over, into the sun and dust. In the long grass the spiders capture flies and spin them tight, for later. The hummingbirds stroke the flowers with beaks as long and fine as a surgeon's lance.

In the field Paul is too far away to hear me if I cried, if I cried out, if I needed him. If we fell out of luck, into shadow, tomorrow, today, we would fall alone. The solid earth is as dizzy with dancing as the sea, moving me on past the farm and Paul, moving Paul past me. Even then, Paul was sick, and I didn't know.

The mere thought. The glimpse of so much loss is all it takes; it rakes across us like a knife, raises the truth up loud. The mere thought makes us, finally, more than willing to speak, to tell, tell the truth, our truth, every secret we know—to admit that flesh is meat and meat is flesh and the world spins on. Luck separates. No one gives it up without a fight.

The porch stays shaded all afternoon, the line between bright and dark. Below, dimness—below, where the roots are, sweat falls and blood falls and luck falls away; below, days end. Over and over, the world is made whole from its broken parts, over and over my hand holds the cold wet glass, Paul plants in the field, and the earth fills with singing all night long; all this without end, winter and summer, day and night, all this beneath the earth's curving beam, the water right beside me, the world's weary head in my lap. Love itself is what breaks our hearts; we fall into its rushing waters and tumble away, knocked breathless, cloven in two.

And the day goes finally by. A cradle rocking, rocking to stillness. I sit in my chair watching shadows growing tall and dark, like young sons coming forth. Our friend David drives straight to the steps in his dirty white convertible. David comes to visit almost every day; this week, he and Paul are fixing a truck. He grabs a toolbox climbs over the windshield and the hood of the car and right over the porch rail, to stand beside me. He is big and bare-chested and never seems tired.

I look at David again, quiet beside me with a toolbox in his hand, and I see the rough gray along his temples, the slight sag along his neck, and realize with a start that David is old. David is beneath the earth's curving beam with all the rest of us, a body, a shadow, dying. "What's wrong?" he asks, and I shake my head, and he looks at my strange face, and the world spins to summer with a gasp of gratitude.

We talk about the wheat going in tomorrow. We talk about the little maple tree, still alive. We don't talk about how our lives are fettered one to the other in the perfumed soil of the spring. Then, I didn't know even that much.

A few years after today, the century-old farmhouse is taken apart. It's not in Paul's hands; he tries to stop the ruin and he cannot. Dozens of people come to help him one summer afternoon, to save what can be saved, to salvage what remains. And when the siding of the big bedroom where we used to sleep is removed, Paul finds an antique cache, a child's secret treasure—a book, a comb, a tiny tin, generations old. "Here," he says, giving me the tin, "you keep this," and we go back to work. And a few years later, Paul dies, seeing it coming, almost ready. I wish I could tell him what I've learned since then; that grieving is a lifelong gift, that grieving is our one chance to cherish another without reservation.

But that was later. For now, today, Paul is coming home. I can see him getting closer, step by step, coming back to me, twenty years ago. Another car turns the corner too fast and feels the pull, taking the curve of the world too sudden and fast. Paul stops to watch the car go by. After a while David goes into the dark house and turns the radio to another station, and then it plays only cool jazz in the darkening sky.

Secrets, Left Bank #9, 1996

Another Left Bank story, for a collection called Secrets. *The events took place when I was seventeen, and the initial draft was my journal from that time. I'd dropped out of college and moved to Eugene, Oregon, to find a place in the longhaired world of community activism. Also, because I fell in love.*

Big Ideas

I MEET STEVE. HE IS DEPRESSED.

"How are you?" he asks. "Are you writing?" This is often the first question we ask each other.

"Yes," I answer, and even I am surprised at the exultation in my voice—the lust.

"That's good," says Steve, and his own voice is like the confession of disease. He isn't writing. He is fifty years old, a good poet, a poet with decades of work behind him. He says he has forgotten how to write, has lost the simplest lessons of construction and sound, and wakes in a rage. When he was gone last summer, he sent me some of his oldest poems to read, and before I could reply, another letter came.

"Why haven't you said anything about my poems?" he wrote. "They're my heart."

MY SON'S BEST friend's mother calls me for advice on her memoirs. The bank clerk tells me he's taking a class in the novel. The carpenter I hired to build a closet says shyly that he is writing a children's book. My neighbor says, wistfully, "It seems like everyone wants to be a writer but me."

I wish I were a painter. I haven't the slightest talent for line or color, so I dream of painting. I imagine the room I would have: a big, empty studio, with light falling on an empty canvas, tilted and ready. I would work on the grand scale, with big ideas and splashes of surprising color. I would be organized and deliberate and keep everything clean. Instead, I work in a collection of debris—most of it invisible, all of it mine. Sometimes I'm happy in my study, and then I'm very happy. Happy as dogs and babies are happy—stupidly content. My cat watches a bird on a branch above his head; "bird," his body sings, "bird bird bird." Sometimes I write like that, staccato words forming on the page like the twitching eyelids of REM sleep, the sign of new dreams. I wake up and there they are, hinting of lost wisdom, and I don't know how they got there and I don't know how to make it happen again. They are someone else's words.

I climb slowly back up the scaffold of old work, yesterday's good sentence or two. I'm stuck with the chore, the workaday rhythm, like pulling rocks from the soil, a job never done. I run the pen across the page just to make the shape of letters, massage the knots from a single sentence, then stare at the page until, thank God, the doorbell rings and I can leave. I sweep or look at maps or file letters, and then come back to fluff the story's pillows, make it tea. I want it to like me, but we aren't friends yet. Finally, Steve calls.

Without saying hello, he asks: "What's the point?"

"You're a good writer," I reply.

"If only people would stop saying that," he says, and hangs up.

So I hang up, too, and go stare at the page until the debris disappears and the paper turns into canvas, big and empty and clean. One sentence appears and is followed by another; everything is syncopated, punctuated high fidelity, and I'm singing "bird" with my whole body, bird bird bird.

THE GLORIOUS SURGE comes to a halt. For weeks, nothing comes. Everything I write is sinful, full of lies, especially the big one, the one you go to hell for: pretending not to be a fool. I argue loudly with an editor who wants yet another draft of a story I barely remember writing. "Make it more left field," he says, and I haven't the faintest idea what he's talking about. I'm afraid, afraid all the time, afraid and I can't tell anyone: that I did too much at once, put in too much, wore out the gift. Life's big surprise.

At first, I don't call Steve. I call another friend, a novelist who's writing for money these days, magazine stuff, anything cool and nonchalant she can find. The raw memoir that makes her cry at the dining table is buried in a drawer. "I'm in deadline hell," she says. "I'm having a breakdown," she says. "Did you know Baudelaire died of caffeine poisoning?" she asks. We hang up at the same time, and I stare at my desk and leave the room.

Finally, Steve and I have coffee and slices of gooey day-old pie in the middle of the day, surrounded by the other unemployed, the students, the rootless, the old. I cuss at the restaurant and all that surrounds me, distracts me, reminds me. Steve is solicitous, full of advice. The oblivious waitress cleans the carpet, and the vacuum cleaner roars in the narrow room. She runs the hose right beneath our table and I find myself shouting through the noise at Steve, who has just told me he's started writing again. "Don't you dare!" I yell, but he can't hear me.

I have to leave town, go teach for six weeks at a giant university where no one knows I'm an impostor. It turns out no one, in fact, wants to know me at all. Budgets are tight, jobs threatened; visiting writers are not welcome here. Most of the required writing classes here are taught by computer programs. I pass classrooms cluttered with silent students facing screens and hear only the clacking of keys and the occasional reedy beep when the Macintosh issues praise.

I am given half a borrowed office heaped with dusty books and Xeroxed syllabi from 1989. The office belongs to Professor Baxter. Professor Baxter teaches Classics of English Literature once a week for the ten-week term; three of the nights are spent watching the BBC production of *Pride and Prejudice*. He shuffles in and out, calls me a different name each time he sees me. He is the only professor who speaks to me. There are no welcoming notes in my box, no handshake from the dean. No map, no roster, no syllabus. The department secretary tells me to stop making so many copies.

I move into a blank apartment by a shimmering pool no one uses, the land in all directions flat and fallow and dry. The students are my only hope.

I don't know where to begin, exactly; I have clearly been mistaken for someone else. The only writing I've been doing myself is in my journal late at night, brief fits of irritation and quavering Dutch courage. But the students don't know this, and I decide they don't need to know.

I talk about what holds us back—the ungentle voices in our heads, the secrets waiting to trip us up. You must have no morals, I tell them. You must use everything. You must be quiescent, patient, willing. I stride the room, cheerful and firm; they watch me and take dutiful notes. Most of them are writing majors, and at first all they give me are commonplace essays and short stories about the tribulations of earnest college writing students. They want to know how to get published, and how I grade.

What are you afraid of? I ask one day. After a silence, a young woman says, "Sentimentality." And another says, "Being thought young." Mariano, my oldest student, almost middle-aged, names anger and Catholicism, not necessarily in that order. Anna, a pale young woman with short blond hair who wears men's neckties, tells us wearily that her father is a well-known writer. When she was raped, he wrote a poem about it. She writes about cooking.

A tall boy in the campus uniform of shorts and tank top and baseball cap comes in for office hours. Like many of the students, he wants me to tell him what to do, what to write, who to be. Their days are filled with fords of choice, little wavelets in a surging sea, running forward much too fast. "I don't think I want to be a writer because I don't want to think too much," he says. "I want to stay normal."

I have them do timed exercises, and write about each other, spy on strangers, invent sex scenes, violent scenes, stories about things they don't believe in. Phoenix wears very short shorts and stretches out her long thin legs covered with thick, feathery, golden hair. She is thoughtlessly athletic, and wears a Dallas Cowboys cap squashed down on her long blond hair. Her scenes of southern California girlhood are devastating and sad. "Last term I was, like, I'm going to be a writer because it was all I was doing all the time," she tells the class. "But now I'm, like, there's a lot of stuff out there, and I'm not ready to settle down." She draws stick figures on her stories, petroglyphs bending, running, jumping high.

I make them write letters to their writer's block, draw pictures of it. Lori makes a cartoon of herself whacking her children and husband on their heads with a book titled *Me*. One boy draws a monster with gleaming red eyes. Carol, alone in a corner, spends an hour covering a page in black crayon and then writes across it in red ink: "I will be judged and found wanting, and jettisoned from the circle of warmth."

Stephanie, gawky and disheveled, is easily the best writer in the class. After a few weeks I realize I'm half in love with her, with her scary ideas, her absolute fearlessness, and I come to class hungry and ashamed, wanting to hear her read, wanting her to ask me for advice. She is only dimly aware of her talent. She's not a writer, she tells me one day. She's a painter. She likes big canvases with solid blocks of color, and writes only "for fun." Her wild stories, her willingness to say anything, anything at all, are the blessing of not being a writer, of having nothing to lose. The other students, the rule-bound ones who want to be writers very much, are startled into attention.

Over the weeks, the stories get better and better, softer, unpredictable, surprising. Anna stops being polite. Mariano gets mad. Phoenix throws her gorgeous legs across the table, and writes a story about her mother's affair. One of the handsome fraternity boys reads a masturbatory fantasy involving corn on the cob and the students applaud and cheer. I begin to wonder if I'll be fired, but the fact is no one but my students and I care what we do or say. No one ever asks, no one ever comes to see what happens between us here. But I realize that what happens is enough for me.

Outside class, I'm God's own forgotten gimcrack, sitting alone by the sparkling pool. The story in front of me is as light as the wind, it means nothing, it flies away from my hands. I'm fighting panic, the fear of having nothing to say, praying, *Please,* and lie all night with nothing but the steady tick of the clock and the murmuring seashell roar of my ear against the pillow. All I want to convey is what happens to ordinary things, the journey of grime and wonder through the world, that's all. And I can't. At the end of the term, so soon, I leave my students and the blank apartment and go home.

STEVE GIVES ME his manuscript, at last, with an air of grand tragedy. It's badly typed, full of punctuation errors and missing words. He hasn't put his name on it. I read it, and call him up to say: "It's good. It's good, but it's not enough. You need to put more of yourself in there, you need to give us more."

If I have one good day, a good hour, even a single good sentence, I turn into a world-beater, the ice queen. Make my day. I lie in bed and imagine waking from a worthless sleep, crawling to the study, starting in the middle of the sentence that ended in exhaustion the night before, typing until the electricity goes off because I forgot to pay the bill. I imagine being a famous narcissist who abandons her children and dies for the holy flaming book, who gets her face on a postage stamp and doesn't live to regret it. Then I fall asleep, and waking up, I don't know how.

I've been told what I told Steve: this isn't the story you meant to write, this isn't how your story really ends, this isn't what you mean to say. I know what a childish grief this is: *I don't know how.* I know the rage, the rising cry, *How dare you,* I know the terror, *I can't,* I know that often nothing matters the way this matters. He listens to me and then he says, "It's all I've got, the whispering demons filling the air."

I tentatively begin again, circling the desk like a boxer pacing a ring. One night, after two glasses of wine, I get up at midnight to scribble in pencil on a sheet torn out of a yellow legal pad because the pressure is so strong I don't want to take time to sit down and type, the words are big and cockeyed on the page, veering sideways, getting smaller toward the bottom where I run out of space and turn the page on its end to write in the margins. This is the half-heard, faraway roar, the mumble of voices too low to distinguish the words. I can suddenly hear *language*—the rise and fall of conversation, the fading in and out of whispers and confidences and narration, and oh, this is how it begins, how I start to be allowed to be able to write. This pressure of *words coming, words coming*, like a train in the distance, the first hint of the whistle. The chuffing roar. I'm unsettled and restless, all I know is *words coming* and no idea what the words might be and now it's just a matter of time, getting ready, ready to pounce.

Steve isn't writing. We can't have coffee because he won't leave his apartment, won't even answer the phone. The last time we talked he said he was too small for all his big ideas. I had said to him, brutally, *"It's not enough,"* and he replied, *"It's all I've got,"* and the words bounced off his work, his walls, his world. How could I ask him for more?

And finally, I start writing by just writing, putting one word after the other on the page, and then all at once I'm writing like a rabbit going to ground, with a sudden leap.

I remember Baudelaire, dead of too little time, and Flaubert, who paced his studio weeping at the beauty of his own words. The sky is a dark dark blue, powdered lightly with thin high clouds, and the moon is a pearly chip thrust into fine blue sand. From that direction I hear no sounds. Shadowed by the world, by the stubborn focus of the words, it seems I can see everything, I can see the lines of gravity holding the moon against the sky, I can see its spinning and resistance and the correct position of the most ordinary things, against the spotlight of our ordinary lives.

I call Steve to tell him that all our ideas are big ideas. Everything is too much. He doesn't answer the phone, and I imagine him standing in the center of the room, alone, watching it shiver with every ring.

Antioch Review, Summer 1997

What is there to write about writing? In a way, there is nothing to say— and yet writers talk and think and write about writing all the time. Steve Tyler and I have been friends for a very long time and have talked a lot about writing—and about not writing—over the years. Long after he'd quit, done, never going to try that again, he was surprised by words. He recently published a book of good poems called A Hole in the Sun.

The Hounds of Spring

MONTHS AGO, WHEN IT WAS DANK AND COLD, THREE weeks teaching writing to high school students seemed a short enough commitment. In April, it's not so easy. Not on fragrant, mild mornings and warm afternoons full of light. I am the fourth writer in this experimental program funded by a distant foundation, the last visiting writer for the year. I follow a playwright, a poet, and a novelist. Each of us took over the same four classes, the same 110 students, divided between regular freshmen and sophomore honors.

I run into the poet at a party a few weeks after his session ends, and he is sly and self-satisfied. "They're going to eat you up," he says, with enthusiasm. "You've gotta get right in their faces," he adds, getting right in my face, "and show them what's what."

So I call the novelist who preceded me, a mild man with a grown daughter and years of classroom experience. "It's the hardest teaching I've ever done," he tells me. "And I'll never do it again."

I'm confident, even in my spring fever. I've taught only adults for several years, but I have three teenagers of my own. I've been rearing children for almost twenty breathless years, and for much of that time I've lived and worked half a block from the big inner-city high school where I'll teach. It's a huge campus, a handsome brick complex covering almost two square blocks next to a city park strewn with the teens' discarded cigarette butts. The campus is "open," and every day several hundred of the 1,800 students walk by my house on the way to their fast-food lunches and return a short time later, tossing Burger King and McDonald's wrappers on my lawn. I think I know teenagers and their animal energy—their explosive pleasures, their dark grief, their eternal restlessness, their springs.

The two freshmen classes are full of loud boys and inattentive girls, daring me to interest them. Several set themselves distinctly apart. Anna, heavy and plain, surrounds herself with yards of empty space, crouches behind purple lips and raccoon eyes. Damon is seventeen, making his third and last attempt to pass freshmen English. He is tall and coolly handsome and self-conscious. "I've got a big penis," he tells me on the first day, when we're doing introductions. Most of the freshmen disappear in the crowd. Pairs and trios huddle together in the back. They call me "Yo!"; they blend together, mouths hanging open when I speak.

The sophomores are calm, obedient, tranquil. Whether this is a difference between freshmen and sophomores, or bonehead English and honors, I'm never quite sure. The sophomores worry about my grading system and call me "Ms. Tisdale." The young men are lanky out of all proportion, taller than me and quick to blush, easy to praise. Josie and Sandra ("that's Sondra") have wild hair and long skirts and sit together, self-consciously mature and outspoken. There are dozens of slim, button-nose girls with shoulder-length brown hair and schoolgirl skirts and short-sleeved sweaters. They are all tediously polite.

"The hounds of spring are on winter's traces," for me as well as them, and I'm surprised at how difficult it is to stand under fluorescent lights in front of this sea of staring faces all day long, these 110 faces all seemingly called Megan or Tyler or K'Shanti. I'm surprised at how difficult it is for me to see each one separate from the others, to meet each one, to simply remember names in the institutional havoc of high school.

Before I started, the classroom teacher gave me a paper listing the six separate schedules used, and a schedule for the schedules; every day before I walk the half-block here, I have to consult my schedule to find out which schedule we're on that day. Sometimes there are forty-eight-minute periods, and sometimes there are thirty-one-minute periods. Sometimes there are assemblies or faculty meetings, and sometimes the entire school opens two hours late. I can't get used to the giant hive's obeisance to the chaos. It is all so far from the day I keep at home, the long silences and self-determined hours in which I write.

The bells ring and ring, two before and after every class. Bells ring, and the empty halls fill with 1,800 handsome, healthy young people wearing a variety of fashion mistakes, the air thick with sweat, pheromones, and a hundred kinds of tension, like some three-dimensional model of chaos theory. They appear, a human tsunami, and disappear a few minutes later. During class, the phone rings. Unspecified "warning" bells ring. Staff walk in and out of the room, other students walk in and out of the room, carrying messages, asking questions. The daily announcement sheet is delivered. Almost every day, a half-dozen students stand suddenly in the midst of a period and grab their packs. "Where are you going?" I ask, and they say, "Field trip," or "Track meet," or "Yearbook meeting," and leave.

The starting bell rings and they are still wandering in, to find their way into the semicircle of desks, chatting, yelling, shoving each other; they put on makeup, draw cartoons, sleep. Every day Jessica spends sixth period patiently scraping the silver lining out of pieces of chewing gum and rubbing it on to her binder cover, filling her mouth with a wad the size of a baby's fist. When the second bell rings, I walk to the front and they turn mercilessly upon me, like a crowd awaiting the verdict, ready for anything.

My focus for these three weeks is a twisted autobiography, a memoir of their futures, looking back. For the final assignment, I want them to do a short scene from the book they might write when they are old—and it takes days for me to explain this.

First, imagine your future, I tell them on the first day. Any possible future. Outline it. The freshmen stare at me. "How am I supposed to know what's going to happen?" one pretty girl asks, all innocent stupidity. The sophomores want to know how it will be graded. "What's an outline?" ask several freshmen. "When's it due?" ask the sophomores.

I start again. Imagine your future. From where you sit, I tell them, almost anything could happen. Almost anything. You could be rich or poor, happy or sad. You could become an interstellar traveler, a bum, an inventor, a criminal. What might happen that will affect you? Who will enter your life? What will you choose?

Make an outline, I say, drawing a form on the blackboard, my hands sticky with yellow chalk—events on one side and your feelings about them on the other. Think of love, wisdom, terrible mistakes, illness, luck, learning.

"You mean two outlines?" asks a freshman boy.

"Is this legal?" asks a sophomore girl in the next period.

"Legal?" I ask.

"I mean," she says, "is it legal to write about something we don't know anything about?"

The next day, a dozen freshmen scratch their heads in bemusement when I mention the outline. "What outline?" goes the chorus—that day, every day that week.

Meanwhile, I have to fill thirty-one minutes, forty-two minutes, forty-eight minutes, four times a day. We do free writing ("What am I supposed to write about?") and make lists of people who have influenced them, places they've been, things they've learned, and what people and places and skills might come in the future. Quickly I find another surprise. The boys are wilder writers—less careful of convention, more willing to leap into the new. I start watching the dozens of vaguely familiar girls, who seem to have shaved off all distinguishing characteristics. They are so careful. Careful about their appearance, what they say and how they say it, how they sit, what they write. Even in the five-minute free writes, they are less willing to go out from where they are—to go out there, where you have to go, to write. They are reluctant to show me rough work, imperfect work, anything I might criticize; they are very careful to write down my instructions word by word.

They're all trying themselves on day by day, hour by hour, I know—already making choices that will last too unfairly long. I'm surprised to find, after a few days, how invigorating it all is. I pace and plead for reaction, for ideas, for words, and gradually we all relax a little and we make progress. The boys crouch in their too-small desks, giant feet sticking out, and the girls perch on the edge, alert like little groundhogs listening for the patter of coyote feet. I begin to like them a lot.

Then the outlines come in. I am startled at the preoccupation with romance and family in many of these imaginary futures. But the distinction between boys and girls is perfectly, painfully stereotypical. The boys also imagine adventure, crime, inventions, drama. One expects war with China, several get rich and lose it all, one invents a time warp, another resurrects Jesus, another is shot by a robber. Their outlines are heavy on action, light on response. A freshman: "I grow populerity and for the rest of my life I'm a million air." A sophomore boy in his middle age: "Amazingly, my first attempt at movie-making won all the year's Oscars. So did the next two. And my band was a HUGE success. It only followed that I run the country."

Among the girls, in all the dozens and dozens of girls, the preoccupation with marriage and children is almost everything. They are entirely reaction, marked by caution. One after the other writes of falling in love, getting married, having children, and giving up—giving up careers, travel, college, sports, private hopes, to save the marriage, take care of the children. The outlines seem to describe with remarkable precision the quietly desperate and disappointed lives many women live today.

One girl writes of her future—and I feel this way, too—"Long awaited depression will fall on me, and I will be ready for it."

FOR THE SECOND week, while I repeatedly remind them of the chapter they must write and then read out loud, we do exercises. More free writing, more lists. We make a list of childhood playground games, a rousing twenty-minute shoutfest, and write scenes about them. We break into small groups. I bring my big box of crayons and a pad of art paper and have them draw maps of a familiar childhood place and try to remember everything that happened there. "More crayons!" they all shout the next day, and so we draw personal symbols of the future when our social security number will be replaced by logos.

I get to know a few students in the changing crowds. Anna turns in every assignment, speaks up in every discussion. Joseph, with his peroxide blond fade and unreadable neon-orange pen, Joseph who never listens and never shuts up and drives me crazy, seems to genuinely care what I think about his work. Skinny little Hunter, with an opinion on everything, who loves to take the least popular position and start arguments, tells me his parents would be angry if they knew he did something as wasteful as "writing stories." He sits next to Rebecca, pretty, plump, smart, and they fight constantly. Karen, quiet and self-contained with a perfect silver hoop piercing her left eyebrow, is a strong-minded and clear thinker.

On a quiet Wednesday in the second week, discouraged by the girls' outlines, I talk to the sophomores about self-censorship. I should have done this earlier, I see now; I thought perhaps they wouldn't need it yet, the way adults usually do. I thought maybe they wouldn't understand it—but I was wrong about both things. I make lists on the board about what we're afraid to write about and who we want to please and suddenly everyone is talking at once, Josie and Hunter and Rebecca and even a few of the Megans, tentatively raising their hands, arguing about censorship and offensiveness and politically correct speech, what is obscene, who decides.

But the next day, the real agenda returns. It is almost time to read the stories. The other writers, they tell me, didn't make them read. I'm not making them, I reply, only giving higher grades for it. The other writers read their work for them—I won't. One of the other writers read their work anonymously—I steadfastly refuse.

Instead I buy potato chips and pretzels, jelly beans and red licorice whips and M&M's and come to class on the first read-out-loud day with overflowing grocery bags. The first reader chooses the first treat, I say, and Isaac surprises me by going first. Isaac is smart, shy, with one crossed eye, and Isaac knocks everyone out with his account of how he fell from grace as world chess champion, became a bum, and finally rose to new fame as a Central Park hustler.

After class, four girls stop me and say all at once, "We can't read!" They can't read, they say, because Isaac's story is so good and theirs are so boring and his is full of adventure and theirs is not. They are afraid to read out loud, fearful of being thought stupid or foolish or—what? I ask them. Girlish? Boring, says one Megan. (Which Megan? I can't remember.) This is a terrible fear, I know—this fear of not being interesting—of being trivial, not special. It is almost as great, I think, as their fear of standing out and being special. I give them a little pep talk, but they aren't consoled.

After a few days of the bravest students coming to stand in front of the class, showing everyone their personal symbol, reading their stories, and then staying put to hear comments, one girl begs me to let her read while sitting at her desk. I list again the reasons why I want her in front: you'll read better standing up; you need to claim your work; you'll be more confident in the end. "Please," she begs, but I'm tough and say no. Read in front or not at all.

"Slowly, clearly, please," I say, and one by one they hunch over their papers and read: nervous, sometimes joking, sometimes stiff, smiles plastered on their faces, a few with ripe pimples and big feet, a few blossoming in perfect spring bloom.

And I am surprised again, to tears. There are bad stories, dull stories—and beautiful stories, better than the stories some of my adult students write. I close my eyes and listen to the voices, deep and high, fast and murmured, and sometimes stumbling and thick, and images appear, people in a London flat, a busy airport, autumn leaves skittering across a wet sidewalk, a bitter whispered fight, a sour resignation to mediocrity. The technique seems to leap beyond all they've shown me, the maturity beyond their years.

(Later, line-editing the stories, I see the misspellings and incomplete sentences and misshapen construction I fail to hear in my delight at their voices. The freshmen spelling! "This Japanise undeground fighting areana is one of the dingist raggity places I have ever fought in." And the fatal danger of the sophomores' dependence on spellcheckers: "I gazed upon a pear of muscular biceps." "She turned summer salts." And my favorite: "I raped the package carefully.")

But the differences remain, more obvious than ever. The boys write about war and fame and money and alien contact. Damon writes about setting a world record in the 100 meters. It's not a great story, or even a good story. But it has a beginning, middle and end, and he stands in front of the class and reads without laughing. Lots of the boys write about marriage and love and hard choices, too, layered through their scenes of movement and action. The girls write about marriage and love and hard choices and no more. Sandra gives me a technically proficient and strangely passive story about a friend's pregnancy, and refuses to read. Jocelyn—loud, obnoxious, obscene Jocelyn—writes about her prayer to God to help her get a job. Anna, purple lips and raccoon eyes in place, reads an intensely detailed story about giving birth.

The exceptions occur even inside the rule. Nancy describes murdering her husband's lover in a gothic tale of madness and imprisonment. Desiree imagines becoming a pro basketball player, and in the end, quits to be with her children so her husband can continue to work for the team. Rebecca is the only girl who writes a story primarily about her own professional accomplishment. She describes running for president, and the entire story revolves around the stress of her campaign being focused on makeup, hair, and clothing.

I don't know what to expect from Cindy. She's beautiful, delicately featured, slender, with a soft voice. She's beautiful in the way that makes adults coo and behave weasely. I suspect she's been stared at and coveted by strangers since her birth. She reads an explicit story about a businesswoman caught in the equation between power, money, and sex, leaving the room dead silent. It is too knowing for comfort.

And the best story to come out of all the classes—110 students—is written by quiet Rose, who is fat and plain and a stutteringly bad reader. It is mature, complex, layered, subtle; there is almost nothing I can write in the margins to make it better, this tale of a compromised marriage to an unfaithful layabout.

Toward the end of the three weeks, I have lunch with a representative from the foundation. She wants to know what could be done to make the girls more "confident." I rattle on, about girl-only classrooms, giving them room away from the boys, time to talk, permission to question and complain without being afraid of being seen as whiners, complainers, bad girls, tough girls. But I know that all of them, boys and girls both, are still only partly formed, soft as Play-Doh. They are like golems—their bodies in full flower and everything else a work-in-progress. I don't dare say there are essential gender differences here, though I wonder more and more.

"But girls have so many more role models now," the foundation representative says. She is a petite, elegant, beautiful woman in a black suit, perfectly coifed.

More role models. Which ones, I wonder. An increasingly impossible physical ideal? A clear-cut choice between career and family? They've seen their mothers suffer from trying to do both. They know all about the "second shift" of endless work. When I was fifteen, my role models were burning bras, marching in the street, starting clinics, passing laws, and getting arrested. Role models now are selling diet books and making music videos.

The simple fact is, I don't know. I don't know how to help them. I know that I have to keep checking my watch during lunch and rush off to make the final bell for sixth period, and that all of these children who are almost grown have spent their entire lives ruled by a clock and the demands of strangers. They have grown up in a fragmented and chaotic place over which they have no control. I know they've rarely thought about the possibility of getting out; they don't see any place to get out to, anywhere to go not ruled by bureaucratic entanglements and someone else's schedule and somebody else's plans. If girls are somehow wired toward pliancy, then the helpless role of student in the shadow of the institution is the worst place they can be. If we want to teach them independence, the first thing to do would be to give it to them.

I'm sitting in the hallway at the end of third period, with three girls named Megan and one silent morose boy named Dave, trying to have individual conferences, which is of course impossible. There is simply no time, and no place to go but the hallway floor.

The Megans are all getting A's, good, competent I-turned-everything-in-on-time A's. Dave is flunking without apparent remorse, having done nothing, said nothing, for weeks. I tell the stocky, brunet Megan that I want her to read out loud and she says, "It's so hard to read. I hate to read my stuff. It seems so boring." And what I can't tell her is that it is, a little, sincere and earnest and predictable and boring. So I give them another little pep talk about the way women writers have been demeaned for writing about the domestic and how it's a great subject and great domestic stories have been written by men and women both, but especially by women, and how they're going to have to cope sooner or later, whether they write or not, with this dismissal of the female realm. And they nod, good students, good girls, silently acquiescing to authority.

Dave sits cross-legged, staring at the floor, in dour sleepy silence. He will never write anything, but I will miss him anyway, this lumbering boy. I will miss them all; I miss them already.

So I say it again: "I'll be listening to you. I'll listen." And what I want to say, long to say, and don't, is: Dream a little. Oh, my girls, dream.

Then the bell rings again and the human ocean spills into the hallway like breakers in a storm. We scramble up off the floor before we're trampled by the hurrying sea.

Salon, July 1, 1997

For several years, I taught for Writers in the Schools, a terrific program pairing writers with high school classes for several weeks of focused writing. At the time, my own children were teenagers. They had all had difficult years in school, one way or another, and teenaged energy had been a significant part of my home life for a long time. I taught at the neighborhood high school a few years after my middle son had dropped out for a brief career as a juvenile delinquent. I was startled to discover that trying to cajole noisy classes into writing a little bit turned into a heartbreaking study in how we turn girls into victims.

Temporary God

FROM THE TINY BALCONY OF MY DREARY HOTEL IN MARINA Del Rey, California, I can see a sprawling shopping center, a busy freeway, and a small kidney pool glittering in the dirty light. A half-dozen people drowse or read in the plastic chaises by the water.

I'm alone, out of town on business, and I have two hours free—two hours to pretend I'm alone in the world with no place to go and no one to please. I go out to the pool with a soda and a book and find an empty lounge, its vinyl strips still sagging in the shape of a departed bottom.

Three chubby girls with identical black hair and ill-fitting swimsuits are playing Double Dare in the shallow end.

"Dare, or Double Dare?" the biggest girl says to the smallest.

The smaller girl flips her heavy, wet hair. "Double dare," she says, without hesitation.

"I dare you to stand on your head under water."

"Eeeaaasssy," drawls the girl, jumping in and flipping over.

A heavy, self-conscious woman bobs in the deep end, watching the dark-haired girls.

Nearby, a pair of prepubescent sisters compete for the attention of an older boy. Their swimsuits bag on their attenuated bodies as they shriek and call; the boy, his bony chest puffed out like a mating frog's, takes turns flinging them away from him so they can splash and scream.

A slim Japanese woman in a black tank suit silently leads her timid little boy down the steps.

And weaving through, as fluid and oblivious as the water, slide two teens.

The girl is blooming, about fifteen years old, unblemished. Her shoulder-length brown hair is pulled back and clings to her small head like a cap. The boy is a bit older, perhaps, gawky and thin, and his shoulder-length brown hair is disheveled and loose around his long neck. In the tiny pool, in the noisy L.A. haze, they fold themselves together like gliding swans. He holds her for a moment like a man carrying a child, or a bride, then she turns slowly and wraps her arms around his neck. He comes in close to her ear and whispers, she turns her back to his chest and leans her glistening head on his shoulder. He pushes off the bottom and they float backward to the pool's edge and pause against the deck, beside each other. He turns and she lays herself on his back and he slides forward; she ducks out of his reach for a second and he stretches after her, she laughs and rolls back to him, they bounce gently face to face, murmuring.

This goes on for a long time.

I read my book, drink my soda. And all the time, I watch. People slowly, sleepily come and go. The dark-haired girls are called away. The boy demonstrates his skateboard moves to the sisters. A young man arrives with fresh towels. Trucks rumble by. The boy and girl slither through the water together without a thought, seamlessly drifting between the changing swimmers. I watch from behind my sunglasses, and suddenly she catches me watching and returns my stare, stony, self-contained. The difference between us is simple. I am just another voyeur, dismayed by the distant object of desire. She is not dismayed. She is a universe of Two.

I've left behind my thirteen-year-old daughter, my youngest child. She is young at thirteen, younger than her own body, interested in books and soccer and her pet turtle. She is still very interested in me, in my position of safety and control between her and the world. She likes to sit behind me when we watch television and mess up my hair and tell me stories that invariably begin, "Guess what?" and eat big, messy bowls of cereal right before going to bed. She misses me terribly when I'm gone, and this time I wrote a note for the kitchen bulletin board to remind her when I'd be back: "Mom, Sunday, 12:30." If she was here, she'd be winning Double Dare; she'd lie beside me drinking soda and dripping on her mystery novel in the sun.

But that will end like everything else.

I remember how it feels, their dizzy height of obsession, the centering of the universe around Two. I remember how all else fades like a weakening signal, to a blur, how when you are together, all the world is the world made by Two, and when you are apart, there is only waiting to be together. I remember when love and sex were one thing, as unbroken as this moist ease in the sunlit water. I remember how one falls in love and longs for the body of the other and, longing, believes in love.

And I remember, oh I do remember, that the ghostly adults around you have no idea, because they have never felt like this, and so there is no reason to try to explain.

Many years ago, when my daughter was still toddling around with a ragged bear in her arms, I tried to explain to an old friend how it felt to be her mother. She was my third child and I was still trying to find the words.

My friend had no children, had no interest in children, tolerated mine with poorly disguised impatience. I wanted her to know why they mattered to me.

I pointed to my daughter on the floor beside us, and said, "I'm the giver and taker of the world to her." I was trying to explain this enormous responsibility, the weight that sometimes feels intolerably large. "I bring good and evil whether I mean to or not. I might as well be God."

My friend sneered at me. "Well," she said, "aren't you special?"

The boy and girl slide through the water. I watch, furtively, and think: Her mother. Somewhere her mother watches them make their smooth way through the water. He pulls her close to him, a large hand claiming her smooth belly. She strokes his cheek. I actually lean forward off my lounge, almost speaking, wanting only to beckon her to the poolside for a moment and whisper, "Be nice to your mother." But I say nothing at all, and pretend to read.

I see the accelerating future approach. I've done this already, after all, with two boys—grieved for the silly three-year-olds, the gap-toothed six-year-olds, the willowy nine-year-olds. They've died and will never return, and I grieve. She ruffles my hair when we watch television and my back actually arches, like a cat, pushing into her hand, asking for more. She brings goodness to me and makes me fear evil; she gives and takes away the world. There are so many mysteries ahead.

I remember the world fading into the universe made by Two, and I remember how it shatters when that ends—and then, how it begins again, brand new. So much to do, so many mistakes to make for the first time. And what is there to regret? This is how the world goes, this is how it must be. I don't grieve for her—I grieve for me, sitting by some poolside in a few years, pretending to read so my sunglasses hide my hungry, tearful eyes as she glides by, oblivious.

I haven't seen my childless friend in many years, but I've replayed that conversation again and again in my mind. I hadn't thought I needed to say to her that it's terrifying to be God. I thought such a thing goes without saying. The risks are so enormous—the losses so sharp. For years, I've wanted to tell her how powerless that power feels. How it is to be a voyeur, subject to the most pleading of desires. I wish my friend were here, and I could say: I dare you to try this. I double dare you.

Salon, September 16, 1997

I wrote a column for Salon *for a few years, called* Second Opinion. *(It was part of the regrettably named section* Mothers Who Think.*) I consider this essay as one of a pair with the next story, "Crossing to Safety." They are two ways to think about the way we lose childhood—the enormous gift of being young and healthy and unafraid for a time, the inexpressible small deaths of growing up, and the stupefying losses of simply watching this happen.*

Crossing to Safety

EVERY SUMMER FOR SEVEN YEARS, I CAMPED WITH OTHER
Girl Scouts beside a lake, in the shadow of a mountain in southern Oregon. A cavernous lodge stood above the shore, and we had endless acres of tall pines and dusty trails to ourselves. In all those years I never found the camp's boundaries.

We were divided roughly by age into several groups and assigned to airy cabins, each with its own campfire ring, its own name, its own quality. I remember the days as being almost without variation and filled from morning to night with songs of all kinds, funny and sentimental and silly and sad. Each day meant waking to "Reveille" played on an invisible trumpet, to bright, cool air and pine perfume, to the clattering of battered plastic bowls heaped with oatmeal and the dull thunk of arrows hitting hay bales. And each day ended with a chorus of high girls' voices singing taps in the sudden dark. When the last note ("safely rest—God is night") faded, *niiiiiigghh*, like a melancholy kiss, we would stay silently by the fire a few moments, each of us with hot, dry eyes toward the flame, backs cool in the rising forest night.

I've never gone back, unwilling to break the spell those summers cast upon me, an enchantment with the whole and its many parts under which I still dwell. Each thing still has power over me: pine scent, canoes, wildflowers, the popping of firewood under a starry sky, and girls. Those summers are part of why I still live in the Northwest, part of every camping trip and hike, part of every swim in its cold rivers and mountain lakes.

A few years ago, I volunteered to work at a camp my son attended. It was all much tamer than mine had been: a pool instead of a lake, a small town complete with Dairy Queen nearby, wide grassy spaces instead of corridors of trees. It was a pretty place, with big poplars and a few snakes and house martins and bats swooping at dusk. I made pipe-cleaner animal figures and painted faces on river rocks on hot afternoons and doled out Band-Aids. But I was uncomfortable inside my thick skin—conservative, withdrawn. Adult.

The campers under my care seemed mulish and bored, and instead of singing they listened to the radio, and it seemed to me they thought smaller, more local thoughts than I had. Boys and girls were mixed together there, in a hot, explosive herd, and the girls were especially careful, unwilling to swim races or chase balls or cast a fishing line. At their age, I would take a canoe alone into the swamp at one end of the lake to sit in silence and wait for beavers and consider things. They sat together, fettered into a constant group by fear and liability insurance, heads tucked together like birds on a roost.

I missed the lake. It was mostly the lake where we did things—where we floated, swam, rowed, paddled, raced, and dived—in that round, deep, black pool a true mile wide.

I swam across the lake once. It is one of the measures of courage by which I have weighed the rest of my life.

There was a lake swim every summer. Each girl could try, if she could prove herself first in a test of endurance by swimming fifty laps, swimming for an hour or more without stopping. Those who dared came down to the dock on a chosen evening, when the light had begun to yellow and the mountain across the water was turning black with shadow. Counselors—those large, strong, tall women who ambled through the woods like an admired alien race—sat on the dock, their big legs dangling in the clean water. We swam without rest, forward and backward, pacing ourselves into the darkness.

A few days later, the half-dozen of us who had passed the

test were awakened before dawn. I pulled on my swimsuit and clothes—whispering, hurrying, shivering, thrilled—and walked through the forest to the shore with the others, no sound but our own padding feet. Six girls, six counselors, six rowboats set out with the swish of oars into the empty, flat lake in the dark, and crossed.

It was a long way, that mile, so far from the safety of the camp that we could barely see its shore, and all the cabins on the other side were hidden in the hovering trees. On a tiny spit of sand under the mountain, I took off my jeans and sweatshirt and shoes and put them in the rowboat, where the counselor sat, bobbing, watching me. The group dissolved, no one spoke above a whisper, there were no longer six girls, but only one, only me, alone. I hit the icy water and swam.

I swam for a long time, the counselor pacing me in silence, through black water and black air, in the shadow of the black mountain, and watched the dawn.

Small splash of beaver's tail far away, the sound carrying forever into the day, the cattail silhouette of the swamp small in the distance, tendrils of mist rising to surround us in fine veils as the colors of the world appeared. Blue water, blue air, blue mountain; golden light, green trees, the red roof of the lodge ahead, a tiny patch. I swam. I pierced the glassy surface of the water like an arrow pierces the air, and watched my pale hands disappear into the blackness below.

I swam and finally came to ground near the lodge, applauded by a smiling crowd, a hero's welcome home.

On the last day of my son's camp, a hot, parched, shimmering day, I watched the boys and girls drift sleepily off to bed while tiny bats darted across the sulfurous porch light of the lodge. When all was quiet, when it seemed all the children were asleep, someone turned the lights on around the pool, and suddenly the whole staff was there on the deck—all the crotchety adults, worn out from the past weeks. We broke the pool rules, we ran on the deck, threw balls at each other, we floated, paddled, raced and dived under the tall, black trees. I shed my thick skin. Near midnight, someone slipped into the shed and turned off all the overhead lights and all that was left were the bulbs underwater, casting a shivering aqua cloud onto the side of trees. I floated on my back beneath a milky spray of stars in the August night. And then I rolled underwater, turning the world upside-down, and watched my pale legs pierce the glassy surface of the water and disappear into the blackness below.

Salon, August 7, 1998

Recording

I'M NOT REALLY EAVESDROPPING ON THE CONVERSATION in the backseat. I can't help it.

"I think the mistake I made with David," says Kristen, her eyes hidden underneath a baseball cap, "was to let him have internet relationships while we were dating. As long as he didn't become emotionally involved."

Cody, her ostensible boyfriend, soft of face and with a blond ponytail as long as Kristen's own, nods sagely. I watch them in the mirror, my eyes darting back and forth between the highway and their reflected faces.

"I've made lots of mistakes in relationships," Cody says. "That's why I've had so many."

"You haven't had so many," says Alison, Kristen's best friend, squeezed next to her in the backseat.

"Yes he has," argues Kristen. "We've both dated lots of other people and we've dated each other three times. This is the third time we've been together."

We are driving up to the mountain to go snowshoeing, into a winter world seventy miles from the city and valley, where it rarely snows. Three cars, three adult drivers, twelve students on a mid-week field trip, and it was my idea. This is Project Week, with days full of field trips, and I am enamored of snowshoeing and wanted to get the kids outside. Though they are all from my daughter's small school, I have never met these particular students before. They are polite—courteous in a way that seems only reasonable when dealing with a strange adult—but it is obvious from the first few minutes that they are also completely uninterested in me. My earnest attempts at conversation are gently deflected, almost ignored, and quickly I lapse into silence and let them speak. Which they do, without cease.

Kristen regales Cody with tales about David. "I can't stand this girl Stephie who David says is his best friend. She stayed at his house one weekend."

"Were they together?" asked Alison. This is the code word, simple and potent. You are together, or you are apart.

"Nooooo," says Kristen, thoughtfully. "But she's too old for him."

A while later, Alison is complaining about her own boyfriend, who hasn't come on the trip and, it seems, has little time for her.

"Alison, you know you have to get him to a therapist," Kristen says forcefully. "He has to learn how to talk to you."

They are thirteen years old.

IF THIS WERE television, Cody would be the Cute Guy (subset, Goofy Cute Guy). Kristen—slender and blonde, in a faceless, cookie-cutter way—would be the Cute Girl. Alison is the Cute Girl's Fat Girlfriend, saved from purgatory by this single thread. And next to me in the front seat is Ryan, the tragic character—the Fat Boy No One Likes. He alternately plays with a Game Boy in brief bouts of concentration, and eats. Now and then he laughs at the conversation he is carefully following, trying to turn his bulky body around in the seat and take part. He is treated with much the same courteous lack of interest with which they treat me.

I find myself thinking of my passengers this way, in capital letters outlining roles, within a few minutes. Their conversation is a script, full of catch words and cheap ideas, the irony entirely unconscious. Where did they learn to talk this way? They seem saturated with image, imitating not only behavior but response as well—living through the imagined conversations of imagined selves. This is how people talk on television, in the movies, this is what the magazines say. Is it that simple—that blunt? Do they inhabit these iconic roles because they have grown so familiar with the formula—or do I see them as icons because I am?

Kristen is still talking about David. "If I wasn't dating you, I'd still be dating him," she says to Cody. "But he wanted to know how old you had to be to get married and I said, 'Yeah, right.'"

"That's why I broke up with Billy," agrees Alison. "He said he wanted to be together forever."

Ryan is eating peanuts with a steady hand. Quietly, so that only I can hear, he says, "I've never had a girlfriend, so I wouldn't know."

Cody swears and then looks up suddenly and catches my eyes in the mirror and asks innocently, "Is that word allowed?"

"I don't care," I say, looking back at him.

"How about kissing?" he asks.

"A little kissing is okay," I say. But they don't kiss. Perhaps it is still more idea than fact.

A single untutored word blends in with a hundred rehearsed ones; mediation is the norm. This is the normality of adolescence: a wild anarchy of selves. Young people try on points of view and habits of speech like clothes, leaving the discards in a pile behind them. Sometimes there seems to be little but imitation and disguise at this age; at times, the self of each adolescent is little more than a successive mimicry. Chameleons.

I wasn't so different. I dressed the way people I admired dressed, talked like them, parroted their ideas. Young people always have—the culture of youth is obsession with the culture. And still I think it's different now. These teens live in a world of mirrors, in nothing but mirrors, endlessly reflecting themselves.

Even as they try to live the lives played out before them, the lives they do live are recorded constantly; they live recorded lives. They are always on stage. Every event I attend is a sea of camcorders. Dances, soccer games, dates, picnics, slumber parties—all are photographed and videotaped, spliced and edited, and then copied and mailed off for distant viewing. Every classroom has computers; every break involves a screen. They can add special effects now, and music, subtitles, narration; their lives are shot across a world wide web in living pixel color. Nothing is more real than what we see made up.

They start talking about celebrities, a favorite topic. When life is an artifact, a recorded event, recorded lives are the most real. "I'm related to that general guy, what's it, Patton, like through my great-grandmother or something," Alison says, and Cody says that he too is related to Somebody Famous and Kristen notes that she is also distantly related to Somebody Famous and adds that even Edmund, crazy Edmund who is the school scapegoat, is supposedly related to Britney Spears.

Ryan, who is eating potato chips now, says to himself in the front seat, "I'm not related to anybody."

"Maybe you'll be famous someday yourself," I tell him, with a note of maternal encouragement that horrifies me as soon as I hear myself speak. "Then everyone in your family can claim to be related to you."

And already I'm wondering why I think it should cheer him up to imagine that he'll have to be famous before his family would be glad to be related to him. But he nods thoughtfully, chewing.

WE REACH THE ski shop. The kids in my car are the youngest, the "seven by eights," in the lingo of this small school, which houses kindergarteners through high school seniors. The middle-schoolers, acutely conscious of each nuance of the high school students, are themselves ignored by their models.

We fill the shop in the massive, floor-to-ceiling way only teenagers can achieve. Everyone gets snow shoes and most get boots, and I count how many of them are wearing jeans after being carefully instructed not to wear jeans, and then we all line up in the parking lot for a quick how-to-put-snowshoes-on lesson and then pile back in the cars and keep heading up. Soon the road is lined with tall conifers sprinkled with snowy confection, and with each curve the deep tree-carpeted valleys appear further below, sprinkled white. Smoky fog swirls across the road, shot with sunlight.

"Wow," the kids say, and seem genuinely surprised.

"It's beautiful!" Kristen breathes, eyes wide open for the first time all day, and she pushes the baseball cap back on her head. None of them are regular skiers, none have been snowshoeing before. Ryan has lived here most of his life but he's never been to the mountain at all. For a moment, the screen of the world fills their sight, a Panavision view as breathtaking as every SUV commercial they've ever seen, as pretty as any backdrop in their video games.

"Don't go in the caves," the man at the ski shop told everyone, referring to the early spring caverns opening in the deep drifts. I look up from the crate of snowshoes in the parking lot and count the feet sticking out of the caves and march over to be a grown-up. Slowly they assemble, complaining good-naturedly, suddenly remembering everything they were supposed to bring but forgot at home—sunglasses, lunch, gloves. I pass out extras of this and that, to the Handsome Guy, his Petite Girlfriend, the Tall Girl, the Skinny Guy With Glasses, the New Girl—I can't stop; I look around and each has a place, a perfect fit. Conversation surrounds me, a blend of rhetorical sophistication and the blunt concerns of teenagers—sex, power, yearning—a wave vibrating across a web of relationship. The politics of relationship they recite to each other sounds as familiar as nursery rhymes.

We march off, a ragged group spread across a plain of deep snow as smooth and unbroken as the blue sky. They form a body, organic and shifting in the Brownian motion of youth—busily swimming close and then far away, aggregating and dissolving, speeding up, spinning in place. They make a lot of noise, and spread farther and farther apart. Several boys compete to see who can mess up the most snow, who can run the fastest before he falls down, who can come most perilously close to the bank of the river before I yell at him. Two girls march stalwartly ahead, as though they can march forever. They stay side by side, steadily walking in a straight line toward a distant stand of trees across a featureless sheet of soft powder.

I've forgotten my camera and for a minute feel guilty—I, the adult, will fail to record this event. But suddenly out of the hundred-dollar backpacks come the cameras. Light flashes across the snow, but they aren't taking pictures of the snow. They are taking pictures of each other, singly and in groups, and of themselves, the camera held shakily at arm's length. All, that is, except Ryan. He walks wearily along in a group of one—now trailing behind, now slogging ahead, now slipping sideways—and he takes pictures of the empty snow, the unpeopled trees.

I have a lot of photographs of myself as a baby—sleepy or wide-eyed in the arms of my smiling mother, and with Aunt Lois and Aunt Lucille and Aunt Beryl and Aunt Ruth and Grandma and even a few with my father, who always looks like he's about to yell, "Get this baby off of me." And I have quite a few color slides from childhood—summer vacations, shivering at the beach, standing in anonymous parking lots, nervously watching the Christmas tree. I have only a few photographs of me in adolescence, all taken at our summer cabin—several distinct pictures of me in a swimsuit with a diving mask on, or half-buried in sand.

All these pictures were taken by my parents, and so I have no pictures of the life I lived away from home. No photographs from five years of Girl Scout camp. No photographs, bar the posed class pictures, from ten years of public school. Nothing of friends, long summer days, field trips, teachers, the county fair, my first job. No photographs from college—though I remember a few being taken, like distant clicks of someone else's idea while I disappeared into the moment before me.

There are years of my life from which I have no images at all outside my own mind.

I have many pictures of myself as a young mother, first holding a baby and then suddenly surrounded by three children. I have a lot of pictures of the kids when they were small, and I still take their picture whenever I think about it—which isn't very often. We made a videotape once, when my daughter was three and my sons in grubby late childhood. We borrowed a relative's camera, a heavy and uncertain piece of equipment, and I interviewed them—what did they want to be when they grew up, could they sing us a song? I loved that brief slice of their moving, laughing little selves. We watched it at Christmastime, until my middle son recorded over it when he wanted a copy of *Friday the 13th.*

WE HIKE TOWARD the place where the river comes in against the cliff. The skies have changed from blue to gray and suddenly a squall lets loose and we are enveloped in thick big flakes blowing sideways in a wind. The girl in the lead, a distant speck, breaks through the snow, sinking up to her thigh and dangling briefly over the freezing water hidden beneath the snow. The snow is already covering our tracks, and everyone looks the same—dark lines wavering against the shadowless white. The kids in jeans are complaining of the cold. We quickly get them turned around to head into the shelter of the trees, and they are without concern. They are immortal; this is only snow.

Back we go, hill by hill, and the sky suddenly clears again to blue and yellow light. We eat lunch in a hollow of small evergreens, each with its hat of snow. It is again a lovely day, lovely and fresh, white and soft and clean. Ryan stands apart, slowly rolling a giant snowball with his feet. Kristen and Cody and Allison are in a dell, out of sight—far from the danger of eight potentially contemptuous high school students.

After lunch, we slowly trudge back to the parking lot.

When the obligatory mess of snowshoes and gloves is finally cleaned up and mostly sorted out, and we've made the obligatory stop at Dairy Queen for french fries and shakes, we head home. The kids begin to roughhouse in the back seat. Kristen punches Cody and he shouts, "Ouch, I'm going to need that when I turn eighteen!" and everyone guffaws wildly, and for a few minutes, they're really thirteen years old. Cody chortles and shouts over

and over until I tell him to stop, and he stops all at once, his eyes
a bit shocked by all the random firings of his own head and skin.

Kristen says to Alison, "You have to stand up to Billy."

"Stand up to him?" says Alison. "He's twice as big as I am."

She is a big girl, and at first I wonder if this is her way of pretending that's not true. Then I wonder what she's afraid of—is this
more imagined life, this anxiety about a young man's rage? Is it a
little docudrama, a little bit of primetime? Perhaps they are mutat-
ing toward the furthest extremes of each type they inhabit—to the
edges of the continuum where there is the least overlap and thus the
most coherently defined shape. Perhaps our screens are filled with
these few almost mythically charged roles because so many people
fit them—because there are finally so few ways for us to meet each
other, so few types of people we can be. When will the roles solidify?
At what point is it impossible to take the mask off again?

Divorced, divorced, divorced: every child in my car comes
from divorce. I ask them leading questions; they are tired now
and more willing to let me ask. Kristen says she thinks her parents are thirty and thirty-two—which means they were young parents indeed. But maybe she has no idea what thirty years old really
looks like—certainly, if she gauges life by television and film, she
can't know. All the people on television look younger than they are
supposed to be. It occurs to me that it is not only Felicity and Ally
McBeal who have given her the lines she should say, told her how
to react to life's big moments. Perhaps she has been listening to
Mom and Dad.

Middle-aged divorced parents, dating. Perhaps she listens
as they get ready, worried and anticipating, and listens when they
come home and unwind. Perhaps she has spent long hours watching her mother dress and take care with her face and hair, wondering aloud what to expect, whispering in her daughter's ear what to
beware of and what to dread. My generation, so determined never
to grow up, has turned parenting upside-down.

I never once thought of my parents as my friends, or as anyone I would want for a friend. They couldn't enter the world in

which my friends lived. This, too, has transformed into *The Partridge Family, The Brady Bunch*—and a long parade of family sitcoms. Goofy Dad and Exasperated Mom, their struggles played out in the living room. The intimacy of my mother's life was not only separate from mine in a crucial way, it was of no import to me. I took her for granted, which is a different thing altogether from taking her for a friend.

I wonder if my passengers can take anything for granted. They live on shifting sands. Alison tells Cody about another e-mail boyfriend, and he wants clarification of a point: "Is that before or after you fucked each other blue on the web?" he asks.

Ryan is eating his third Odwalla meal bar since leaving Dairy Queen.

LATER THEY DISCUSS ways of harassing David. I have finally figured out that Kristen never actually met David, but conducted the romance entirely by telephone and e-mail. "My father liked him because he was so far away. 'I like this guy David,' he told me. I said, 'Why?' And he said, 'Because I don't have to see him.' But David used to call me at five a.m., I mean really at five a.m., and say, 'Are we still together or not?' and I was trying to sleep and that really pissed my father off."

The girls consider sending David envelopes full of grass clippings, toenails, or dirt, and then discuss whether they could insert themselves in a picture of Everclear and tell David they were hanging out with the group.

"I need a digital camera so I don't have to pay for film and processing and all that," says Alison.

"Well, you need a computer," I say helpfully, but Alison looks at me in the mirror and says, "I *have* a computer. I also *have* a scanner and a printer and Photoshop and a CD burner."

Of course. I recently attended a wedding of a couple in their mid-twenties. The old-fashioned, expensively engraved invitation included a traditional reply card, a tiny return envelope, and a CD of their favorite love songs with their photo on the label. This startled me. It seemed so—it is so hard to explain why or how, but this slice of their courtship was at once too private and too casual. I felt I'd been invited into a place that belonged to no one else, by mass mailing. I am getting a bit older, and perhaps that's all that's going on here. Alison's pronouncement startled me—not the laundry list of expensive toys, but the withering suggestion of technical prowess. These are people of experience, masters of their world. And they are not illiterate, exactly: even fucking on the internet is a matter of writing down the words. She knows how to do this—how to invent, how to manipulate. I'm just not sure if she knows anything else.

A group of affluent parents in a town on the outskirts of the city have banded together to start a private school for their children—a school without computers of any kind. There is plenty of time for that when they are older, they explained to a reporter. Now is the time for fairy tales, art, music, and books. The parents all work at Intel.

When everything is recorded, when we can watch everything as soon as it happens, then every possibility lies before us. Every kind of life is visible, even as real life disappears behind the stage. We describe ourselves most easily as *like* someone else, our experiences like a story, a movie, a show. We are offered so many things to be like now; life slides by, surface by shiny surface. Teenagers may be doing nothing more than they have always done, but the world in which they do it is not the world it was.

Threepenny Review, Fall 2002

At first glance, any essay about how technology is changing experience—especially one from the point of view of one generation watching another—is stale by the time it is finished. But this essay feels more relevant to me as the years pass. My grandchildren are now the age of the young people in this essay, and the same conversations occur. The same divisions in what we value and fear exist between us. I imagine they have always, in their way, existed between generations, and always will, but the risks of what we can lose, the investment in what is already lost— this feels enormous to me at times. And at the same time, I am one with these young people, longing for and inventing and demanding my future.

Violation

MY SISTER WRITES TO ME OFTEN THESE DAYS, THOUGH
most of our communication is business. Our father died several
months ago and she is his executor. Back and forth my brother
and sister and I go about annuities and armchairs, social security
numbers and thank-you notes, the debris of death. This kind of
business, weighing the heft of memory, is never indifferent. The
armchairs, the thank-you notes—each leads us back to something
else, things of vaguer shape and sharper meaning.

She is angry. She is especially angry about my newest book,
and she is also just angry. A river of old pain long staunched slides
out easily now, in brief fragments, disjointed rambles, long com-
mentaries. In the dismantling of houses and bank account, we dis-
mantle long decades of false courtesy, too.

Almost all this talk, these complaints and sorrows, come to
me by e-mail. E-mail is a strange construct for such strong feelings, but these odd missives are what I have. In the midst of her
coded address at the top of my screen, I see the time she sent the
note. Often she writes to me after midnight. I imagine her alone
at the desk in her dining room in the poised silence of the night,
her eyes intent, while her teenage daughter sleeps and the jittery
dog shifts at her feet. I imagine the pool of light reflected on the
French doors behind her, blanking the empty yard, shading the
day's dishes, the dog's bowl, the emptiness. I imagine this, knowing the room, the dog. The night. Knowing her.

She has no idea, I think, how artless her words are, how

revealing, and so she sends them into the ether assuming they will never return. They slip in a series of resentful taps onto the screen shimmering before her. That screen, that dim room, seems to be such a private and solitary place. It is exactly this privacy, this solitude, I violate.

She hates my "nasty little book," she writes one night. "You are airing family business in public—like it is the truth, when it is your opinion." Later: "That book really hurt. Those were your thoughts, not necessarily truths." Another day: "I have to live in this town, not you. I don't think a lot should have been said, whether true or not." A few days later: "Don't use my name in a book again without my permission."

She is sixteen months younger than I, truly my little sister, still half a head shorter than I. When she is angry, she moves, and her words roll across a room or the page in one long, unpunctuated injury. They arrive in my study heavy and solid, as all words are. With what she believes to be vapor, she protests the permanence of what I say.

FAMILIES ARE DREADLOCKED worlds; they tangle together so finely one cannot always get through. It is not easy to have a writer in the family; I understand this. Nor is it easy to be the writer in the family; writers charge themselves with the burden of a family's unspoken story. We can bury it in fiction or parse it into poetry, but form doesn't hide as much as we might like. No matter how plain or muted the source of our material appears to be, the people in our lives know themselves to be material. We who write know them to be, and knowing can make a writer shake with terror. If we aren't careful, it can make us into monsters.

For the memoirist, for those of us doomed to the first person by our cracked talents, the obvious questions of disguising characters and shifting locations shouldn't arise. Our questions are simpler, perhaps harder. The territory of what we have experienced is a restricted one for a writer—but so full, so rich, so slippery and unclear. The intimate and hidden interest me; the ordinary inter-

ests me, because it is so strange. I've never wanted to write anything else, never begun to mine the vein of what just happens each
day. But being bound to experience as a source of material doesn't
save me from betrayal. Writing about myself, I betray my past and
everyone in it; I am betrayed in turn by the limit of my memory, my
small, human needs.

Like many others, the chorus of my family has several inter-
locking lines: *How could you?* whispered as quietly as thought.
That's not fair, intoned in a young and injured voice. *That's not true.*
For how little we talk to each other about what really *did* happen,
or about what is happening now, our arguments seem always to
be about exactly those things.

When I have allowed myself to consider, even a little, what
I do from the point of view of my characters (that is, portions of
manuscript, narrative devices, people I love), I am wrapped in
worry. Is it true? For a long time, this was my rigid concern. Every
word, the tone, an adjective: is it true? But simple truth can be a
terrible harm. I began asking: Is it fair? And fair to whom?

I sometimes hesitate even to say I write memoir these days.
The current fashion in the genre is for extraordinary detail in a distinctly fictional voice, and what I write is nothing like that. Looking backward, it seems to me that I've written very little about my
family—either family, the one I came from or the one I made. I've
crept so cautiously around them that several people—including
my sister—have complained that I left them out of stories where
they belonged. Several readers have assumed I was a recluse of
some kind. There are many kinds of recluses, of course. Part of
me is a plain coward. Part of me is constrained by notions of duty
and integrity. But I am also constrained by my own reserve, which
comes partly from the knowledge of exactly how untrue and unfair
all writing is. The book is not the life; the writer is not the person.
The mask is not the self. So who are the characters?

My sister's anger now is rooted less in my recent book than
in the vignettes themselves, and all they imply. My few, carefully
shaded words loom large to her: a passing reference to my father

drinking his "hair of the dog" each morning, how he irritably waved the carving knife at me during dinner. Clues, hidden—but, like me, she knows where the bodies are buried. There is nothing oblique to her here. My brother, the eldest and most likely to remember what I remember, has never said a word to me about my work. Craven, I haven't asked.

In 1995 I wrote an essay called "The Basement" for the anthology *Home*. I sent my sister a copy last year after long consideration, and she has been coming slowly to the boil ever since. In that story, I describe her at age six as "squeamish, chubby, pale, and black-haired—she's the one left out, the baby." She is aggrieved over this line; she has been wronged. Every word chosen creates a world. Selection is all and only what writers do; nothing is neutral. Objectivity is the biggest lie a writer tells. My sister's anguish is that of the silenced defendant, listening to the eyewitness tell lies. We all know how unreliable eyewitnesses are, but we listen anyway. We believe—we condemn. "I was *not*," she says now. "*Not* like *that*."

The real betrayal of all nonfiction writers is that we forget. Days pile atop each other, knocking things out of the way—and we forget. In the end, it's not our parents' criticisms or our siblings' anger that breaks us, but our own—our own endless punishment of ourselves, the grand and self-absorbed masochism of people who struggle to say it just right. We will inevitably fall into the cracks between every possible solution—every safe place. We fall between cowardice and kindness in our desire to be fair; between courage and cruelty in our need to tell the story. We are betrayed by our own amnesia, by the fact that one can never be sure. I don't believe, though, that our greatest fear is being wrong. We're afraid of speaking at all. We are more afraid of what others will think, whether they will still love us after we speak, than we are of being wrong when we do.

For years, students in my writing classes have asked me the same questions I continue to ask myself. In an elementary school classroom on the Oregon coast, the small desks shoved to the side in the cool, sweet air of a summer morning—in a basement meeting room of the Unitarian church, the walls covered with cheerful slogans about kindness and honesty—in a humid conference room in upstate New York where the heat lies upon us like wool—I am asked the same questions: "What if I don't remember exactly?" "What if people disagree about what happened?" They have begun to worry about fragments and dangling plotlines, the gaps like broken typewriter teeth in the stories they want to write. A few already have the nagging suspicion that the fragments aren't in the writing, but in themselves. When the conversation gets rolling, there are other questions: "Isn't it okay to make up the details?" "Isn't memoir better with dialogue?" "Why not fill out a little?" Why not?

Nonfiction—not false. But nonfiction is never exactly true—the writer's own perfume lingers on every word, gently and insistently filling the reader's head with one person's singular world, shared by no one else. Easy enough to take what we do remember and fill it out, fill it in, with period detail and nicely timed entrances and inner monologues. This is the stuff of good drama—exactly the kind of drama my students want to write into their own memoirs, the kind they hope to get past me. They admit that they don't really remember things in great detail. The details they add just *feel* true, and therefore must be.

I say no. I always say no. Essay and memoir writers don't mess with plot or chronology, don't invent dialogue or combine characters. One wrestles with words, molds language, atmosphere, tone, suspense—not history. The bones of the story are already there, laid across the table, and to bare it exactly is the writer's role. Nonfiction is supposed to tell the truth—and telling the truth is what people *suppose* us to do. I have been stricter, even puritanical, about this than many writers I admire. (It does not escape me that obsessive concern with facts is an antidote to chaotic childhoods. Finding one's secret turmoil to be the mundane anecdotes of psychology textbooks isn't quite a cure.)

My students are disappointed when I answer their questions. Many clearly not only want me to say yes, they expect me to say it: yes, you can create, invent, conflate; yes, you can fill in the details. They are surprised when I say no.

Instead, I tell my students to write down all they *can* remember, all of it, to put everything in, all the chaff, all the crap, all the garbage. Only then do you find the wheat, the treasures. Wheat and chaff are entwined and must be thrown to the wind in order to separate. Put it all in because you may be wrong about which is which. Figure out your agendas, your vengeance, your grief and desire. Use the confusion and forgetfulness, the sound of crickets in August twilight, the thud of a heavy shoe stopping outside your bedroom door. So goes my lecture, and my students nod and write it down. Wheat, they carefully note. Chaff. Sound of shoes.

Our lives are uncertain, I tell them. Make that uncertainty part of what you tell. Believing that, taking it as my own measure, I am a liar, too.

A FEW MONTHS after my father died, my brother and sister and I were cleaning out his house. My father had lived alone for the last twelve years of his life, shrinking in on his grief at my mother's death and his fifth decade of alcoholism. His house was not dirty, thanks in part to my sister's regular visits, but it was as untouched as a crypt. A layer of dust covered almost everything—my mother's books, his record albums, the cans of soup in the pantry, all gray with a fine, silky silt. His suits were wrapped in dry-cleaning plastic years old, and his bedroom was piled high with mail-order travel and history books still in their cardboard packages, books he couldn't be bothered to refuse. When we began cleaning his house, we were literally dismantling it. I gathered up an armload of books from the position they'd been in as long as I can recall, and I half expected the house to come down around me, its structural integrity suddenly gone.

I bought my siblings lunch at the brewpub where the Sambo's used to be. Perched up on teetery bar stools, we finally began talking about the furniture, the old dusty house, and what to do with it all. On the rare days when we are all together we are in a web made more of the tension between us than the strengths of our bonds. I hold each of our quiet conversations or pleasant hours as though they were ancient papyrus about to dissolve; I hold them with great care because they are so few. I was glad to be there, to be doing this, eating bar food next to the shiny vats of ale in the building that once upon a time had been the orange diner we hung out in after high school. The change from then to now measured the arc of my life. I was more than ready to tackle a project that had begun to seem more like archeology than grief. Do you want the green chair? one of us asked, and the mood was generous, without rancor. Do you want the kitchen table, the circular saw, the car?

Then this happened. We go back to the house and into the kitchen. I lean over the tiny kitchen table with its uncomfortable wrought-iron chairs and ask my sister, "Do you want this table?" And she loses her hold all at once, flaring like a gas main, and stomps past me as heavy and hard as my father had stomped, knocking the chairs aside. I feel a strange peace. I am standing at last in the DMZ of my own history, the small neutral territory where enemies meet and no one is right and no one is wrong.

"I already *told* her!" she shouts to my brother. "No one ever listens to me!" Together they run out to the yard. I'm standing in the kitchen door watching through the window as they yell at each other. I can't hear the words. Then my sister peels out of the driveway in her Ford Explorer, almost taking my brother's foot off where he stands, broad-shouldered, hands clenched, watching her go.

HOW CAN I tell my sister that I'm not writing about her at all? I'm writing about me—who she is in my life and work is not who she is in hers. The me you see is not the me who sees you. My students ask over and over again. I answer them. But I don't believe what I say. My sister would tell a different story about that day; a story with a different moral, a different wound. How can I blame her? (Do I pretend that I am above blaming? What a comfortable place to be.) Alexander Smith called the essayist "a law unto himself."

We've heard it all before—we've *said* it all more than once, to each other, to our angry sources. Grist to the mill.

When it is my turn, I am like a pitcher facing a hard drive straight back to the mound; the ball so assuredly flying away shoots back, with no time to prepare. I have carefully avoided reviews of my new book, delicately stepping past them, whatever they may say. I've learned to shield my writing, when I can, from the work of being published; they are sometimes quite different things. But by accident I come across a brief review in the back of an influential national magazine. A bad review—mean. I flinch, read sideways, don't finish. I call my editor, a friend, other writers. They commiserate—it's really not fair. I have long conversations with my bedroom ceiling: defense, summation, resounding acquittal—and no one to tell. I can't resist, and go back to count up: four or five short reviews in this magazine every week, and for months all are kind, a growing mound of genteel enthusiasm. Except for one review. Except for mine. It is so not fair.

"Writing, I explained, was mainly an attempt to out-argue one's past," writes Jules Feiffer in his novel about identity, *Ackroyd*. One tried "to present events in such a light that battles lost in life were either won on paper or held to a draw." I don't get to talk back. No one ever does. But I write, and own the truth of every story I write because I write it. In writing it, I make it the truth. Complaints are impotent—competing versions of the story I've already told, and much less likely to be believed.

MY FRIEND MARIA Dolan has been working for years on an essay about her relationship with her parents during their divorce in her childhood. She has long been stuck somewhere in this tragic, funny memory of her girlhood. This particular block is partly my fault; I once told Maria not to think so much about whether the story was true, but whether it was fair, and now she can't write at all.

"My desire to be fair means I never think it's finished," she tells me. "Since I keep interacting with my parents, I don't want to freeze them in the way they used to be. I struggle to tell the story in a way that reveals them as people who can and will change."

In the last few years, I've begun to tell my students that we can only say so much about the truth, and the facts, vital as they are, are not exactly the point. What we really want to write down are the unprovable facts, the experiences that can never be defined but demand to be considered, truths that seem to contradict each other and therefore can't be true. One wants what I call the felt truth most of all. How easy to rationalize hurting people. How easy to say that our feelings count more than the facts.

My friend Deborah asks what I'm working on, and I describe this story I am writing now, and she tells me about something that happened when she was eighteen. It was the late 1960s in Los Angeles, and she was about to move into an apartment with her boyfriend. Her father often wrote her long letters of advice, and he did so then, carefully explaining why he thought this was a mistake. But her father also happened to be an editor at the *Los Angeles Times,* and after mailing Deborah her letter, he printed it on the editorial page.

He meant well, she added. She has not quite forgiven him.

Are we foolish enough to think others can rely upon our goodness of heart? Let us trust each other, our hope of redemption, our best use of words. But most of us don't know ourselves well enough to know how good we really are—else we wouldn't be writing so many words about what's happened to us and what we've done, and how it felt and what it might mean in the end.

I REMEMBER MY childhood as though it were a silent movie with the subtitles removed—made out of black-and-white snapshots and the jerky 8mm whirring in the background. Bend and pick up an Easter egg and hold it up for the camera. Pose on the sled in the soft snow falling like a fog across the lens. The most vivid moments are recorded nowhere but in me, and yet they have the same quality, this mute and almost self-conscious quality of being recorded somehow. I am swimming across a silent lake through a dawn mist in the shadow of a white mountain, at first fearful and then exultant as I've never been before. I am sitting in the crotch of my grandmother's black walnut tree, listening to the ratcheting of the blue jays above me, and there is nothing in the world but blue jays and walnut bark and nothing else needed at all. I am sitting at the dinner table when my father explodes and grabs my sister and begins spanking her, and she is yelling and my mother is crying and I leap from my own chair and shout at him to stop, to leave her alone, to leave us all alone. And the film fades out into black and the rest is unknown—after the lake, after the tree, the shouting, what?

For a long time after I left my parents' home, I was drawn to simple stories—ones with obvious narrative devices and clear morals. That was how I told my own story, explained myself to me— in starkly defined characters with set roles and explicable motives. As time passed, these stories were less satisfying—less true. But the conventions of storytelling have a strong pull. We want neat endings and known winners. We want to answer that question— what happened next, what did it mean?—with all our hearts. We want to answer it so much we make out of the fragments a kind of whole cloth.

Memory is terribly uncertain, made as it is out of callow ignorance and youth. We invert the chronology, combine characters, reorient the compass of our lives, until it is like a vaguely remembered dream with potent and cryptic elements in random order. It is up to the dreamer to decide what each element means. We can only know this moment and try to see it clearly, this moment of remembering those moments then, a world long gone in which someone I used to be used to live. The very best we can hope for is the ability to tell *a* truth, some truth or other, some portion of it, and tell it as close as possible to the moment of its being true, before it changes into something else again.

I find now that a lot of my questions can't be answered at all. Not being able to remember exactly is a story, too. And the story doesn't end, doesn't really have a moral, sometimes the crooks have good hearts and the heroes are corrupt and sometimes I can't tell which is which, and that has to be the story I tell.

CLEANING OUT MY father's closet this spring, I find a grocery bag filled with color slides dating from the 1940s. In among the weddings of strangers and blurry backyard luaus are hundreds of pictures of my brother and my sister and me when we were young that I have never seen before.

We are often together here, if nowhere else. From year to year, in summer and winter, by the riverbank and the Christmas tree, we stand beside each other—the kids, only a few years apart, bound together.

My brother leans toward the camera, grinning, perfecting self-confidence. By the age of five, he is a sturdy and seemingly fearless boy. At three, I am hardy and strong. He and I almost look like twins, except he smiles widely and I face the camera with composure—a rugged girl in jeans, giving nothing away. My little sister is pretty and dark with charming bee-stung lips and black hair falling in big, natural curls.

Photographs are false truths, too. My brother's confidence is shallow, brittle. My composure is deeply cracked. And my sister, who is almost dainty, is crying or beginning to cry or has just finishing crying. She sits on our mother's lap, with big eyes, because we have left her behind, forever ditched in the backyard when we want to climb trees. She isn't plump; I was wrong; how could I have remembered it that way? I was wrong and I was right, for this is what I meant by that word—this fragility, this girlish weakness in a world where weakness was lethal. These are the chorus lines beneath the singers. Beneath *it's not fair* and *that's not true* runs this river: *I was strong. You were weak. You walked away and left me behind. You stayed behind, and I survived. You—we're not sure about you yet.*

MOST WRITERS APPROACH a new story like a boxer circling the ring—with a certain reluctance to engage and break the spell of *what might be.* To write memoir is to live in what is—not only the truth, but the story one is capable of writing and not the great story of which we dream.

I was excited when I began to write "The Basement." The anthology was a good project—a dozen or so writers were each assigned a room; we had only to write a true story about something that happened in that room. I wanted to write about my grandmother's basement, where we spent a lot of time as children. I could revisit that world where my brother and sister and I were together, a gang of three. I would write about driving to Grandma's house in the old station wagon, how we would run through the living room and down the basement stairs and play all day long in a child-driven world while our boring relatives visited upstairs. I began there, and then I was paralyzed for two months. I could write nothing at all. I played solitaire for hours, read mysteries, took naps.

Toward the end of my writing workshops, when everyone's guard is down and little secrets have slipped out, when the room is as safe as rooms of nascent writers can be, I sometimes ask students to fill in the blanks of this sentence: "I can't write about ___ because ___." I give them only a few minutes, time for a few words.

Then I make two columns on the blackboard. On the left, I list the first words they wrote: *A car accident. Sex. Parents' divorce. A crime I committed.* This is hard for the students, to say out loud what can't be written. Then, on the right, I list the reasons: *I feel guilty. Feelings will get hurt. It's embarrassing. No one cares.*

Finally, I erase the column on the left—the events, the memories, the ideas. The stories. All that matters is the reasons. Those are the stories—this is what you write: how it feels to commit a crime, to be afraid, to not know how it ends. This is what all good stories are about. Start there, I tell them. Start there.

I sank for two months into the lassitude of unspent words until I started to ask myself that question. "I can't write about Grandma's basement because—because—" Because. Because I was so lonely there it was as though I'd already died. Because childhood is a dangerous place. Because we were ordered into that basement and it seemed to me that we might never be allowed to come out, that the whole world was filled with sunlight I would never see. Because I hated my grandmother, and you are not allowed to hate your grandmother. Right before me like a ghost in the room was that poor little girl with her solemn face and her jeans and dirty t-shirt—right before me stood that poor thing who is not me and has not been me for a long, long time, and I started writing like crazy.

So I wrote the truth no one but me knows and no one but me can tell. I rewrote history: down, down to the basement we go in the story, again and again, and at the end of the story, up I come, and fly away. That is the moral of my true story, that I did fly away, on wings light as the summer, wings I made out of words like these.

My friend Maria says she is unwilling to freeze her parents in their mutual past. I tell her that the story will also freeze her, in its telling. We fear getting stuck with the claims we make, with any day's untidy thoughts. It isn't just the people who live on; the story also lives on, its narrator lives on—forever the same, saying the same things, the writer's ghost. When I look over books and essays I've written, they were clearly written by someone else. I could not have written these stories—that is not my point of view, these are not my beliefs, this is not my voice. It is not me, they are not true, and it is not fair.

One of the few things I wrote about my father in the new book is that my mother brought him a Bloody Mary in the morning. It was part of her ritual day, and meant to say as much about her as him. What I didn't say, what my sister called family business, was known by the whole small town: his decades of drunkenness, just keeping his job, sleeping much of the rest of the day away, the sudden snapping of temper like a hurt dog, the kind of drunkenness that makes morning such a trial my mother had to bring him a drink while he still lay beneath the covers, and after he'd taken it he'd totter slowly into the kitchen where we were eating our Frosted Flakes and reach behind me into the cupboard to pull out the whiskey and pour himself a neat two fingers, his hair uncombed and his crumpled pajamas sour with the night, and then shuffle back, like an old, old man, to dress for the day.

I didn't write that. I didn't use the bare words. I told myself it was tangential to the story. I told myself there were too many musty confessions of alcoholic childhoods out there, it was a too-familiar territory. In fact, I could see my brother's face, my sister's face, wanting it not to be true. Most of all, I could see the composed face of that plain little girl, who was such a tough cookie and loved her daddy after all.

"Please don't use my name without my permission again," my sister adds, late at night, alone in her room. And the *please* makes my heart flip over. It is so plaintive. But I don't stop. I don't have the right to tell these stories. How could I have the right to the lives of others, to their former selves and hard losses? These stories are like slamming doors. No right to speak unprovable truths. Life's not fair. It's all so not fair.

Tin House, Summer 2001

I imagine some essayists don't worry much about the questions of rightness and fairness and whose version wins. I know many memoirists don't. I'm familiar with the trend toward blurring the lines between fiction and nonfiction—the insistence that we write what is true to ourselves and nothing else matters. But of course what we do matters to those we use as material. "Violation" is an attempt to grapple with the ethical dilemma of writing about people who have no say in what we write.

Second Chair

IN FOURTH GRADE WE WERE PUT ON A READING "SYSTEM," a box of color-coded cards with stories and questions. Each color represented a grade level, and I finished the twelfth-grade cards—dark purple—by November. All it meant was that I had nothing to read for the rest of the year, and spent that time with my head down on my desk. I was the first girl to wear glasses, the first to wear a bra, and the last to get a clue. When we put on a play about a beautiful princess with long golden hair, I waited to be picked. When Mrs. Hurley announced that Charlene, the pretty girl with long golden hair, would be the princess, I was actually surprised.

So the next year, I tried band.

At home, I took piano lessons from a fussy German man who wore a bow tie and rapped my knuckles with a ruler. For band, I picked the clarinet, sleek and pure. Several times a week I walked past the teachers' lounge, where my mother smoked cigarettes with other teachers behind a closed door, and into the upper wing of the school, the one set aside for sixth, seventh, and eighth graders, to the music room, a warehouse of lousy acoustics, bad lighting, and a rat's nest of scattered metal music stands, risers, and chairs. The music teacher was a tall, skinny man with a mop of black hair, big glasses, and pockmarked skin named Mr. Hutchinson. He was one of the youngest of the faculty, intense and kind to the mob of middle-schoolers that made up band. He didn't conduct so much as wave his long arms at us in patient exasperation. We called him Mr. H, teasing, because we liked him.

I rented a clarinet from the little music store on the main street of town, and I had to go back every few weeks to buy mysterious bamboo reeds, an errand I imbued with as much status as an assignation. New reeds were stiff and tasted fresh and grassy, but day by day they softened with my spit into something all my own. Walking there and back along wide small-town streets, I drifted from dream to dream, drifting toward something just my own, toward music, or a life.

Both my parents were schoolteachers; they met in what was then called normal college. My father taught industrial arts at the high school. Most of the kids in the county attended there, some traveling an hour each way through ranch land or down logging roads. My father reigned over a small village of modular classrooms set apart from rest of the school, a noisy, male world filled with welding torches, voltmeters, and table saws. The industrial arts classes were forbidden to girls; I rarely saw the inside of his classrooms, and he seemed only rarely to notice me.

So I helped my mother, who taught fifth grade and lower-section music. For a long time I didn't think anyone worked in the summer. The seasonal ecology of public school was my world—rhythmic shifts from crowds to solitude, from noise to quiet. From school to everything else, and back again. Our town was the small center of a wide territory—a lot of fine, empty land and not many people. So I saw my teachers at school, and I saw them in my living room and at my parents' barbecues and New Year's Eve parties. Mr. H somehow became pals with my hopelessly square mother, who called him "Hutch." There were teachers everywhere: Mrs. Meamber lived across the street, Mrs. Hurley and Mrs. Cramer and Mr. Noonan were my parents' friends, and Mr. and Mrs. Herfindahl were my godparents. Straight A's were the least that was expected and the last thing noticed in a world where the lines were as blurred as this. I didn't even need to bring home my report card. My mother got it early.

From late August, when we made new bulletin board displays, until June, when I helped her take them down, I spent a lot of extra hours in school with my mother. We often arrived before the first bell and left after the last, and when I was tired of her room I wandered the wide tiled hallways painted in muddy greens and browns, sneaking peeks at other classrooms, with their walls of windows and blank chalkboards waiting for words. On empty afternoons, cutting up scalloped construction paper borders, I thought that I quite liked school.

I was a child with passions—intense, unbudging, irrational passions, inevitably strange and confusing to my mother. She was a plain, shy woman all her life. I realize now that she longed to feel accepted as much as I did; this was our shared secret and we kept it from each other until she died. I was unable to grasp the subtle and terrifying nuances of classroom politics. She encouraged me to read *Seventeen* magazine so I could figure out how to be like other girls. And I wanted to be like other girls; for years I thought I was. In fact I was a sideways creature, and not really at home where other people lived. I was uncensored and a little primitive and tunneled through my mind like a mole who didn't know the light. I perched in trees, waded culverts, and often refused to wear shoes. I read adult books and wrote odd stories, the kind that lead to parent-teacher conferences and visits to the school counselor to take interesting tests. Sometimes I disappeared for hours, scrabbling up a fifty-foot cedar to chew on sap while the wind swayed me back and forth in its cradle, forgetting time.

CLASS PHOTOS WERE taken in the spring, on breezy sunny days, each class perched on bleachers set up on the front lawn of the school, 1965, 1966, 1967—second grade, third grade, fourth: I look at them now and can tell you who's headed for perdition already. So young, and each of us jammed in place like pegs under a hammer.

Steve, the class clown, cavorting in the middle of the top row with his retinue, Randy, Ryan, Jim, Mitch. In the front row sits Charlene, with her long golden hair in a neat bun on top of her head like a movie star, and her friends, Danette and Tracy and Lori, with their neat braids and white-ribboned socks on neatly crossed ankles. On the edges and in the hidden middle are the rest of us: the fat girls like Dee Dee, skinny ones like Ramona with her wild carrot hair and flagrant freckles, Joyce in her second-hand clothes. In second grade I sat near the end of the front row, my legs crossed and hands resting on my knees in the kind of casual, sophisticated pose Grace Kelly might strike. A few years later I am back in a corner, wearing sky-blue glasses with pointed corners decorated with fake diamonds and a homemade dress I'd talked my mother into making out of psychedelic fabric from the discount store, all bright green rhomboids and yellow swirls. I look like a before ad in the back of *Good Housekeeping*, but I am smiling because I think that I look pretty cool.

The band was the only place where the poles of social relation met, a curious mix of the popular and the picked-over. Steve played trumpet, which even today seems obvious. Ryan chose the trombone. Lyle, who looked a little like Tom Cruise in his early years and was wildly popular, played the drums, but so did Jean, who hit six feet tall in seventh grade and moved with a kind of bovine assurance between snares and the lone tympani.

For a year, I took clarinet lessons with Ida and Eileen and Mary, squeaking and shrieking in arrhythmic hoots and sudden, startling flights of music like little birds surprised out of a tree. Any music we managed to make was punctuated by the constant scrape of chair legs and the rattle of the stands knocking whole rows over like dominoes in a frantic tumble, but we practiced our scales and tried to follow Mr. H's swaying baton.

I never liked the slim B-flat clarinet, after all; it made a small nasal song and I wanted more. I bugged Mr. H to let me play the bass clarinet instead, which I longed for like a dog wants a bone, with a simpleminded need. I wanted the profound dark-chocolate notes of the big reeds, the perfect satisfaction of its large silver keys and the big curved bell at the bottom. The bass clarinet was so big I could barely lift the case. That was what I wanted—that heft and burly weight.

Finally, Mr. H let me switch. Overnight, I left the crowd of chubby clarinetists to be the second-chair bass clarinet, next to Sue—a year older, academically gifted, a natural musician who could sing and play several instruments well. For a time I followed Sue's lead, practiced regularly, and drew the big sleek body of the clarinet intimate and near. I loved its low, still sound, like the sound of small round pebbles falling slowly through a dark deep pool. I was genuinely happy in the making of that sound, alone or in the band, at home or at school. For a time, the music was enough.

All the instruments were divided into sections, rows, and chairs. Populated sections like flute and trumpet might have two or three full rows, each row a hierarchy of first and second and third chair and down, assigned by Mr. H. Such is the subtle strength of an orchestra, of course—the complex supporting frames of row upon row, each section holding up a piece of the whole. But the first row, which led the section solos and set the standard, was the only visible one, and to be lodged in second and third row was to labor anonymously. First chairs held the kind of deadly power only children really understand. For a few of us, first chair was what it was all about.

Our seats were assigned, but sometimes we moved—by Mr. H's royal directive and by "challenge." If there was a coup—if a player moved up a whole row, for instance—alliances were broken, players shifted forward and back like gypsies shoved along the road.

Any player could, at any time, throw down the gauntlet to another player. Challenges were wars conducted in private. Mr. H picked a piece of music, each player performed it, and Mr. H decided who would sit where the next day. You won or you lost and there was no appeal; we believed Mr. H was fair and we knew he was God. It was his lot in life to know how well or badly we played, to know what would happen in a challenge before it started. He knew in fact how well or badly we managed to live through any given hour or day. His particular curse that he had to tell us what he knew.

One day, I challenged Sue for first chair, and I lost. I was a little surprised. I practiced more, dragging the heavy instrument home every day, and I challenged her again a few months later. When I told Mr. H I was ready to try again, he looked at me a moment without a word and then said, "All right, you can try if you want," and I knew then and there I would lose.

IN SIXTH GRADE we switched wings. I left my mother's room behind and entered the world of lockers and homeroom, white lipstick, sudden shocks. It was 1969 and I had big breasts and grew my hair long and started wearing a fake cow-skin miniskirt and boots. Nothing quite fit anymore—clothes and parents and school had begun to chafe, raising a faint bruise beneath my skin. I took advanced math and won the writing prizes, and these things counted for about as much as straight A's.

All year long, I challenged Sue again and again; it became our ritual, an almost friendly duel. I always lost. The worst of it was that I had come to see Mr. H was right. I loved my music, I held it as tenderly as my fantasy dates, but what I wanted was to be the first. I was a teacher's kid and the second-chair bass clarinet and it should have been more than enough, but it came to mean only that I was last. The bruise spread. I would never have said it out loud; it was a betrayal to feel it, a betrayal to say, but deep in the lightless tunnels I thought to hell with Dee Dee and Ramona. To hell with Sue, heading off toward her music scholarship. It was Danette and Tracy I wanted to be; they were the bright ones, and it seemed they would forever burn brighter and hotter than me.

Eighth grade, 1971. Bright patterned shirts on the boys, whose hair was getting shaggy. I put mine in tiny braids while it was still wet, and when I combed it out the next day it filled the air around my head in a dusky halo, eyes lost behind a curtain of hair. I began to push backward through the river of school, shoving aside the waves of girls with their neat ponytails, the boys with their wide-lapel polyester shirts who hardly knew my name. After the last bell rang, the empty hallways of school were as airless as a small cell, as doomed as hunger strikes, and instead of staying late, I cut out early. I allied myself with Danny and Don, the shortest and the tallest boys in our class, two gay boys of awkward teeth and lonely hours. We spent long spring afternoons in Danny's garage, trying to play "Revolution #9" backward on the tape deck, making sandwiches in his empty kitchen, walking through the town from one end to the other, and doing nothing much at all. We were waiting, mostly.

Perhaps the worst job a teacher has is as witness: to watch the bucktoothed kids with bad clothes scramble up like Sisyphus, to watch the easy climb of the Steves and Tracys who peak at sixteen and tumble down inch by inch for the rest of their lives. In such a way, every child is abandoned, left in tears beside the road, and all any of us can do is watch. What else can we do? Here is the sour-smelling girl who lives in a trailer, and here the boy with a limp who smiles all the time as he lurches madly through the crowded halls, and here one of the tightly wrapped little geniuses who will manage to shoot herself in the foot if she only has one bullet.

As high school loomed over us like a shadow of wings, I spent my breath on sarcasm instead of the bass clarinet. I drove the teachers to distraction and more, until one day Mr. Castor threw me against the wall as I stomped between classes, my big smart mouth talking all the while. Mr. Castor held me up against the wall of the tired school in front of a hallway full of people, shoving his crew-cut blond hair and thick-necked wrestler's rage in my face, and I smiled. I knew he was just another also-ran.

The way so much ends, band ended, fading out, *pianissimo*. Grade school ended. I quit piano lessons and a year later, took the clarinet back to the store. I gave up on making music, but I called it something else. I called it knowing better. I walked away, and called it wising up.

I was still disappearing for hours—and not up cedar trees. I was under the bleachers in the empty high school football field, kissing a boy I didn't particularly like. I was cutting out of class to ride back roads in some rump-sprung convertible with a bunch of dropouts drinking jug wine. I was lying to my mother and shouting at my father, and riding on the back of chopped Harleys with men years out of high school, leaning back with my long hair flying. As a girl, I loved to swing; I swung in wild arcs up and back, legs pumping and blood roaring, straining for height. At the top of each crescent curve I would throw all my weight to one side and fall back and up in another gathering spin like pleats of a skirt—swirling, swinging, a helix of weightless flight. In such a way I leaned back on the sissy bar on hot afternoons. No helmet, no shoes, no hands. No hope, no plan.

A few years later, I left. I left, I left, I went away to be an adult before I was ready, because I was so ready, and I destroyed more villages and burned more bridges than I really want to think about even now. The problem with being second chair is thinking, *I could do better than that.* Sometimes it's true and sometimes it's not; the problem is when you go on saying it all your life.

WHEN MY MOTHER died, I went back to my hometown for several days. I ran into Tracy working behind a cash register at the Safeway on the edge of town. She had dimmed. The day before the funeral, I walked the short blocks that had once stretched so far— home to school, back again. It is a curious dream, the place we live as children, like a stage set from a half-forgotten play. The houses that seemed like Tara in the wastage of my early years were a bit shabby, and I could smell the stink of wood smoke over the whole town, the nothing much that once seemed to be a world. I worked my way up behind the school, to what used to be a broad wild meadow pocked with mysterious rabbit holes and fine purple thistles. It was a dull and empty park, a false green lawn under a gray sky.

Half the town seemed to come to my mother's funeral. My God, she was loved, and I sat in the front row of the church and wept, lost. We invited her closest friends to the house afterward, and I found myself sitting beside Mr. H in our backyard, sitting side by side in twin chaise lounges and drinking whiskey together in the dark. He was old, or at least that much older than me still, and he moved with the steady patience and mild disappointment of someone who knew he was exactly where he belonged. We talked of this and that—of her, of me, of town. The next day, he was going back to work again, earnest and willing to try, to raise his voice over the scrape of metal chairs on dull linoleum and the dreadful squeaks of beginning clarinetists. To witness.

So we leaned back in the summer darkness and looked at the stars hard above us in a black sky, in the empty sky of a small country town. He had a weak radiant sorrow about him, and it took me a while to realize how much he was going to miss my mother. Of course they'd been friends. She loved music, and she wasn't so old—just one of the shy, plain people who need friends in a lonesome world, and I didn't even know that I was one of them for a long time.

For a moment I envied Mr. H his impossible job and the small town sky and the gift of resignation. It is something like a real victory to not have to fight in the first place. I began with appetite, which has no enemies. Somewhere along the way it turned, like bad milk. I caught the world in a big lie—the one that claims we're all lined up in sections in some kind of fair order, holding each other up. Whatever contest might be going on isn't played by fair rules, and it has nothing to do with appetite—nor with passion, music, swinging, stars. I was the last to get a clue, but finally, I did. I rarely play the piano now and never the clarinet, but I listen to music all the time. Sometimes I still think, *I can do better than that,* but I know the only thing I'm doing is me.

After everyone had gone, I stood in my old bedroom in the dark, gentled from the whiskey, tears all gone and so far gone I thought I might never cry again. "Dint of long longing lost to longing," wrote Beckett. "And longing still. Faintly longing still."

In the middle of the street below was a young girl, rollerskating all alone. It was late; the neighbors' houses were already dark. But she crossed the asphalt for a figure-eight and her skate wheels grated and rumbled, low and then louder, higher and fading away again and again. She was under a streetlight in a pool of yellow. I watched her dip and spin and slide suddenly backward in perfect control, the way a flock of birds moves high in the sky without a sound, in grace. Her hair swung with the rustle of wings. She looked up and seemed to see me in the window, and stared as though I had no business there at all.

Antioch Review, Fall 2002

A memoir is a distillation of the past. A simple memory like playing bass clarinet in the school band becomes a prism through which a much greater subject is refracted. I set out to write a story about longing and loss. I intended it to be sad, and I'm sometimes surprised that people assume this is the whole story. You can never tell the whole story.

The Birth

BELLE PRESSES HER HEAD AGAINST THE WIDE BARS near where I sit, between a hay bale and a stepladder. My smell is uncommon here; her questing trunk slithers toward me like a snake sliding out of a basket. The tip hangs in the air snuffling, a few feet from my lap. She fixes me with a flecked, amber eye, resting like a stone in a pool of wrinkles, blinking slowly.

There is a sign on the wall beside me, in faded yellow letters: DANGER DANGER—the word repeated, to drive the point home.

She exhales in a great whoosh at my feet, to let me know my place in things, and the hay on the floor spins away in the wind of her breath.

This is not my first time inside the elephant barn at the Oregon Zoo; when I wrote a long story about their efforts to protect and propagate the endangered Asian elephants, I got to know most of the keepers, and the elephants as well. Still, I'm a stranger here, snuck in tonight by friendly hands for a special event. The keepers, a few in coveralls and boots, and most in pressed uniforms now soiled with sweat and dirt, enjoy sharing their hard, anonymous work. Mike, the veterinarian, wanders in and out, looking for something to do.

Belle is the old woman; she looks old, her hips sunk like a dowager's shoulders. She is Sunshine's grandmother; Pet is Sunshine's mother. Pet was an orphan, taken in her childhood in Thailand to be sold as a token to the Americans. Here they are made into a family, bound together. Pet is in labor, coming toward the delivery of the twenty-fifth calf to be born here, after almost two years of pregnancy. In the big, cold room, they stay close together, often touching, always in reach. When our voices die away for a moment, I can hear a rumbling stomach, churning carrots and hay. Belle rocks slowly against the wall, rubbing her crinkled rump with the sound of crumbling tissue, all the while flipping the end of her trunk back and forth against its own length, so that it slaps itself, whap, whap, whap. They move like hills walking, like tectonic plates shifting, oceans pulling moons. Their power is potent and occult; they never seem to hurry. Sunshine presses her broad forehead against the iron bars as thick as my arm. She has two dull, short tushes, nerveless teeth almost mistaken for small tusks. Her wide, flat ears are giant fans of skin, speckled pink, flickering, enormous gingko leaves. One ear has a little tear in its edge, like ripped paper. She is a teenager; she acts like a teenager, slipping her restive trunk out into the water trough beside the bars. She is a bit of a rascal, a rule-breaker. Her trunk climbs seemingly of its own accord through the trough and out, reaching for me. Her inquiring nostrils blossom and flicker, a foot away. Jim strolls over and leans on the wall beside her. He swats her trunk fondly, and she walks the tip up and down his arm while he massages it.

A spasm of labor roils along Pet's side, a shifting, asymmetrical bulge. She lifts a leg, swinging a foot. The soft curve of her mountainous body is marred by the muscular contractions, the fetus rolling in its tight bed. I watch with a careful nonchalance, taking notes, trying to hide my pleasure at being allowed inside tonight, where I am not really supposed to be. I'm afraid that if I half begin to show my thrilled appreciation, it will suddenly be time to go. I want to be part of the casual, abbreviated conversations, the insider lingo, the easy motions of working men who've worked together a long time. But they are all as full of tension as I am, their jokes a mask for a barely suppressed excitement.

There's not really a good reason for us to be here. There's not much anyone can do to hurry the process along or solve any problems that might arise. Elephants are so outside the size of things, their biology still unknown in many ways, that we are rather help-less here. Pet has had several babies already, and the cows know what to do; they practically choreograph the event.

Sunshine steps up behind Pet and sticks her trunk inside the pendulous lips of her pink vagina. They stand still a moment, in repose, a moment of pure and intimate biology. One of the blessings of being near animals is their confidence in their own nature, their freedom from the bewildering questions of identity that plague human beings. They are incapable of being embarrassed by this event; to do so would be outside nature, and only humans try to function outside nature. Sunshine inhales Pet's scent, and with a slow and infinite grace, swings her trunk out, under, and up in a particular inverted curve of an arc known as the flehmen. She presses the quivering tip against her palate, where there are two small oval openings leading to a gland called the vomerona-sal organ. I am not blessed with this organ, and neither are you. There she reads pheromones and hormones, a succinct report on the labor and the baby to come. Then she yawns, dangling her vast lower lip, and lets the pink loaf of her tongue hang out.

ELEPHANTS ARE EARTH, loam, soil; they are doughy and firm; they are "the nearest thing on earth / to a cloud," in Heathcote Williams's words. They are at ease doing what animals do, except for how we've messed everything up. Nothing can ever be as it was.

People are restless; elephants are restless. The air is thick with dust from the stacked bales of timothy hay, and over that is an unrepeatable perfume I know as the smell of the barn—a little urine and manure, the sweet hay, and especially the savor of the animals themselves—a ripe smell, mature and pleasant. Outside the glass wall in the viewing area are layers of people ignored by the elephants, who are long used to people there. The visitors lean on the window with a yearning I recognize, a kind of murmuring hunger for something none of us can quite name. Pet raises her tail for a moment and I can hear a collective, "Aaah!" from the crowd, a moment of hope to be present at this rare birth, to have that bit of luck and enter, just like that, a totem magic.

Bang! Bang! Wood slamming on metal, a crashing door; a gigantic whoosh like a miniature storm passing. This is the father, Hugo, a tall, scary circus elephant who joined the herd a few years ago. He is temperamental, dangerous; he knows tricks. Today he is demanding to know why no one is paying him his due. Bang! And he crashes his dissatisfied head against the bars.

The three cows ignore Hugo's outburst, and instead eat mouthfuls of hay one after the other in an easy, swinging rhythm—tossing it into their huge mouths, and lightly onto their backs to coat themselves with straw and the greenish pollen like old women covering themselves with shawls.

Pet urinates in a great splash on the cement floor, as much liquid as a tub of water emptied and thundering across the floor and foaming like a tide. Then she stands stiff and still, squeezing her sides, rear legs planted and tail stiff. Belle slowly slides her trunk along one of Pet's swollen human-shaped breasts, which point toward the floor and are swollen tight, slowly leaking fluid.

The regular keepers, unable to sit around any longer, come to the bars for a visit. Charlie brings Belle a chocolate chip cookie, a tiny bite in the delicate grip of her trunk. She downs it rapidly and asks for another; and then another. Jay playfully tosses apples to them, to "the girls," and one after the other is caught and disappears into big, dark mouths. Now the three elephants are leaning on the bars in a row, heads together, their three trunks rooting through the keepers' khaki uniform pockets, pushing into their dirty hands, all six ochre eyes watching. Suddenly they start rocking back and forth as though on cue, trunks swinging like the Andrew Sisters snapping their fingers in time. I lean against a wall caught by this collision of the strange and the ordinary, the familiar and the unknown. The impossibly unknown, impossible to understand—impossible not to convince yourself that you understand.

People come and go, new faces, greetings, farewells. Someone brings sandwiches, a thermos of coffee is passed around. The keepers take turns with their regular chores, with the rest of the herd. The big hydraulic door in the back slides open, and one of the bull elephants goes by, trotting. I hear the distant plop of straw-thickened stool, and Roger and Jim enter the cage to sweep it away, very small men in a forest of gray flesh.

Pet turns around, presents her huge, ovaline rear to my view, and I can see the knuckling of the labor like a thundercloud rolling across her back. A big plug of mucus, ivory-colored, thick, hangs stickily from her vulva. She flicks her trunk at it, annoyed, until it drops to the floor. Sunshine strokes Pet's vulva a moment, then returns to the food.

I NEVER TIRE of watching them—never. They are elegant, strapping, healthy, unafraid. Bristly black hair sticks up through the hay snow on their backs. Their faces seem to me to be Egyptian faces, defined and sculpted into spare planes. Their almond eyes are like whale eyes, calm and deep, set into skulls full of domes and bubbles, great billowy vaults of brain and air-balanced upwellings of bone to protect big, whorled minds.

Jay leans on the wall and Pet plants a sudden wet kiss on his cheek. Snort. Snuff. A series of blips, a rumble, silence. Then, outside the yard, a single, long, trumpeting cry. Belle lifts a leg and holds it there, as though she were waiting to try on shoes, or step up stairs, or have a pedicure.

The sky is turning white in the early evening, milky through the high cathedral windows. Jim, tall and thin, comes over to visit with Belle; she thrusts her trunk at him and he whacks her as though she were a freshly waxed car, and then gives her another apple.

The overhead lights come on. The zoo is about to close and I'm waiting to be thrown out, when the curator comes in. But he only says hello and asks me if I have ideas for the baby's name. He is glad, nervous.

"I don't suppose you know the Thai word for twenty-five,"

he asks, watching the cows. This baby will be the twenty-fifth one born here—the first in years, a rare and celebrated event.

"I hope it's a girl," he adds. The herd needs a girl—all the world's herds, all elephants, need a girl, a fertile, healthy girl. Elephant births were, in a strange way, almost routine here for a few magical years. But it couldn't last and now each one is profound—apocalyptic. We people, who can't contain ourselves, have hunted and harried elephants to the ground; they run before the nets like hares before the hounds. Except for people, elephants have no natural predators, but one is enough. Each calf is a beauty, a pearl, a prize.

A sudden squeal, and the keepers who have been half-dozing on chairs and hay bales look up with interest. This is how elephants sing near calves—a long squeal, colliding with a squeak, a mew, then whirring, rumbling, beeping in a stew of noise. Yet the elephants appear not to have moved at all. They aren't posturing or seeming to do anything. It is simply an invisible room of sound filling every corner; from several directions, bouncing around the high cement walls. It stops as suddenly as it began. In a few minutes people drop their heads again and lift their legs back up onto chairs.

THE ELEPHANT HAS always had a place among humans, always been a source of story, pregnant with meaning. The elephant has been considered an egg—from which was born the Earth—and a rain cloud, bound to the Earth. Elephants were assumed to have once had wings; are still thought to worship the moon. They were—they are—sacred beasts, rotund angels. Not little cherubs, not baby angels, but the massive and demanding angel of the Old Testament—beings full of jealousies, duty, and reluctant love.

I imagine the bars gone, the cement floor as grass, the walls as leafy trees. I imagine Belle coming at me, a stranger in her territory, blowing her authority in my face. Even here, they are barely contained. The air is filled with their unapologetic scent. A herd of elephants on the move, wrote Frank Buck, "is regarded as an elemental force that is not to be disputed. The thing to do is to get out of the way as when a storm comes."

Are they vast, emotional angels or more like demigods, the half-holy divine offspring, not quite perfect but filled with power? Or are they a kind of elfin fold, giant pixies, like the imps and trolls of tales, but stranded in a shrunken place? An elephant can pick up a dime off the floor with a slight twist of the lip. They can open doorknobs. They are flibbertigibbets, sprites as big as hills.

In fact, I have sometimes thought of them as the tragic descendants of aliens—I imagine a roaming galactic species, large and wise and full of strong feelings, trapped here by some cosmic accident a long time ago and since devolved from their technology to a simple life of peace, food, sex, and family. They are certainly humanoid, oddly enough; perhaps in the lost reaches of the past, we had an unknown common ancestor. Humans are aliens, too, after all, trapped on this difficult planet. We would be wise not to disdain what seem to be their lesser ways.

Eyes like stones in a pond, where I sit out of harm's way. Out of love's way, stung by acute envy for the men who lean casually against the walls; quick to alarm but warmed by a peculiar trust. The love between two species is not like the love within one.

Whap, whap. Belle slaps her trunk. Night has taken hold; the lingering volunteers are shooed out against their will. A security guard leans on the doorway to the main viewing room, watching the cows with the same fascination as everyone he sent away had done.

Bets beckons silently, and leads me up a hidden spiral stairway beside the bars, to an aerie looking down on the cage. Everything is coated with layers of cobwebs and dust, years of it, fine and sticky and musty, draped over the pipes in veils, and over lights, boxes, forgotten tools, lidded white pails.

There is one yellow globe on above the cows, and all the other lights are turned off now. People are quiet, keeping to themselves, settling in for a vigil.

Bets and I, moving as quietly as we can, watch from the aerie.

The cows seem smaller and more contained up here; but I can also see the complex, stealthy shifts of relation between them, their constant touching. Then Pet walks into a far corner, her back to the room, and her vulva swells outward. We can see the perineum bulging, a shiny curve. Then she relaxes again. We throw a towel over the railing's netted cobwebs and lean cautiously over.

"She knows we're up here," Bets whispers, nodding her head toward big Belle, who gazes up into the darkness for a moment. She could reach us if she tried.

Bets is silently exultant, reaching for her camcorder again and again to capture the nuances of labor, never before recorded. How Sunshine tastes Pet's mucus again and again. The way Belle so slowly leaves the hay and walks over to stroke Pet every now and then. Suddenly the cement wall on which we lean begins to vibrate and the air fills with a thudding, seismic shiver; a boom so distant and deep sounds that it seems to come from underground. I question Bets with my eyes, and she confirms—it is only Packy, the patriarch and Sunshine's father, ramming his great skull against the wall. He is the largest Asian bull in captivity; when he complains, the whole barn dances to it.

Later, when I'm in my chair again, Mike comes to lean silently on the wall, urging Pet on. He whispers to her, simple exhortations, cheers, like a parent watching soccer. He is her doctor, after all. Belle checks his pocket and tries to grab his coffee cup; he whacks her trunk with it and she kisses his ear. All this is happening above where I sit; Belle turns from Mike's pockets to look down at me a moment, with royal disdain.

They move together into the far corner, tapping each other, huddled. Below Pet's flicking tail a bulge rises, and she squeals, ponderously shifting her weight this way and that, then there is only the rustle of skin on skin, a distant fan, the occasional, muffled thud of a bull banging on the wall.

Her legs are streaked with creamy, sticky mucus. This is the time; this must be the time. We hold our breaths. Then she turns

around, quite relaxed; and to the keepers' general disgust begins
to eat hay, working her fat cheeks in and out like a bellows.

Finally, Jim climbs to the top of the bales, twenty feet above
the room, and goes to sleep. Jay pulls two chairs together and curls
up. Mike stretches out under a blanket on a bed of straw. I nod off
in my chair and jerk awake, watching the shadowed motion of the
cows through tired eyes. All at once, Sunshine folds her front legs
beneath her, rolls onto her side, and falls asleep. I turn my head
into my own shoulder and smell my hair, thick with scents of dust,
hay, and the ineluctable perfume of elephant.

I wake up suddenly shaking, lost, wild. Pet is flapping her
ears wildly, squeaking; she craps and pees and lapses back into
silence. The big echoing barn is black, all shadow, except for the
sulfurous light of their room. Am I sleeping or awake? Is this a frag-
ment of dream, am I suspended between worlds? I seem to float in
a small pool of yellow light, a bubble floating in darkness through
the drift of tiny particles. Far away I see the black silhouettes of
ponderous bodies swaying, bodies ten feet high.

THIS IS WHEN I should tell you about the birth itself. But I wasn't
there; no one was there. Pet's labor stopped; she closed it down.
Even when we all finally fell asleep, she held tight to this calf. I left
in the middle of the night; the next morning, everyone left, left her
completely alone, and then she delivered. She was attended by
Belle and Sunshine, the soothing midwives. We had usurped every
other moment, including conception; this one was kept apart.

The baby died. It was a boy, all wrong—eyes too flat, skull
misshapen, one leg deformed, an odd angle of spine. He couldn't
stand, a misbegotten product of too few genes. Mike moved him
away from Pet so she wouldn't grow too attached, and milked her
melony breasts himself, squeezing out the milk by drops, by hand,
and fed the calf through a tube for a day.

"It's just one of those things," he said to me, after he'd put
the calf to death.

Just one of those things.

One day while resting, God fell asleep and dreamed of a fantastic creature—strong and delicate at once, powerful enough to hold up the world, graceful enough to move silently through the jungle. God woke up laughing and decided to make the elephant.

The elephant held up the world. Now the elephants, God's most amazing dream, are dying. And I fear the world, bereft, will sink of its own weight, out of sight.

Portland Magazine, Spring 2003

I stayed in touch with the scientist Bets Rasmussen for several years after I wrote about her discovery of the elephant's reproductive pheromone in the New Yorker. *It was my great privilege to be invited to kneel beside her in the loft of the elephant barn one evening and watch one of the cows in labor. This story is both joy and tragedy to me, not because of the birth but because of what it represents—the successful breeding program is largely over, the victim, in part, of limited genetic material. What we have done to elephants—to orangutans, whales, lions, polar bears and to so many of the other great, bright, powerful creatures of this planet—should haunt us all.*

Scars

1982
*Wound (woond) n. [OE. Wund]: an injury in which the skin or other
tissue is broken, cut, torn, etc.*

FOUR YEARS AGO HE WAS BORN AND EVERYTHING CHANGED.
Daily we leave jobs, friends, lovers, but the child always comes
along. When the going gets rough, my son and I can't call it quits
and cut our losses. I can't pack a bag, make a break for it, find a
more compatible child. The contract cannot be broken.

We are strangely entangled. When I wake from a bad dream
without a sound, he wakes in the next room and cries for me.
Between us there is no shame, no holding back. I take risks with
him I wouldn't dare take with anyone else. I treat him with rough
impatience, with all the bile I hide from friends and lovers for fear
of losing them. I am less tolerant of deviation, more injured by separation. We fight, and then make up with a tentative, weary kiss. I
demand so much: loyalty, obedience, faith. And he gives me all I
demand, and more—he thinks me beautiful; he wants to grow up
to be just like me. And I am bound to fail him, and bound to lose
him. Strangers' hands will stroke where I stroke now, and already
I'm jealous of this secret future apart from me.

I quail at the mistakes I'm bound to make, what I'll saddle
him with, what the price for each of us will finally be. For nothing is free. Daily the gap between us grows, in tiny steps. He is not
mindful of it—but I am. Oh, I am. I'll give the world a son, heavy

with the grief of giving him at all. Then and after, he'll drift in and out of my view, keeping secrets, neglecting me, while I watch from a distance, unrequited.

My mother shows up, startling me, when I speak to my son. I repeat what she told me, the phrases and platitudes, in the same tone of voice and inflection I heard as a child. She is my forebearer; I am his inheritance, and will prevail despite his efforts. Years from now I'll show up, a sudden surprise.

Could my own mother have felt this fierce love for me? I treat her so casually. If she ever felt this way it seems she should be grieved—bereft by my distance. Can it be that she misses me? We don't speak of such things: our closest contacts are narrowly averted, sudden swerves from danger. Will it be the same for my son and me, the boy who now crawls like a spoiled child-prince across my lap?

"When I grow up," he tells me, "you'll be my baby."

1986
Dehiscence (de-his'ens) [L. dihiscere, to gape]: a bursting open, as of a wound …

HE'S TALL NOW, and lean: when he comes running toward me, breathless from some grand injustice or new idea, I see his ribs pressing against the skin, light and shadow. He takes deep, thoughtless breaths, free of blemish, taut and promising. He has my brother's face, a handsome face, and he wears his lucky muscles with negligence and not a whit of gratitude. He is eight years old.

Sudden sufficiency. What binds us is less visible, as though we'd been cloven in two. I would not have thought it possible to feel so halved. I can wonder now what it is like to be him—wonder and know I'll never know. What does he think in a privacy I can hardly bear, a privacy that seems entirely unfair? I am still the dictator of this tiny country; he is still my subject, but he dreams of revolution.

I may not kiss him in front of others anymore. He holds the car door for me, calls me "Ma'am," with a giggle. He has great white teeth, dark circles below his eyes, a scratch on his cheek, dirt in the lines of his neck. He wants his hair cut "like Elvis Pres-ley," he wants it cut "like Michael Jackson," he wants a Mohawk. He sings commercial jingles for hamburgers and jeans and toothpaste while he builds elaborate block constructions; he strews his room with View-Masters and action figures ("They're not *dolls*, Mom," he says in irritation) and books and dirty socks and sheets. He is, above all, busy; I am tired.

"You are," he tells me, "more beautiful than the women in *Playboy*," and he's out the door before I can ask where he saw *Playboy*.

How does he know the exact inflection? He has the same disgust and injured dignity I felt all those years ago, dying a thousand deaths in the face of my mother's twittering concerns. He comes into his own and it is my turn to be out-of-date, to be shocked, to drone on long after he ceases to hear me.

I am, he tells me, so *old*.

The neighbor boys tease him and he runs home in a paroxysm of despair: "No one likes me," he sobs, and lends to his crying a thorough attention. What courage children have. I lead him to the dentist and he climbs shakily in the great chair, looks at me and asks me to spare him this. I won't; seeing my refusal, he turns away. He wants me to keep him a baby, he doesn't know that I would if could. Already *I* am separate. He looks at me and sees—only me.

He is an infant again, arms around my thighs, moaning with love, whining for cereal, a story, my lap. But he's too lanky, too long, for my lap; his elbows get in the way of the book. Then he looks for the mysterious pleasures of adulthood: freedom, mobility, explanations. But his brow furrows when he calculates the cost.

At night he is drenched in protest. He licks his teeth clean, stumbles out of the bathroom in a dirty t-shirt and yesterday's underwear; crawls over the mess on the floor of his room, and hides his stuffed bunny shamefully under the covers. I wait. And when he falls into the humid sleep of children, that greenhouse dark, I slip stealthily in beside him and stroke his honey hair. He sprawls out, clutching the bunny; I balance on the edge, listening to the ruffled quiver of his breaths. I stroke the fear; my fear, of his life, his death. When I contemplate the space he takes up, how vast its emptiness would be, my heart shakes like a rabbit in the jaws of the wolf. I watch his face turned soft with sleep, the smile that skips across his face as he turns smug and safe, and I can see that he's dreaming. He dreams without me now; we dream different dreams.

The balance is shifting. I withdraw sometimes; I want to read my book or be alone when he craves my attention. He will always live with me, he says, or perhaps next door. A transparent gift of beauty is evolving in his bones and skin, beauty made of equal parts grace and pain; I see that he will have a face of triumphant perfection if he wants. And I see the bruises rising under his skin from life's blows. I know he won't live next door, and I'm glad. I don't think I can bear to watch. Right now, I can't remember life without him—I can't remember myself without him, but the time will come.

I put my book aside and wander to his room to watch him play. I find him reading a book, curled in a corner.

"Would you mind leaving, Mom?" he says, hardly glancing up. "I feel like being alone."

1993
Inflammation (in'flema/shen) [<1. inflammation–see inflame]: redness, swelling, pain, tenderness, heat

I WAIT IN the car in the grocery store parking lot, watching the bright automatic doors in my rearview mirror. It is almost ten o'clock at night, much later than usual for me to be out shopping. For fifteen years I've been confined to childish hours. But everything changes.

I see him walk out the middle set of doors, which slide silently apart and then close behind him. He is tall, several inches taller than me, slender, graceful, arrogant. He wears his thick hair in a high tuft, dyed boot-black, and his black leather silver-studded jacket swings open with each long step.

I used to have crushes on boys like him.

We all have blows—we learn to expect a few, to roll in the force of life's first. That awful job, that last paycheck, the broken heart, the broken nose. All the broken promises no one has even made yet—wounds that can't be helped. I don't have to fear failing him anymore—I already have. What's done is done.

But I hadn't expected this.

I hadn't expected to be knocked to my knees in grief when he marches out after I tell him to stay, when he slams the door and disappears, and I drive through dark streets seeking him, and find him smoking in the park with the silent, leggy girlfriend who won't speak to me at all. I draw myself up, demand *decency, respect*; they stare, and whisper to each other.

And I hadn't expected the sorry business of petty crime. He's been arrested for shoplifting—for stealing candy bars, for stealing cigarettes, for stealing condoms. I drive to juvenile hall again and face the disapproving eyes behind bulletproof glass, and sign the papers, and wait outside until I'm joined by a raggedy, rude, foul-mouthed boy I hardly know. We drive home in silence and as we walk in the door I tell him to wash the dishes and he says, "No," and I say it again and he refuses again and then adds, mockingly, "And I don't want to have to say it again." And suddenly I'm soaked with white rage, a face-slapping high-dive, and I'm inches from his face brandishing the nearest object, yelling, "Don't you dare, don't you dare, don't you dare speak to me that way."

When we're calm, I can see he thinks I miss the point, the urgent momentum of growing up. I seem to have no ground, nothing to rely upon. He calls me a "disagreeable old hag" at the dinner table and suddenly it makes me laugh. It's so absurd. I saw my parents' anguish in my own small crimes from a cool distance; I remember their stupefaction. I drew up painful words for them deliberately like poison into a syringe. Children grow into strangers who disappoint and perplex us, having long wakened to disillusionment with us. They seem oblivious to our loss—after all, they've lost nothing.

We are their parents. And now it's my turn and I am so sorry now for what I did then.

He disappears for three days and I cannot find him. The fear is horrible, sickening; the remorse and guilt meaningless, confused. Then his girlfriend's mother calls me to tell me he's staying there because we "kicked him out," and I try to tell her it's not true, to send him home so he will work it out with me, and she refuses. She believes him, his tales. I ask her not to shelter him from this.

"I'm going to take care of him," she tells me. "I like him."

When he finally returns, we fight round after round, and there's no bell. Every victory is a Pyrrhic victory. *Baby*, I want to say, *baby love, I don't know what to do. Show me what to do.* Harsh words again, the stomp of heavy boots up the stairs. From two floors above me he lets loose a deep-throated cry, an animal cry, and then the noise of something heavy thrown with what seems an irrevocable, rending crash.

1997
Scar (skar) [<MFr<LL. < Gr. Eschara, orig. fireplace]: a mark left after a wound, burn, ulcer, etc. has healed

LIKE ALL THE other scars, this one is slowly filling in, closing off. Scars may be tender, or numb, but they are always there. Scars change the shape of things—they wrinkle, tighten, shorten things. I brought this person into the world and everything turned upside-down and all that's happened since has been in some way connected to that event, his birth. The parent-child bond, I know, is truly bondage, and its end is in many ways a liberation, an enormous relief. Here he comes, hat in hand, to claim himself and go.

He is nineteen, towering above me, his voice booming on the telephone. He is gorgeous. He is not a virgin; he admits that he is in love. He is kind to his little sister, worries about his carefree brother. Every day, changes: he drops out of high school, grabs a quick diploma at the community college, makes plans, finds a job, is shockingly responsible. He gets a checking account and an 800 number and big ideas: conspiracy theories and politics, tales of hidden alien artifacts and government cabals. His union goes on strike and he walks the picket line with all the other working men. He is righteous, indignant, a defender of the weak, and I bite my lip not to laugh and cry at once; oh god, it's the way I was at nineteen, it's exactly the way I was.

He absents himself delicately from my life.

One day he stops me in the hall, without warning, dragging his foot and looking at the floor, and mumbles, "I'm sorry," and I ask him for what and he says, "Because I was so hard," and without meeting my eyes he reaches down from his height to hug me awkwardly and adds, "I love you, Mom," and dashes down the stairs and is gone, again.

Portland Magazine, Winter 2003

The first section of this essay is one of the first essays I wrote, at the age of twenty-two. I added to it—and subtracted—over many years, and finally found a way to put the pieces of my son's life into an order that made sense to me. Into an image that made sense to me—because even now, when he is in his late thirties, I can run my hand over the scar and feel its shape and texture. That skin is not the same as it was before he was born.

On Being Text

I MAKE A LITTLE MONEY NOW AND THEN BY REPRINTING certain of my essays in college textbooks. Most such books are simply collections of essays, stories, and the occasional poem, interspersed with lessons and exercises. They are the bones of undergraduate literature and writing surveys these days; there seems to be no end to them. I have to assume it's a happy business for all involved—writers pocket what feels like overdue royalties, and the editors don't have to struggle through first drafts. It's a devil's business nonetheless.

For a time, I was content to sign contracts and bank the money. I would glance at each book when it arrived and then add it to the shelf. I started to pay closer attention several years ago when I read a brief biographical note attached to my essay: "Sallie Tisdale, a nurse, not a professional writer, doesn't structure her essay in any formal way." Well, excuse me, I thought, and promptly wrote to the editor, Judith Summerfield. (Judith graciously apologized, and we began a pleasant personal correspondence that lasted for some time after that.) I began to look much more closely at the long row of thick paperbacks I'd collected.

What I found in many of these texts astounded even as it bored me. They present a world of writing and reading unlike the one in which I've been living for more than forty years.

By the time I got to high school, I was a back-talking troublemaker, driven to sin by my complete lack of interest in my classes. I read constantly, though without plan, and had been writing for years; I was filled with the hunger to know. I was a natural student, and natural students often don't belong in school. By adolescence, I knew I loved learning, but I had given up on being taught.

In my freshman year, a new and idealistic teacher saw my small grief in a way no teacher ever had. Mr. Huffman pulled me out of his English class, gave me a long list of books to read, and sent me to the school library. Day after day for that entire year, I spent an hour each morning alone in a room filled with books. I sat on the floor between the metal stacks and read work I had never heard of before and wouldn't have chosen for myself: *The French Lieutenant's Woman*, the letters of Napoleon and Josephine, *Day of the Locusts*, *A Thousand Cranes*. All Mr. Huffman asked of me was that I come see him now and then and tell him what I thought of these books. We didn't talk about rhetoric or syllogism or parallel structure. We talked about books the way readers do—what we liked and didn't like, and why.

He was gone within a year. I left the year after that, essentially quitting before they could fire me. With the luck of the naïve and the help of a kind professor I'd met, I talked my way into the state college near my home. I stayed for two years, happier than I'd ever been before.

It took me ten years and three universities to get a bachelor's degree. I took semantics, philosophy and ethics, physics and bacteriology, religious studies and algebra—all of which were thrilling—and I took semesters off to learn a few other things and to decide that what I wanted to be was a writer. I took only two writing classes and no literature classes at all in that decade. What I had, instead, were countless conversations and debates about writing—about books, stories, words, about poetry, voice, and ideas. What I had was readerly comradeship with my peers and with teachers, in classes and over coffee and late at night—the intimate meetings of people who traded books with each other and really wanted to talk about them. Most of those books were good, some were great, and a few changed my life.

So I was never taught how to look critically at text, how

to diagram a sentence, or tell the difference between parataxis and hypotaxis. I learned a lot of this by experience and intuition, without knowing the terms, though I've picked up a lot of the terms and definitions over the years as I found use for them. But I learned to write by reading, and I learned to read well partly by writing—though mostly I read for reading's sake.

These collections of literary criticism on my shelf have different aims, not always clear. (One does honestly state, "The text's organizational structure facilitates easy syllabus design.") Some are for readers, some for writers, a few for students of contemporary culture. They don't stint on good writing, provocative ideas, or strong voices. I'm usually in excellent company, in part because the same writers (and often the same stories) appear in one such textbook after another: Raymond Carver's "What We Talk About When We Talk About Love" and Tillie Olson's "I Stand Here Ironing" and E. B. White's "Once More to the Lake." Where else but here and on the remainder table could I cozy up to John Berger, Virginia Woolf, and Roland Barthes?

For the most part, the literary criticism here is not at the level of Lionel Trilling; it's for beginners, often presuming certain gaps in the student's education. (One book includes the Declaration of Independence. At the end, the editor asks: "What conclusion are readers of this document expected to reach? In what way are the truths listed in paragraph 2 'self-evident'?") Most include little lessons on persuasion, "process analysis," and contrasting. Some define the essay, name its parts, and lay out the exact steps one takes in writing one; this, I read, is to help you, the student, "expand your repertoire of writing strategies so that you can adopt and use methods you encounter in a wide variety of texts." Then there is this kind of thing: "All the activities a writer goes through before actually beginning to write are part of prewriting." I find it hard to imagine that we really need a word like *prewriting*, which would have to include making coffee and playing multiple games of solitaire. But my main objection to this whole genre is how it kills the story.

Life Studies includes James Thurber's "The Secret Life of Walter Mitty," a story designed to make you cringe and chortle at the same time in the uncomfortable humor that Thurber mastered. The student readers, however, are given no time for discomfort. They are instead required to explain in five hundred words or less "a few implications of Mrs. Mitty's statement, in the next-to-last paragraph, 'I'm going to take your temperature when I get you home.'"

One of my favorite short-story writers, Toni Cade Bambara, is represented in the new book *Reading Rhetorically* by her story "The Lesson." Bambara wrote in a child's voice, tinged by false bravura and righteous indignation—a wonderful voice, unique. "She been screwed into the goalong for so long, it's a blood-deep natural thing with her. Which is how she got saddled with me and Sugar and Junior in the first place while our mothers were in a la-de-da apartment up the block having a good ole time." And lots more like that of a poor black girl's awakening to the vast, unfair world, enough to break your heart by the end of a few thousand words. Bambara's observations are so devastating, her awareness of inner grief so acute, there is nothing left to say by the end. But students must answer nevertheless: "Since plots usually involve some kind of conflict, how would you define the conflicts that set this story in motion?" Oh, how to begin!

We live in an abridged culture. We are surrounded by broken pieces of meaning: vaguely familiar melodies on television commercials, classical paintings cut up for coffee cups and t-shirts. A lot of my own work, like that of many other writers, has been pirated on the internet, where it is sliced, plagiarized, sold, and rewritten, sometimes one paragraph at a time. The everyday world college students live in can seem to be nothing but parts, a world without gestalt. In such a world, the purely imagined lives of Bambara and Thurber are blessed wholeness. And the moment the students finish reading, they must start to dissect. I'm afraid that what the students of these books are really learning is what college students learn about so many subjects: how to take things apart, but not how to put them together.

The introduction to *Conversations: Readings for Writing*, edited by Jack Selzer, includes an exhaustive analysis of E. B. White's "Education." The analysis is longer than the essay itself. Selzer aims to prove that White was not writing an "objective, neutral appraisal" of schools but a "calculated argument," and that his voice is a "created pose, an attempt to create a genial, sympathetic, and trustworthy speaker" through "rhetorical sophistication."

To be sure, White was a master of rhetorical sophistication. I suppose I read him for that reason, but mostly I read him because he is funny and sad and anxious and wants to be a good person, and reading him makes me want to be a good person, too. It never occurred to me that he was neutral about anything. Taking apart his choice of words doesn't change that, and it doesn't help me write like E. B. White. But it can spoil the essay for good.

Maybe the best thing we can hope for from books like these is simply more readers—though I doubt that is a result. There are admittedly noble goals here: better writing, better thinking. I'm all for better thinking and for helping young people to be less susceptible to propaganda—the soothing tones of the evening news moving smoothly from tragedy to farce, the panoramic seduction of advertising, the buried content below a misleading headline. To the extent literary criticism can help a young person navigate those treacherous waters, I'm in favor of it. But if that's the hope, White and Thurber and Bambara are not the best examples. The essay is not the problem.

What I'm quite sure this kind of analysis cannot do is explain how writers write, or teach students how to write their own stories. To take apart a composition requires one to presume a kind of construction that may not actually exist. The construction may not be, as it were, discoverable. If you take apart a house to find the walls and roof, you just end up with a lot of wood. Without walls, a roof doesn't exist. Writers find effects as often as create them; like all the arts, writing is a combination of spontaneity and technique. I write in bursts—intuitively driven torrents—followed by careful repair. Some words are discovered, others deliberate. The result is always a combination of the found and the chosen.

How does one parse intuition, outline discovery? Literary analysis begins by presuming that writing can be understood by understanding its parts. The process is, in fact, called dissection, a term usually applied to dead things.

No matter how carefully constructed a given work is, its writer will always have had more than one intention. Explaining these byways is the goal of deconstruction—to find and then surgically expose a writer's multiplicity, his hiddenness, insight the writer himself may not have. Writing reveals the writer even when it hides her, because sometimes what it is revealing is a disguise, a mask, a lie. (Lies are also a kind of truth, for all our multitudinous intent.) We speak of "glossing" a text when we read it part by part. But when we speak of glossing anything else, we're adding—and in glossing literature, we add our own multiplicity and hiddenness, whether we know it or not.

My work has sometimes been criticized for rambling, for a non-linearity, for structure sometimes buried a bit deep—what Judith Summerfield saw as a lack of "formal" structure. But as often as not, this criticism has been leveled precisely at the parts of a book that I had most carefully constructed to be just so. I sometimes break up direct narrative for a subtler, more layered effect. I am striving for a totality of story, made up of shifts and slips of tone and mood as much as events and plot. I am not consciously concerned with what these books call "strategies" or worried about the conventions of narrative. (Whether this is for better or worse I leave to my own readers, taking comfort in the words of Jean Cocteau: "Note just what it is about your work that critics don't like—then cultivate it.") Reading my own critics has taught me a little bit about my work and rather a lot about certain critics.

That is not to say that literary analysis is without entertainment value. It's just more fun when applied to someone else.

Life Studies: A Thematic Reader, edited by David Cavitch, contains my essay "We Do Abortions Here." Each essay is followed by study questions. "In the detailed description of an abortion, what does the author want the reader to recognize?" That description includes an image of the fetus as "an elfin thorax, attenuated, its pencilline ribs all in parallel rows with tiny knobs of spine rounding upwards."

I wrote this essay a good many years ago, long enough to regret any piece of work, but I'm still mostly pleased with it. I've always liked *pencilline*, a word one hardly ever needs but which seems just right here—a single word to imply a specific, prosaic shape. "Elfin thorax" works—the word *elfin* all wrong for something pretty, but effective in the vaguely violent context here, with "knobs of spine" attached.

Did I think these choices through when I wrote? No. I just knew they worked. And I don't really know how I knew.

David Cavitch also asks of my essay, "What is the author's outlook on humanity? What generalizations does Tisdale assert or imply about the human race?" I laughed out loud when I saw this. How can anyone answer it fairly? With apologies to Mr. Cavitch, there is something fundamentally silly about this question. A thousand words due on Friday isn't going to scratch the surface. My outlook on humanity is the entire theme of my work—of any writer's work. What else can we write about? Even if we determinedly avoid the human realm and write instead of birds and stars, humanity is our ground, our air. (One text includes Annie Dillard's essay "Living like Weasels." Question 6: "This essay is not really about weasels but about ways Dillard thinks people could live. What does Dillard find attractive about how weasels live?")

The Longwood Reader has an excerpt from my essay "Meat," which is partly about the butcher in the town where I was raised, and partly about my father, and also about firefighters, summer, adolescence, and justice. The editors not only removed the few sentences about sex from the essay but also retitled it "Sins of the Flesh," giving away the game entirely, if you ask me—which no one did. There must be some irony in the fact that the authors of a text on literary analysis feel no qualms about rewriting the texts they analyze. But it makes me tired to think about it.

"Meat" began with nothing more than a memory of my mother's freezer, filled with packages of meat wrapped in butcher's paper, like white rocks scattered among food. There was no more to it than that at first. Only this image, and no idea what it meant or where it would go—and then I wrote around it, opened it up, found more details, a story. "Note how the verb tense changes in several paragraphs, helping to quicken the action," the text explains. "Why does the first sentence in paragraph 7 begin in the past tense—'Buying meat was like this every time'—and then immediately shift to the present tense—'I *am* with my mother ...'?" Italics and grammar theirs.

I can answer that one, in fact. The style follows and leads at once: A child opens the freezer to see the packages of meat, so the voice is ruminative, meditative, with the conditional *would* and *could* scattered through, and occasional repetitions, as in, "I grew wings like angel wings"—the kind of repetition editors and writing professors tend to cross out with red pens, common in my voice. Certain scenes seem to recur again and again, almost like ritual. There are unanswered questions posed, ambiguous scenes, mistakes. I want to convey the point of view of a strange and isolated child, a hidden and sensual child, who doesn't try to explain herself to others—observing without understanding.

Most of a writer's decisions are unconscious. A stroke of paint here, a switch to a minor key there, the use of *flaccid* instead of *soft*. At this level, expression simply appears; it is expression expressing itself, images, ideas, states of mind, and feelings being acted out, evoked, displayed. An idea appears, connects to another, a layer appears and then another—suddenly there is a leap— Ah-ha! This connects to this, this idea hides under this idea, and if I move this detail to the end, then suddenly the whole tone becomes suspenseful. Later, in revisions, with careful polishing, the impulsive choice is reconsidered, sometimes rejected, sometimes improved, tightened, expanded anew. So we go on, version to version, tweaking, shifting, hemming, primping. I don't know how one knows the right word or the right tense, how exactly I know when a sentence needs two fewer or one more syllable. I can go on about rhythm and prosody, about mood or tone, but sometimes one just has to take the gifts the world gives us.

What none of these books does is celebrate—shout with the fun of Ian Frazier's marvelous "Canal Street" or cry at Brooks's "The Mother." They tell the student to make an outline instead of to share a passage with a friend. Critical reading doesn't laugh, doesn't snort in disdain or slam itself shut in frustration. When I recall those midnight coffee-shop huddles, I remember the intensity of feeling we shared. I remember how much the books mattered. These textbooks don't ponder the way a reader ponders; they ponder the way a textbook ponders, which is ponderous indeed. And I'm afraid that, less than halfway through any of them, the benighted sophomore will be thinking of changing her major to biology.

Anything not to read George Orwell's heartbreaking essay "Shooting an Elephant" and then have to answer the question, "If he had believed in the goals and values of British imperialism, would his actions have had more integrity?" Anything not to read Denise Levertov's poetic shout of exhausted rage, "The Mutes," and then have to answer the question, "Would you call this poet hostile to men?"

Recently, in one collection, I came across an essay called "The Miracle Chicken" by my friend Bernard Cooper. The editor asks, "What is Cooper's purpose here? Why do you think Cooper tells us about his father's affairs? How do you think Cooper feels about his father?" For once I can answer these questions with some confidence, partly because I know there are no simple answers to these questions. His father has long been one of his favorite subjects and their relationship a fertile field of sometimes mutant flowers. He is a careful and patient writer, and there is much more to any story he writes than what he tells. Like all serious writers, he controls the appearance of his stories—seemingly spontaneous and unguarded here, a bit artless there—but every word "a created pose." That's not—or shouldn't be—a surprise. That's writing. Study questions about the work of friends remind me to be careful reading the work of strangers—careful to remember that much is hidden, that I can't know what is accident and what design. Artlessness is one of the most difficult effects of all.

The plain truth is, I don't really want to know. Reading between the lines means reading a lot of blank space, and there aren't any words in those blank spaces. I've occasionally been complimented as a brave writer—but I know what I didn't say, what I was too craven to include. Only I know how carefully I've held the light so that the shadows fall just so. Perhaps others can say, "Here are shadows; here is light." But they will never know what the shadows hide. Sometimes I recognize my own lies only later, when the work is done.

How would I change college literature classes? I still think Mr. Huffman had the right idea. Read, read, read, and then try to explain how it feels. Read a book because someone you like tells you it's a good book. Listen to other readers when they react. Read some more. I believe that one reason I learned to write is that no one ever really tried to teach me, or rather, one reason I became a writer is that no one ever tried to tell me what a writer was supposed to be like. I had nothing to rebel against and nothing to measure myself beside except the stories in my mind. Writing classes? Oh, they're impossible. And yes, I do teach writing sometimes, and it too is a devil's business.

I still don't read with a critical eye. A recent textbook says, "For your writing to improve, you must learn to read like a writer." I believe it would be better for me to write like a reader. Most of what I know about writing I know from reading—but reading whole, as a reader reads, lost and unfettered, wandering in another's world without a jaded eye. Wandering free of all jaded things is part of the joy of reading; how dare anyone take it away? We can surrender to a master of rhetorical sophistication without any need to wonder how or why. Maybe literature lives only in the reader—born in the changing life, taking its breath in the reader's changing life, a different story for each person who reads it. If a tree falls in the woods and no one hears, does it make a sound? Who cares? Until I open the book, there are no words inside.

Creative Nonfiction, 2004

I am a reader frantic at times with how much more there is to read. I disappear into the work. I form intimate relationships with authors, assume I understand them, that they would understand—and like—me, and that I know their intentions. I am probably wrong about all of that. As a writer, I don't think about this much. Anthologies give us a window into everything wrong with how we teach writing—and reading—and how one is actually read. It's not pretty.

Balls

WHEN WE WERE YOUNG AND YELLED, "LET'S PLAY BALL!"
play meant more than *ball*. We played all kinds of games, many
centered on running. When we were very young, we played Croco-
dile in the wading pool—one child crawling through the shallows
with teeth bared, the others flailing in rapturous terror. Later we
invented Monster, a frenzied combination of chase and tag. Summer meant vicious games of Red Rover in the sunny field, filling
the quiet afternoon with laconic calls and bone-jarring thuds.

In the days when there was no such thing as exercise, the
game I loved best was football. It was a brutal, gleeful game, best
played in winter mud as sharp-edged as sheet metal. The mob
mind prevailed—sometimes we just called the game *tackle-pile-
on*. The bottom was the best place to be, as it was often better to be
chased than to chase, better to splash away, shrieking, better to be
caught, to be out, to be free.

Balls were just an excuse for the dirt and the running: football,
kickball, tetherball, softball, dodgeball—the ball itself didn't matter much. The hot, winded pounding of our hearts is what mattered.

Later on, the ball mattered, too.

My brother played football and lettered in gymnastics. In
high school, I tried the gymnastics team and track, the only girls'
sports, but they were the wrong things for my stocky, bosomy body
with its odd centers of gravity. So I learned to climb, lifted weights,
hiked, and rode my bike. I liked it all, but these were solitary
things. I wanted games—I wanted balls. One summer I trained as

a New Games coach. New Games are simple kinds of play designed to eliminate even the idea of competition. No score, no points, no losing, no goal. Our t-shirts read, "Play Hard, Play Fair, Nobody Hurt," but they might as well have said, "Nobody Wins." I missed victory. And many of the games deteriorated into a gentle mayhem, tackle-pile-on without bruises or mud. Without tackling. The games got boring fast, and the only ball was a giant inflatable Earth.

In the seventies I joined a community softball league, put together by a bunch of hippies longing for baseball but determined to be counterculture about it. It was softball sprinkled with a little dope dust, but it was also my first time playing with a real ball, a ball with a life of its own. We played hard and often—dozens of us on eighteen teams, with a season running from April through October. The rules prohibited strikeouts and required each team to field at least four women at all times. We had no umpires—or more precisely, we were our own umpires. Most of the players worked in small nonprofits and collectives; long committee meetings were the rule of the day for all of us. Deciding who was safe and who was out by consensus-based discussion had a certain diabolical logic.

My team, the Wild Turkeys, was routinely at the bottom of the league. Coach Ken let anyone play, so we were heavy with beginners, many of them women. I watch the serious girl jocks in the gym today with a pang of sharp envy; mine was the last generation of American women who grew up largely not playing organized sports. Most of the men, counterculture identities notwithstanding, had played plenty of sports over the years. It was not just my first time on a team—it was my first time playing real sports with—and against—men.

The pitchers were required to help the hitter hit, a rule intended to compensate for the wildly varying levels of skill, and also to make the game more interesting—more fun. I loved the no-strikeout rule, because when I started playing softball, I wanted to get a hit more than anything. I was an average beginner, earnest and a bit erratic, but competitive enough to become a serviceable player after a few seasons. All I wanted was a hit and any kind of hit would do—that marvelous sting of bat on ball, the solid glee of watching it fly away, feeling it fly away, as though I were flying, too.

For a few seasons, I pitched for the Wild Turkeys. At least once a game I got cracked in the shin or had to throw myself to the ground to duck from a drive. Some of the men—ponytailed, beer-drinking hippies like the rest, but much more serious about sports—played community ball because it was the only game in town. They missed strikeouts, big time. They missed the umpires. And they groused, not very quietly, about the female quota. These serious men stalked to the plate with the heaviest bat slung on their shoulder, settled into a stance, gave me the evil eye, watched my slow, soft lob come in, swung with all their might—and popped up. They were easy outs, bopping nice soft ones into the shortstop's lap, easy smacks into the glove of the grinning woman confined to center field. The strongest men, the hardest hitters, popped out inning after inning because they only wanted home runs. The women, still learning to play and happy to get any hit, made their bases on dribbling grounders to the infield. They brought each other home, laughing with the strange new calls we'd learned, the *good hustle* and *hey batter* and *slide!* "Lucky swing," the men would mutter.

One day, I figured something out: I was a better player than they were.

AFTER FOUR YEARS, a back injury, and a move to a new city, I didn't play ball in any form for years. I juggled children, jobs, and writing, and had no hands left to juggle balls. Eventually I was lifting weights again, hiking, riding my bike. I learned to dive. But Lord, I missed softball. I knew I really wasn't good enough for the city leagues, and I thought my back was probably past the twisting and sliding of a good game … Still, I wanted that team thing, that gospel call-and-response. I wanted to be playing ball.

I started going to the Wednesday night co-ed volleyball game at the YMCA. Right away, I was back to the well-oiled muscles, damp skin, the sped-up mind of play, this time with volleyball's own soft mantras: "Side-out, side-out!" "Back! Over!" It was a bigger ball, a smaller field, but the same fluid motion until I would lose myself in the metaphysical presence of the ball, the place where the ball might be. Falling asleep after hours of play, I watched myself watch the ball, kneeling, screaming, spreading my arms wide in an iconic plea for help. After playing for a while, I came to know in the moment of placing my body to meet the ball if I would hit it well or poorly, if I would get the sharp tang of a spike or watch it float haplessly over the net. I was back again to the long reaches, the slides—the treacherous ball, the beloved ball.

The YMCA had a lot of regulars: a guy who lifted a ton of weight for an hour before coming up to the court, a short man who carefully combed his few hairs over his pate before stepping out. There were a few women, some very good players; there were a few good men, and a vast abundance, a cornucopia, a veritable feast of pop-fly boys.

I was learning the game; I made dramatic, egregious errors sometimes. Like most of the women, I took the blame when I screwed up and was quick to apologize. It is partly that old conditioned response, the Pavlovian drool of shame women develop around sports. But I also knew when I'd made a mistake and felt the need to admit it. In contrast, in surprise, I watched the men flail about after an error, watched them swear, stomp, pound the posts, kick the ball—the offending ball—as though they'd been cheated. The joyful tumble of *tackle-pile-on* seemed far away from this tawdry, mean court. They didn't love the ball the way I did—they seemed in fact to hate it. They *wanted* the ball, but more the way one wants revenge than cake. They had ball envy—the slicing hunger for the soft, round phallus in your hands. Your hands, and no one else's.

It didn't take me long to figure out that I was a better player than most of them. I wasn't a powerful player, not at all flashy, just what I've come to realize is called a utility player. I made my passes, and if my spikes were rather more like gentle taps than slams, at least they were over the net.

This wasn't the big leagues, but it was a long way from New Games. A man flies up for a hard spike and slams the ball straight into the net, so that it springs right back into his face with a sharp whack. A guy in the back court rushes forward, trying to steal the set from the woman there. She is too quick for him, and spikes the ball. But the other team is quick, too, and returns the spike, right into our back court, right where the hotshot is supposed to be, and isn't. He's still in the frontcourt, out of his zone, yelling at the woman: "You handed it to them, dammit. You handed it to them!"

One night when several men in a row on both teams served hard out of court, and the serve shifted in side-outs back and forth, back and forth with no volleys, I yelled, "It's the boys' night out!" No one got the joke except the woman setting for the other team, who smiled and rolled her eyes to heaven.

My husband used to play basketball with a bunch of other white-collar guys. One night he hobbled home, barely walking, and told me he'd hurt his ankle early in the game. None of the other players, including the two physicians, checked on him until the game was over. He sat on the bench in pain until it ended and someone was willing to drive him home. "Of course," he explained, "if they hadn't been *playing*, it would have been different."

I began to wonder if men were just more appropriately involved than I, just more real sportsmen. Did I misunderstand? Was the vague metaphor of sport as war not metaphor at all? Sometimes I would forget the score and have to ask for it when it was my turn to serve. If a man grew overwrought, I'd say, "It's only a *game*," and they would stare at me as though I'd surrendered to the enemy just as victory was sure.

It was years before I thought to feel sorry for these guys. The men with whom I'd played softball would rather stomp off the field in disgust than pull the ball down a little and find the gaping holes in our ragged field. They didn't seem to know how good an ordinary base hit felt. The mad spikers didn't seem to know how fine was a lofting set, how right a high assisting pass. They never whooped with relief or joy, shouting with delight for bringing someone else on home.

One man at the Y was the champion ball-stealer—my ball,

any woman's ball. He was a bad player, aggressive but without finesse, and he would loudly point out where each woman should stand and tell us to rotate when the serve changed, as though we had never played before.

During one game we played side by side, and with each play he would shift toward me a few feet, too close, harshly whispering instructions under his breath and distracting me.

When I served, that girlish underhand the men disdain, it was low and sleek over the net and we had a point.

He rolled his eyes.

He set to me in the frontcourt because he had no choice. I tapped it over into the opposition's backcourt, someone bobbled it, and we had the point.

"Well, great!" I said, for something to say.

"It would have been *out* if they hadn't *gone* for it."

What could I say? I didn't hiss or sigh. I didn't tell him to back off, I didn't smile and agree. I just looked at him. My daughter stood on the sidelines, cheering us on, cheering everyone on equally with no concern for the score.

What could I say? Finally, toward the end of play, he raced up from the backcourt behind a woman in spike position, reached over her shoulder to steal her hit, and slammed her to the ground. She slid across the wooden floor on her elbows and landed in a heap. I was the only person on the team to move, to ask if she was all right. The offender wouldn't even look at her. But worse, far worse—she wouldn't look at him. She didn't say anything at all. She just brushed herself off and took her place again.

Joanna Russ famously said years ago that men aren't pigs—they're fools. And they are surely fools for balls. The fleshy ball is a bullet, a spear, a knife of the patriarchy, and the team a tribe grimly fighting for the cave. They hunt; we gather. I sometimes wondered what happened when there were no women there. Did they circle the gymnasium, pissing in every corner?

I played a little softball this summer for the first time in years—six of us at a picnic playing pick-up. I was the only woman, playing with five nice guys I've known for a long time, and I walked onto the field with a shiver of delight. I was pretty bad at it. I hadn't thrown a softball for a long time. But we were all pretty bad and no one was in a hurry about anything. I swung and flubbed and swung again and finally got a hit, and lumbering through the dust to first base, I remembered that it is best to be tackled. Best to be under the familiar weight of all the rest of the players than make it to home base all alone.

I STOPPED PLAYING at the YMCA. I joined a women's game at an old community center on Monday evenings. The gym is tiny; the volleyball net stretches from wall to wall and there is barely room behind the line to serve. On hot nights there is no breeze, no air; we prop the door open and the ball shoots out now and then, disappearing into weeds. But the slapping, thwacking sounds of the game, shoes squeaking, ball thudding, is the same, it's universal, like a repeated dream, and the music is all iconic female chant: "Mine!" "Back!" "Good set!" "Good hustle!" "Nice try." We slap hands, slap shoulders. Often we cry: "Help!" We say *help* to mean the ball is too far away, *help* to say we can't reach it, *help* to say we can't do it alone. We say *help*, the way women do in need, and in love.

In that tiny gym, we are always banging into each other— everyone lunging for the ball, racing for it, longing for the ball, just so we can pass it along again as soon as it touches our hands.

Everyone except Julie, small and tidy and quick. She plays like a man. She's always trying to steal the ball from the rest of us. She wants those big *cojones* all to herself.

Seattle Review, 2007

I had to quit softball when I hurt my back, and I finally quit volleyball after two dislocated thumbs and a rotator cuff injury. I still miss softball acutely and think often of those hot, loud nights in the little gym, setting and dreaming of the spike. I don't miss co-ed pickup games.

Chemo World

SEVERAL YEARS AGO, I BEGAN WORKING ON A SMALL oncology unit at Providence Portland Medical Center in Portland, Oregon. The unit, known as 5-K, is shaped like a T and can hold twenty patients at a time. Its small size, the closely knit team, the long relationships with returning patients, felt exactly right. Nurses who come to 5-K usually stay a long time. The work is complex, challenging, intimate. To do it well requires me to be at my best. There is, too, the vague pleasure of feeling competent in a place where most people can't imagine working. The world of cancer is a world unto itself. Double doors at each end shut out the rest of the hospital in a kind of quarantine—keeping germs out but also keeping the cancer in.

So many people in my circle of family and friends have had cancer that not to be one of them feels strange at times. On 5-K, this circle has expanded to include many strangers. Sometimes it seems as if everyone has cancer, that having cancer is normal, and we're all just used to it. I know a lot of healthy survivors, but often the magnitude of the disease asserts itself. My mother's early death from breast cancer raises my risk of the disease significantly, so I have a mammogram every year. Last year, the technician took my films and left me in my drafty gown. She came back a few minutes later and said I needed to go down the hall for an ultrasound as well. She couldn't explain why; I'm sure she didn't really know. The ultrasound technician would only tell me there was a "shadow," and then she left with her own set of pictures. I waited in the dim, cramped room; I waited in a quivering fear that had a life of its own. When the young physician arrived, I almost tackled him.

"Look," I said. "Look, I work on 5-K. You tell me what the hell is going on, right now."

"Oh, we're not thinking a malignancy," he said, surprised. I wanted to hit him. I wanted to yell: You tell me that *first.*

CANCER IS A catchword for a group of diseases defined by the cell in which they originate. Different cancers have different courses, prognoses, and treatments; they are different diseases. Some are fast and some are slow, some are relatively easy to treat and others almost impossible. They all involve abnormal cells without a useful function, cells that are not orderly and are not controlled by the normal mechanisms that manage cell growth. Tumors can double in size in two to three months. By the time of diagnosis, many have metastasized to new sites. The cancer is loose, it has broken free, and the second-generation tumors are often genetically evolved, with new properties. With each move, the cells become more primitive, evolving into a kind of ur-cell. There are cancers called "unknown primary"—the cells are so plain their origin can't be identified. These are cells as psychopaths: twisted, clever, self-destructive, taking victims down along the way.

The number of cells involved is difficult to grasp. By the time cancer is detected, many millions of abnormal cells are present, and they are usually dividing rapidly. Treatment is a matter of killing as many of these abnormal cells as possible, as fast as possible, without killing the patient in the bargain. Most oncologists are reluctant to use the word *cure*, and tend to speak of cancer as a chronic disease. The goal of treatment is remission, a state in which the cancer can't be detected. Remission doesn't mean there is no cancer in the body. Animal studies suggest that millions of cancer cells remain hidden in the person considered "cancer free."

The immune surveillance theory of cancer holds that in a way we all *do* have cancer, that a healthy immune system fights off rogue cells as they appear. (New research indicates that cancer in turn can shut off crucial parts of the immune system, actively dismantling what might attack it.) A person's immune system may be able to eliminate those remaining cells one by one, the way one fights a cold, and the remission will be durable. As with other chronic diseases, in theory cancer patients could simply continue to take anticancer drugs their entire lives—if the drugs were not so toxic.

5-K IS ON the same floor as the Robert W. Franz Cancer Research Center, and at any given time almost every cancer treatment is represented there.[1] Patients are receiving various kinds of immunotherapy and chemotherapy, having radiation treatments, and recovering from surgery. There is often at least one person having a stem-cell transplant. Others are there because of the kinds of problems that tend to accompany cancer and its treatments, like infections. 5-K is a regional center for peripheral stem-cell transplants and one of only a few dozen centers for high-dose Interleukin-2 (IL-2) therapy in the United States.[2]

When I first started in the unit, I was told by more than one nurse, "If you can work on 5-K, you can work anywhere." As a population, 5-K patients are sicker than most in the hospital, skirting the edge of instability and crisis repeatedly. They may stay for weeks at a time and return again and again over a period of years. Quite a few die there. Assignments on the three daily nursing shifts are doled out partly according to the level of care each patient requires and partly on the level of training of the nurses. My training as a 5-K floor nurse took more than a year and will never stop; it includes special instruction in chemotherapy, transplants, immunotherapy, and cardiac monitoring, and studying for my national certification as an oncology nurse.

In the time I've worked there, we've had a wedding, a num-

---

1   Many people with cancer never stay in a hospital, receiving all their treatments as outpatients. People stay on a unit like 5-K because of their general health or the seriousness of their treatment.

2   IL-2, a cellular protein, is currently the only curative treatment for patients with metastatic malignant melanoma and kidney cancer.

ber of birthday parties, some anniversaries, many deaths, many emergencies, several resuscitations, the occasional family fight. There is no cancer demographic, no particular population: this is everyone, from everywhere. This is the musician who hauls her IV pole down five flights so she can play the grand piano. This is the young man covered in tattoos who was turned away from two emergency rooms for lack of money before he came to Providence and was diagnosed with leukemia. This is the young Mexican father who has no papers and has been treated without cost for years. This is the ice-skating instructor who had been a Sweetheart of Sigma Chi, the avid hiker who can no longer walk, the lawyer who likes to have whole pizzas delivered to his room from the joint down the street. They range in age from eighteen into the nineties, are all races, many nationalities, all degrees of wealth and lack of it.

Christa, a forty-four-year-old woman now in remission, told me that when she was first diagnosed with lymphoma, everything happened terribly fast. "I was carried along in this urgent wave," she said. "People kept talking about getting second opinions, but it was so urgent I was just swept along." People with cancer are overwhelmed first by fear, then by information, then by noise and change, and finally by continual tiny losses that etch away at their sense of self like water on a stone. Modesty is one of the first things to go, and privacy hardly exists. People sometimes are admitted to the unit directly from the doctor's office, having just heard the news. There's no time to pack a bag; they are literally stripped before the day is done. I remember a man who buried his wife on December 22, and on Christmas Eve was admitted to 5-K, having been diagnosed with leukemia that morning. He sat up in bed with an unfocused, sagging shock in his face, barely answering my questions. He was facing a brand new life, which had arrived without warning.

I think this is why most of my 5-K patients prefer watching *Animal Planet* to anything else on television. They doze, they watch TV, and they chat desultorily with relatives, many of whom essentially move in for the duration. (We provide beds for them; after a few days, the small hospital rooms are draped with drying laundry, suitcases, family photos, and knitting.) The patients walk the halls in varying degrees of boredom, anxiety, or persistence. Because of their low resistance to infection, many are strongly encouraged not to wander outside the unit's small range. Most wear hospital gowns, women sometimes in nice pajamas or clutching a robe, men sometimes without shirts, all with the same gray slipper socks. They push their IV poles and look at one another: the thinning hair, the fuzzy heads, the bald heads, the occasional surgical mask, the gaunt faces, the reflections of themselves. You can tell which visitors are new: they are the ones who stop to read the inspirational posters with the careful concentration of schoolchildren. The veterans are in the kitchen, making a new pot of coffee.

I read the charts. I know what some of the code words mean, the scan results, the markers. One nurse sometimes wears a pin that says CANCER SUCKS. This is one way to put it. The very idea of what we do here, so peculiarly intimate, so daringly rude—the things we ask are so unfair, the disease itself such effrontery—and it is usually at this moment of reflection that my pager goes off and interrupts me. I don't have the right to know what I know about others, to see what I see of their secrets—how can anyone?—so I try to hold my knowledge as lightly as a fine glass vase, bound to break.

For many weeks, we cared for a young woman, a born-again Christian with non-Hodgkin's lymphoma. She came to 5-K for a stem-cell transplant. She was admitted to the large room usually reserved for transplants, the one equipped with special air filters to reduce contaminants. The night she finished the high-dose chemotherapy that starts the process, she was a bit nauseated but still feeling all right. Her room was madly decorated with drawings and dolls and quilts and flashing Christmas tree lights and signs and pillows. I slid quietly in and out of her room all evening, hanging and adjusting a blood transfusion, listening to her heart and lungs, checking the pump that delivered anti-nausea medication, testing her urine to make sure the drugs hadn't damaged her bladder.

A group of friends arrived with a keyboard and a few guitars, and she sat cross-legged on the end of her bed, holding her face in her hands, while they sang to her. Hardly a word was said for hours, except in prayer.

That's one kind of day. Here's another: a forty-one-year-old woman diagnosed with lung cancer. She was athletic and had never smoked. She and the husband, who clearly adored her, had a toddler. After a month of arduous chemotherapy, her oncologist, Dr. Jeffrey Menashe, came to her hospital room for a talk. He is a tall, lean man and dresses in a pressed white shirt and dark tie when he visits his patients on 5-K. I listened while he told her ever so gently that the treatment hadn't worked. There is a new drug under investigation, he said. I can't make any promises, he said.

"I'll do it," she said, and the tears were sliding down her face, dripping off her cheeks. "I'll do anything to live."

I ASKED CHRISTA, who had lymphoma, what she remembered about being told she would need chemotherapy. "Oh, just the word 'chemo'—just the *idea* of chemo," she said. "You've heard the most frightening things."

Just that word, chemo: an insider's word, diminutive, familiar. *Chemotherapy* actually means any treatment with medicine, but in modern parlance it means only one thing—the cytotoxic drugs. And what a word—the root, chem, has the same Greek source as the word alchemy: the search for a means of prolonging life, a universal cure for disease. The search for transmutation. My friend Sylvia, who survived Hodgkin's disease, said of her chemotherapy, "It's like going to a foreign country you've heard a lot of bad things about and never wanted to visit. And then you have to go there." After Sylvia said that, I began to call it Chemo World.

Cytotoxic means *cell-killing*; these drugs destroy fast-growing cells of all types. They are still the cornerstone of cancer treatment, used before, during, and after surgery, radiation, and other treatments. There are many dozens of cytotoxic drugs of several classes on the market, and more are being released all the time.

To kill fast-growing cells in a living body in order to return it to health is a little like using buckshot to kill a cockroach on the picture window. Cytotoxic drugs can be teratogenic (causing fetal malformations), mutagenic (causing genetic mutations), and, yes, carcinogenic. They also sometimes kill cancer, so most of us view them with trepidation and hungry hope. Jeffrey Menashe imagines a day in his lifetime when we are done with cytotoxic drugs. He says, "The whole discipline of oncology was built up around the fact that you have a class of drugs that is so toxic you need a discipline to manage it, which isn't true of any other kind of drug."

Most cells of the body multiply by division; they are magnificent duplicating machines. When more cells of a certain kind are needed, some of that type create enough material, genetic and otherwise, for two cells, and then they divide—that simple, that miraculous. One of the hallmarks of cancer is that the cells continue dividing without cease, without regard to physical space, available nutrition, or any of the other controls that limit normal cell growth. They just keep multiplying—growing and dividing and growing again.

Cytotoxic drugs are classed by how they affect cells. Certain drugs are "cell-cycle specific," meaning they only kill cells at a specific phase in their growth cycle; others are nonspecific. One type of drug inhibits DNA repair and synthesis; another interrupts cell metabolism in a specific phase; yet another breaks the DNA helix strand in any phase. Some drugs are thought to kill in proportion to the dose—the more drug administered, the more cells are killed—and have a "kill rate" for just what proportion of cells they destroy.

Cell biologists and cancer researchers may spend an entire career focusing on a particular gene expressed at a particular phase in the cycle of a particular kind of cell. They study things like the tumor-suppressor gene Smad4/DPC4 and how gelatinase B affects the growth of tumors' circulatory systems, and they study them for years, from every angle. But for all the time, money, and words spent on cancer, many of the basic questions are largely unanswered. Walter Urba, director of the Robert W. Franz Cancer Research Center, says, "We don't really know how all these drugs work. We *think* we know."

Tumors are heterogeneous, made up of cancer cells dividing and behaving in different ways. For unknown reasons, cancer also tends to become resistant to the killing action of a given drug. To combat tolerance and attack these differently behaving cells, most chemotherapy is given in combinations. Combinations also allow a higher kill rate without overwhelming side effects. Few drugs are used alone, and most are used for several diseases.

Many combinations exist in standard practice. My handy laminated booklet from *Pharmacy Practice News* lists four different regimens for Hodgkin's disease, fifteen for non-Hodgkin's lymphoma, and thirty-two for breast cancer. Well and good—except that with thirty-two regimens in use, which one would be right for me? This is where it gets tricky. The order in which the drugs are given, the rate at which they are given, and the amount of time between drugs are partly a matter of opinion. Any known genetic markers of the cancer and current research matter. But so do factors that can only be called political in nature: where and when a physician trained, the proximity of a teaching hospital, and insurance compensation can all affect the choice of a regimen.

One of the reasons for choosing a specific regimen over another is the patient, not the cancer. The therapeutic index of a drug is the difference between the dose required to have a therapeutic effect and the dose that causes harm. Cytotoxic drugs have one of the lowest therapeutic indices found; there is often a very fine distinction between getting results and causing harm. In fact, taking patients as close as possible to the edge of tolerance often seems to increase survival rates, though some drugs have lifetime cumulative dose limits. A person with heart disease will not be able to tolerate the same doses and drugs as a person with a healthy heart. Moreover, the drugs are given to patients with stressed kidneys and livers, who may be recovering from surgery, who are taking many other strong drugs, who are malnourished, who are still suffering the lingering effects of prior chemotherapy and radiation. (They are given, after all, to people with cancer.) No one can predict how a patient will respond to any given drug; it may be genetically determined.

There have been many disappointments in the research. Interferon, a cell protein, is one; monoclonal antibodies are another. IL-2, which is curative for a small percentage of patients, isn't much help to the rest.

"We're disappointed that we don't have a vaccine yet," says Walter Urba. "But there will be vaccines." Many will be tailored to an individual, at a cost of many thousands of dollars. "If we figure out how to cure cancer," he adds, "we'll figure out how to pay for it."

The hope in oncology is for more targeted therapies using drugs that interfere with cell growth in much more precise ways than cytotoxic drugs. For example, a whole new class of drugs that affect estrogen synthesis has changed the treatment of breast cancer dramatically. A close friend of mine was diagnosed with widely metastasized breast cancer more than two years ago. This disease is generally considered terminal, usually within a year or two. She has not had traditional chemotherapy at all. Her tumors have been controlled by a single oral drug, anastrozole, and one course of radiation. It won't work forever, but right now, with metastatic cancer, she feels healthy and well.

The nature of discovery is surprise, points out Menashe. "We're in the fog still, and we don't know when we're going to break through. It could be tomorrow." Until then, cytotoxic chemotherapy is the cornerstone. The foundation, the bedrock, the core. The whole damned house, for a lot of people.

LIANA MARTIN IS the nurse manager of the oncology unit, where everyone knows her as Lee. She hired me to work on 5-K. She is fifty-five years old and has been a nurse for a long time, an oncology nurse for twelve years.

Three years ago, Lee had her first routine colonoscopy.

"When I woke up, the G.I. specialist said, 'Okay, we need to find you a surgeon.' I looked at her and said, 'Are you saying I have *cancer?*'" As soon as possible, she went to see Walter Urba, whom she counts as a good friend. "I said the worst possible thing I could say to him. I grabbed his hand and said, 'Walter, don't let me die!'"

Lee had colorectal cancer, which was already present in the lymph nodes. Urba prescribed a regimen of chemotherapy and radiation. Even with her experience, she was surprised at the uncertainty involved in the doses and in what to expect. "I wasn't supposed to lose my hair," she says. "It came out in handfuls. I expected to have some nausea, but we couldn't control it—I lost thirty-five pounds. The radiation oncologist said, 'Oh, it's the chemo,' and the medical oncologist said, 'Oh, it's the radiation.'"

She had severe diarrhea. She developed peripheral neuropathy, damage to the fine nerves of the extremities, which causes numbness, tingling, and pain. Then she also developed an unusual side effect called hand-foot syndrome, in which the hands and feet become red, swollen, and burning. The side effects were so severe that Urba had to interrupt her treatment several times to let her recover. On the one hand, she knew the drugs were dangerous. "The nurses hung up a bottle, and I knew it was poison; I was letting them put poison in me." On the other hand, she wanted those drugs.

"It was really hard to stop. It felt like a failure. *My* failure," she says now. "I really was hindering my care in some ways. I had eighteen bouts of diarrhea in one day and I didn't call the radiation oncologist, I didn't tell him until after the treatment. And he was livid. I knew he would have held the treatment. That's how panicky I was." More than once, 5-K nurses called Urba themselves, because Lee was obviously sick and refusing to admit it.

Finally, Urba dropped her doses by 20 percent. "That was really hard," she recalls now. "I wanted it, *all* of it, *every* bit, as much as possible." She wanted that poison, but she was out there, skirting the edge.

PREDICTED SIDE EFFECTS are based on averages and on research, just like doses, and of extremes are averages made. The side effects are caused by the collateral damage of a treatment designed to kill fast-growing cells. Side effects can be immediate or delayed, brief or enduring, but they are almost inevitable. The picture window will shatter as the cockroach dies. I find that many people fear chemotherapy in an almost supernatural way; they have heard so many things about it; they tell one another tales about it, and some of the tales are true.

Unlike most drugs, chemotherapy is hard to keep secret; it makes itself known in painfully visible ways. Losing one's hair is the biggest fear most people have. They know it is an irrational fear—it won't kill them, it's temporary. But hair is iconic and relational, a symbol of youth and sex and status, almost as important to the self-image as the face. To suddenly be without it is horrifying to many people, and to be without it because of a deadly disease is worse. Losing the hair means sickness, it means weakness, it means you are in danger of losing your life, and you see it in the mirror every day.

No one really knows why chemotherapy makes hair fall out, a process called alopecia. The drugs damage the dividing cells of the follicles in ways not well understood, so that the hair shaft weakens and breaks. Alopecia is not confined, as many people believe, to the scalp. People may also lose their beards, eyebrows, eyelashes, the hair under the arms, the pubic hair, even the fine hairs of the forearms and legs. (I've heard this large-scale baldness called "the total Yul Brynner.") We may not be covered in fur, but hair is protective. People get sunburns on their scalps or find they are cold all the time without hair's insulation. Without eyebrows and eyelashes, it's easy to get specks in your eyes, and when you cry, the tears spill out like water over a dam. After treatment, when the hair grows back (rarely, it doesn't) it may be a different texture, even a different color.

I've seen women weeping in grief over this dreaded loss, refusing to leave their rooms, but most people get used to it quickly. Perhaps it is easier when one goes to the clinic week after week, or spends time in the hospital and sees so many others—men and women, young and old—who all look the same.

Nausea and vomiting is the other great fear before treatment and, unlike hair loss, may be more distressing than expected. Some drugs stimulate various, complex neurochemical pathways as they work, leading to activation of what is bluntly known as the vomiting center located in the brain stem. The retching that follows can be violent, sudden, and long-lasting. The surprise for many people is that only some of the drugs do this. Cisplatin, one of the most common drugs in use, causes nausea in more than 90 percent of patients; vincristine, another common drug, rarely causes nausea.

There are good, quite expensive, new drugs for nausea and some old standbys that work well for many people, but nothing is foolproof. Marijuana helps some people a lot. Many patients swear that a joint is much more effective than the pharmaceutical form, a pill called Marinol.[3]

Oregon has a medical-marijuana law, but the law is problematic in ways I didn't foresee when I voted for it. One lymphoma patient, an artist, casually lit up a bong in his room on his first day on 5-K. This was a mistake in several ways—not least that he was sharing it with his friends—but it is how I found out that the entire building's no-smoking rule applies to this legal medicine as well. Since the medical-marijuana law prohibits a licensed user from using it in public spaces, such as the hospital's outdoor smoking area, this patient found himself in a difficult position. One day his girlfriend began crying, begging for me to find a way for him to get some relief—"just one joint," she said tearfully. I called security and explained the situation, and they told me the schedule of their rounds out in the parking lots. I told the patient and his girl-

---

3   It's so difficult for researchers to get permission and material to do tests on marijuana in people with cancer and AIDS that much of the information available is anecdotal, but there is a lot of that.

friend what I'd learned; they took a walk, and we didn't talk about it anymore.

Worse than the nausea for many people is a condition called mucositis. Many drugs damage the DNA of cells in the mucus membranes of the entire digestive tract, from mouth to anus, as well as mucous membranes in the vagina. This damage and the release of inflammatory chemicals destroys tiny blood vessels and connective tissue, creating ulcers. Some patients are in such severe pain from mouth sores that they can't swallow or even speak. They require narcotics and may need days or weeks of what is called TPN, total parenteral nutrition, a metabolically balanced liquid given through the veins. (Now and then, if a patient has a certain sense of humor about his or her dark condition, the nurses will label the big, milky bag: "Steak, baked potatoes, apple pie," changing the menu day by day.)

Diarrhea is common as well and usually has several causes, including changes in fluid and electrolytes and direct damage to the cells and normal enzymes. Christa described the result of her severe diarrhea as "scorched earth," a term accurate in both metaphorical and clinical ways. She was a little indignant even two years later. "Everyone wanted to see it! You don't really want to show it to them."

These are the side effects patients dread, but there are many more they don't even anticipate. Although vincristine rarely causes nausea, it is renowned for neurological complications, one of which is constipation; another is foot drop. Another is peripheral neuropathy, even at relatively low doses.

One class of cytotoxic drugs is the antibiotics. We don't tend to think of them that way, but antibiotics are cell-killers par excellence, and some potent ones kill cancer cells by preventing DNA synthesis. They have a tendency to color the urine—usually red, but in the case of mitoxantrone blue-green. Some drugs cause rashes, or little pustules similar to acne, or itching, or changes in pigmentation, or sensitivity to sunshine. Some drugs cause blurred vision and changes in color perception, or increased tears.

There are drugs that reduce libido or cause coughing. Paclitaxel, used for certain lung cancers, is known for causing severe joint and muscle pain. The drugs can cause sterility. They can cause cancer. I know I've told my patients these things, the physicians have told them, we've printed out the information, read through the list of possable side effects with them, and repeated ourselves, and they don't remember—they can't remember, it's all too much and too scary and too new. So their pee turns red and they think it's blood, or they forget about the sun and get a burn, and they cry, reminded. Reminded of so many things they want to forget.

People want to survive; they are willing to do much more than they would have thought they could. Years later, people who are so happy to be alive, to be well, will tell you this most difficult time was a gift, that it changed them for the better, clarified their lives. But in the midst of it? "I'd rather die than not be able to knit," one old woman said to me, having refused any more treatment because of the risk of neuropathy in her hands. And she did die. I've seen people start puking as soon as I enter the room, hours before I bring the drug, because I am associated with it—my blue scrubs, the faint scent of soap on my hands, is enough. I've seen people so used to pain and so broken by it that they simply lie there, leaking tears, as I hurt them again. I've seen an engineer who runs a busy office, a man of authority, ashamed to silence by his diarrhea, like a bad child who cannot get to the toilet in time.

Woven through all this is what we call fatigue. Cancer causes fatigue, and so do radiation and hospitalization and surgery, and so does chemotherapy. It is not a matter of being tired or depressed but something much more mysterious. Fatigue means a loss of vital energy, what some might call life energy, animation, reserve, or power. If you are tired, you can still run up a flight of stairs in an emergency. If you are fatigued, you may not be able to do that. Wanting has nothing to do with it. Just when you need a little extra, there is that much less.

I wonder sometimes whether this is one way the spiritual distress of cancer manifests in the body. We talk about contribut-

ing factors like anemia and malnutrition; we counsel light exercise
and careful planning. But what about the loss of one's identity?
What makes the self a self? With cancer and its treatments, the
aspects of identity erode like sand in a tide, inexorably, constantly.
You are a person who does things (work, family, hobby, art, sports),
a person who fills roles (plumber, father, singer, tennis player), a
person with an interior life unlike any other, and it all disappears.
Who are you without these things? Who is the person who can't
read a book or tie her shoes, can't make love, cook supper, or follow a conversation—who may never do such things the same way
again?

OF ALL THE effects of chemotherapy, that pesky therapeutic
index is what keeps the nurses vigilant. When people die "of cancer," it is often not the tumor that kills them. Cytotoxic drugs can
cause severe allergic reactions. They can damage every organ,
including the eyes and ears and brain. They can decrease the con-
tractility of heart muscle, make the lung tissue fibrous, erode the
bladder wall so that it hemorrhages. They can, they have to, take
people out along an edge no one really wants to walk.

Most cytotoxic drugs damage the immune system to some
degree by damaging the bone marrow. This is called myelosup-
pression; it follows the active weakening of the immune system
done by many cancers and can be lethal. A myelosuppressed person has too few specialized cells to fight infections, too few red
blood cells to carry oxygen, and not enough platelets for clotting.
Many people need blood and platelet transfusions. Sometimes, at
a certain point in the collapse of the marrow, the chemotherapy
simply has to stop until the person recovers.

Infection is the most worrisome problem. The nadir for
blood cells can begin a few days after treatment or weeks after
treatment, and last a long time. People in severe myelosuppres-
sion can die from the normal bacteria on their own skin and in
their gut, from a fungal spore on their pillow, a bit of mold from a
vase of flowers, from a kiss. Suddenly outside the pale of ordinary

life, they die of themselves, and the world. To protect themselves, people bathe every day, wash their hands constantly, wear surgical masks, avoid fresh produce and flowers and pets and children and crowds. To avoid bleeding, they don't use razors, dental floss, or tampons, or walk barefoot or have sex.

In a neat reversal, this dangerous state is induced deliberately for stem-cell transplants. Stem cells are both parent and child, able to become many kinds of cells, depending on the body's needs. Healthy marrow is always making stem cells. Autologous transplant is used mostly to treat cancers of the blood, like lymphoma, some leukemias, and multiple myeloma. It means harvesting the patient's own stem cells, deeply suppressing the marrow and cancer together, and then reinfusing the cells to kick-start the immune system.

When I first began working on 5-K, I made the common mistake of assuming that the transplant was the treatment, but in fact it's the antidote. The real treatment is the very high-dose chemotherapy given first, the most intense chemotherapy a person can tolerate, a dose that is intended to destroy the bone marrow. Without an infusion of stem cells, the person will most likely die from overwhelming infection or hemorrhage. We call the infusion a "rescue."

A person's cells are harvested by a special machine that filters stem cells out while circulating the blood, and the cells are then frozen. A few days or perhaps weeks later, the person moves into one of the big, specially filtered rooms and starts the chemotherapy, which is tenderly called ablation. *Ablate* means *to remove, to melt, to vaporize*, and with that, the countdown begins: Day –3, Day –2, and so on. Day Zero is when the cells are infused.

On Day Zero, the stem cells are thawed in a saline bath and injected into the patient's bloodstream with big syringes. There is a little tension in the air during the infusion—a kind of excitement, almost of celebration. Day Zero is a long-anticipated, hoped-for, feared day. One woman—the hiker who could no longer walk without an elaborate brace, her bones turned to cottage cheese from multiple myeloma—had her husband videotape the procedure. I tried to imagine watching it at home, over popcorn.

Transplant is a struggle; patients are usually in the hospital for several weeks. It is only after the infusion that the side effects of the chemotherapy really kick in. Day +4, Day +7, and on and on. The patient feels wretched and can do nothing but wait for the cells to settle in the marrow. The transplant rooms are large because people need to stay in there; they have no immune system, so they need to avoid as much of the world as they can. They have big dry-erase boards with calendars on them, and many keep track of their daily blood counts there. They read a little and watch television and sleep, and wait. And wait, watching the numbers.

Chemotherapy can be horrible and it can be a breeze, and it is usually something in between. The side effects I've listed here are horrible; I find them hard to read. Is the life that follows the reward for all this suffering? Or is the difficulty itself a gift? I know that people suffer here. They also survive. Their hair falls out and then it grows back. They throw up, they lose weight, they feel weak, they feel embarrassed, and then they get better. People get better. People get well. People go home.

AFTER HER DIAGNOSIS of colorectal cancer, Lee started weekly chemotherapy and fell into a rhythm of anticipation and recovery. On Wednesdays and Thursdays she'd have treatments and then rest for a few days. "On Sundays, I felt okay," she told me. "Mondays, I felt okay. On Tuesdays, I'd start crying."

All of Lee's boundaries blurred together. She was a patient on 5-K after surgery; the nurses she supervised were bathing her. Her friends were giving her orders. "This is a journey, a path, and you do it with courage and dignity," she says now. "But let me tell you, my courage was dwindling—and my dignity! Now the peers who usually sit across the table from me are looking at my butt! I found it very humbling."

We were sitting in her cluttered office in the center of 5-K when she told me this. Now and then the telephone rang, or a nurse poked her head in to ask a question. Lee had changed with treatment. Her blonde-highlighted hair was sparse and gray under a wig. She'd lost both eyelashes and eyebrows. Her tattooed eyeliner had sloughed off with a lot of other skin, and her face was coarse and spotted with brown pigment and tiny pimples.

"I said to Walter, 'Look, I have to have cancer. Do I have to be ugly, too?'" She smiled grimly. "I woke up one day and thought, *Oh, my God—I look like a cancer patient*. And that's one thing I didn't want to look like. I'd look in the mirror and think, *This person could die*."

"Was there ever a point when you thought, 'It's not worth it?'" I asked. "No," she said, without hesitation. Then she looked into the distance for a moment. "Maybe."

There is a side effect little discussed by physicians and nurses, though it is a topic of much conversation among patients. "For me it started with words," Lee says. "I couldn't find the word, and I'd have to describe something. I couldn't work out if I was confused. I had to write notes a lot more. I'd forget things."

Patients call it "chemo brain." It was dismissed for a long time by doctors as a symptom of stress, but oncologists now accept that cognitive dysfunction after chemotherapy is rather common and surprisingly durable. So little is clear in Chemo World. In unusual, complicated, and not well understood ways, chemotherapy affects the brain. It causes not only changes in function—electrical activity, chemistry—but sometimes in structure, reducing the amount of white and gray matter. The effects are usually subtle; people complain of difficulty finding words, remembering what they've read. Many find it hard to do more than one thing at a time and frequently complain that they have a harder time doing arithmetic. Studies only now being done make it clear that the effects can last at least ten years after treatment and perhaps for good.

At what point are you no longer yourself? What is worth dying for? "Chemo brain is scary," says Lee now. "You think to yourself, *What if it doesn't go away? What if I'm going to stay this way?* We've had patients who we've taken so far out, and it seems

like they didn't come all the way back. It scared the hell out of me.
I'm still a little scared."

CHEMOTHERAPY IS USUALLY, but not always, given intrave-
nously. It may be given over a few minutes, in an infusion lasting
a few hours, or continuously for days. It may be given once, or on
a schedule over months, but it is a ritual act. Because the drugs
are teratogenic and carcinogenic, they are considered hazardous
waste. Nurses and pharmacists who handle the drugs regularly
are at risk of absorbing toxic amounts through the skin or by tiny,
aerosolized droplets. On 5-K the actual drugs are only opened
under a ventilation hood, and once the bags are mixed, they are
specially packaged and carried with chemoprotective gloves. The
nurses hanging the bags wear chemo-protective gowns and goggles as well.

I learned to give chemotherapy over time, first by study, then
by observing, then by being observed. 5-K follows the standard
method set by the Oncology Nursing Society. Patients are weighed
and measured twice before beginning a cycle, and each day it continues. Their most recent laboratory results are double-checked
before each dose, which is usually based on body-surface area.
Many cancer drugs can irritate veins, and a few can destroy muscle
and skin, so the patient has to have a new or central intravenous
line, if possible. (If the drug infiltrates the tissue, we treat it as an
emergency.) The original medical orders, doses, and calculations
are checked by two RNs and a specially trained pharmacist. The
drug vials are double-checked. Everything is cosigned in several
places. Finally, the patient is usually given pre-medications, to
prevent nausea and other side effects.

When I prepare patients for their dose, I always warn them
that I will be all dressed up when I bring the drug. I am sometimes rather formal and serious. I try not to use buzzwords, technical terms, or codes. I try not to say "chemo." "When I bring in
your medicine," I say, "you'll see me in special clothing. This is

because the drugs are very strong. This is a good thing." This is a good thing, I tell myself.

I come in, gowned from neck to knee, carrying the drug—the hope, the fear—in a special bag, carefully check the IV and the patient's name and birth date, and lay out my equipment. Then I hook it up to the pump. Chemotherapy is given in precisely calibrated amounts, literally drop by drop, and so we use pumps that control the flow. I label and tape the connections carefully while the patient watches, waiting. Sometimes we chat, but neither of us is fooled. Later, when the drug is done, I take it down with the same care and dispose of all the equipment in a special container in a locked room.

The ritual changed with a patient with mental illness. She believed that she was allergic to many substances, including normal saline. Over the course of several difficult shifts, I had to find a way to give her a drug that could only be diluted in saline, when she insisted on dextrose. I didn't want to lie to her. I set up an elaborate (mostly dead-end) system of tubing and bags and asked a pharmacist given to incomprehensibly complex explanations to come in his white lab coat and explain it to her. She was impressed and bedeviled and let me give her the drug, and I was pleased and a little ashamed.

Before I was allowed to give chemotherapy, I had to prove my skill. I also had to come to terms with what I was doing, knowing what would follow, knowing people would suffer, knowing many people would die anyway, knowing I was hanging up poison. One of the open questions about chemotherapy is when to stop. Brendan Curti, one of the oncologists who sends his patients to 5-K, says, "Some patients view the chemo as a prolongation of pain. Some patients view the chemo as part of their quality of life. And there are people here"—he rolls his eyes toward the rest of the office complex—"who think that doing everything we can means chemo until the last day of life. I don't."

I had seen my mother die from breast cancer after a double mastectomy, radiation, and chemotherapy. The last year of her life was misery, and she kept hoping for a miracle, doing whatever the doctors said. Part of my job here is honesty, but a lot of it is having the strength not to impose myself. My integrity includes giving other people theirs—the right to make choices unlike the choices I might make in their place. Some patients are in denial, others are not entirely competent. In an important way, whether or not one of my patients wants more chemotherapy when it's probably hopeless is really none of my business.

JEFFREY MENASHE SPENT a summer vacation in Kenya training oncology staff in a teaching hospital, where he saw people die for want of blood transfusions that we do routinely. Menashe specializes in treating hematological cancers and abnormalities of the blood, and many of his patients have leukemia. With leukemia, he says, the first issue is whether to treat at all; by the time of diagnosis, the blood may be more cancer than not, so sludgy with white cells that it can't move through the capillaries. Without chemotherapy, leukemic people can die within a month of diagnosis, but the treatment is hard to take and hard to survive. With most leukemic patients, the line between the devastation of the disease and the ruin of the drugs can be quite fine.

"For a person who might have a 30 to 50 percent chance of being cured, people who are young and fit, you treat," he says. "But for older people with a 10 or 20 percent chance, many say, 'The hell with it, I know I'm going to die.' And some people say, 'If I'm going to die anyway, I'm going to go down fighting.' Unfortunately, the regimen hasn't really changed much in many years. The current treatment is to poison the whole bone marrow and hope the normal cells will recover faster than the leukemia cells."

The first cycle is called induction and will hopefully put the patient in remission. Induction hits like a truck—strong drugs, high doses, long cycles, repeated cycles. Leukemia won't stay in remission long for many people, so they return for what is called consolidation chemotherapy. If they don't go into remission, they return for what is neatly termed salvage.

A few years ago, we tried to salvage a young soldier with leukemia. One night I started yet another cycle of three drugs. By then he was emaciated, too weak to stand. He couldn't bear to have his burning feet touched; his throat hurt all the time, and his hair was nothing but pale patches. He had just turned twenty-one. Almost all of his problems were caused by the drugs, but without the drugs he would have been dead already. When I came in one evening, carrying my gown, gloves, goggles, and the bags of medicine, I saw that he was watching *Team America: World Police* on the unit's DVD player. He barely glanced at me as I went about the familiar task, his gray eyes large in his wasted face, watching the movie with a small, spacey smile. He had been in Iraq a few months earlier. "America! Fuck, yeah!"

SOMETIMES I THINK the doctors don't cry in front of the patients because the nurses do it for them. I hold a weeping woman in the utility room, because she has just confessed to me that her husband won't make love to her anymore. A longtime patient is told he doesn't have enough stem cells for a transplant, there is nothing more to do, and is sent home, and the head nurse cries as he goes. A handsome young man bleeds to death in the arms of a young nurse, and we all cry. We cry quietly, in private, not always in front of one another. There are times when tears seem the correct response.

The mother with lung cancer took the experimental drug and her thick blonde hair fell out. She was too tired to read, too scared to talk, and her pain was hard to control. I still think about her face, other faces, the gradually dawning realization. I remember her pretty, ravaged face as she slowly realized she was probably going to die, and soon, and hard. In lonely silence in a strange room—a face bared, flinching in tiny tics of resistance, ducking this last punch, until it is irresistibly clear: I am not going to get better. I half-expect the earth to move in response, and perhaps it does.

"There are bad and difficult days, trying days," says Brendan Curti. "But you have to be optimistic to do this work. There is something spiritual and uplifting in it." There is in fact joy of a kind—this common struggle of people, undefended and bare. This is one of the flavors I taste in my tears.

So many of them have died. The Sweetheart of Sigma Chi died. The pizza-loving lawyer died, the marijuana-smoking artist died, the mentally ill woman died, the poor man with all the tattoos died, and of course the young soldier died. We all knew he would. But not the pianist. I ran into her sister in a public bathroom, where we stood outside the toilet stalls as she told me my former patient was doing fine. And not the Bible student, who went home after more than six weeks of harrowing struggle. Not the hiker, whose bones healed after the transplant, who can hike for miles now.

And Lee is well, though she still struggles with fatigue sometimes. She looks the way she did a few years ago—her hair is thick, her face dear and soft. She no longer looks like a cancer patient.

"I like the word *remission*," she says. "It means live every day as best you can. I have a 70 percent chance of long-term survival, which means a lot. But a 30 percent chance of relapse seems like a lot, too. I'm just now beginning to think about what's next. And how do you live without treatment? During treatment, at least you're doing something about your cancer. But I felt so good that Wednesday when I woke up and I didn't have to go to chemo.

"You walk in with cancer," she tells me. "He says, 'You're in remission.' And you walk out free."

I don't like to hear cancer patients described as brave. Their virtue is going on, without much choice. How can we speak of degrees of courage here? To be sick this way is to have a kind of existential wound. One's life is taken apart like a motor, screws and facings laid along the table until it is just parts and nothing is left whole. I know I'm not brave, not the way that word is meant— stiff upper lip and all. When it is my turn, if it is my turn—I shake to think of it. I am surprised sometimes to hear the small murmur in the back of my mind, coming without warning. I am helping a trembling man my own age onto a commode, smelling his stale breath, and I think, *I'm glad it's not me.* The thought shames me, but there it is. Being brave is simply a matter of going on, because what else is there to do but this difficult thing—wait for me to come down the hall in my blue gown and gloves, and hang up a bottle of poison.

Harper's, June 2007

Cancer treatment is always changing and there are many surprises— but one of the surprises is how much stays the same.

Twitchy

WHEN I GO TO THE DENTIST, I TAKE MY IPOD AND CRANK it up. The right music is important: big music, strong-flavored and complex, but not too sweet. Piano concertos don't work, and folk songs are all wrong. I listen to the Doors and Art of Noise and Talking Heads. Depending on how the visit goes, whatever music I choose will be tainted for months afterward—a bit dentisty, with the faint scent of nitrous.

I pull off the headphones when the assistant appears. Sharon is my favorite, a sassy, skinny blonde of a certain age who makes cracks under her breath. She shares the same bleak humor I bring to the chair. We chat a little, and then she puts the dark rubber nose mask on me, and the smell is the smell of emptiness, the smell of no smell at all. She wraps a bib around my chin and then gives me big black safety glasses, and finally I put the headphones back on. They prop my mouth open and stretch the rubber saliva dam across my tongue and hang the slurping suction tube on my lip, and then I have a hot flash and start panting like a dog. I know I look like a drunk on Halloween, but it's a passing concern. Fashion's not my worry here.

"We're turning the nitrous on now," she says. I sink back, eyes half-closed, and turn the volume up a little more on "Light My Fire." The empty smell is gone, replaced by a light breeze, and I take it in deeply.

This is one of those modern dental offices, the kind you find near suburban shopping malls. All the dentists are women, and the walls are pink and pale blue and light green, soothing pastel walls with big murals of tropical islands and country roads. There are skylights above the chairs and everyone wears colorful scrubs. The waiting room has a children's play area and lots of good magazines.

I watch a cloud cross the skylight.

Dr. Johnston appears at my side and speaks to me. I mumble, "We've got to stop meeting like this," and then her looming face drifts back and I'm humming to myself again.

She murmurs to Sharon, picks up a silver tool, prods a bit here and there.

I hear Sharon say, from a distance, "She's pretty twitchy today."

"Yeah—why don't you turn her up a little?"

I smile to myself. *Yes, turn me up a little*, I think. I watch a cloud cross the skylight. On nitrous, there is a vague numbness like a line drawn around the edges of my body. Sometimes I feel as though I am gently bobbing in the small eddy of a stream—moving, but going nowhere. I know what's happening, what happens next; I hear snippets of their chatting, something about weekend plans, and I resent it. I want them attending to *me* right now, but my resentment is distant, too, and fades away. I watch the sky, a cloud inflating in an interesting way, expanding into a yellow sheet and then darkening, and R.L. Burnside growls, "Baby done a baad, baaaad thing" and the yellow cloud is gone and all I see is blue.

watch   cloud cross   sky

I HAVE WEAK teeth, and of course I blame my mother, who gave birth to me in 1957 when everyone smoked and drank martinis during pregnancy. My mother's pleasures were few enough —coffee, cigarettes, romance novels, and a bowl of ice cream every evening—but she enjoyed them deeply. A few months before she died of breast cancer, she said out of nowhere, "You know, there are two things I'd do differently in my life if I could do it over." And I'm looking at my father sacked out on the couch, and thinking, only two?

"I wouldn't start smoking"—and that hangs in the air a moment—"and I wouldn't let you kids eat so much sugar."

I'm not sure why the last mattered much to her then. Considering. My brother and sister and I spent a lot of hours at the dentist, and more hours drinking Dr. Pepper and eating popsicles. We used to get sugar sandwiches as a treat—white sugar, margarine, and white bread—Wonder Bread, which builds strong bodies all kinds of ways. Perhaps the Flintstones Vitamins weren't the miracle cure the commercials led her to believe. The inadequate brushing from a childhood lived without much supervision took its toll. But I suspect this is something more buried and intractable—genetics or karma or destiny—something embedded in the whole of me. Either way, this is the result: countless fillings, several crowns, many teeth more false than not, and long afternoons in the chair beneath the skylight.

NITROUS OXIDE IS a mysterious drug, though in part it is antinociceptive; that means it blocks some of the sensory perception of pain, just like Advil. But the lidocaine takes care of that. In fact, I don't mind the shot, the part most people dread the most. I don't need the nitrous to prevent pain. I need it for the fear of pain, for the fear of the drill, for the smell, the grinding noise, the vibration, the gestalt of a world I find vaguely terrifying far out of proportion to my experience. I discovered nitrous many years ago, thanks to a dentist who knew I wouldn't get my teeth fixed otherwise. Unlike my other fears—plane crashes, apologizing—this one has not lessened in time. Everything changed with nitrous; I still hated to go, but I could go.

Why nitrous works this way, no one really knows. Nitrous reduces anxiety and makes people feel happy, and the medical literature invariably describes the effect as "pleasant." People report sensations of tingling, vibration, throbbing or droning sounds, warmth, a sense of being heavy or floating. Patients on nitrous are suggestible, accommodating, with "an indifference to surroundings." Indifference is, above all, what I lack in the chair.

278278278278

I am a connoisseur of dosing. Dentists typically use a 20-percent mixture; I need about 30 percent to get through a procedure, a dose that causes some people to lose consciousness. For me, it's just right. Over the course of an hour, I feel myself fading slightly in and out of the room, separate from the complicated maneuvers going on in my mouth. I am a little removed, but not gone; the tension remains. Now and then I am reminded to unclench my jaw, relax the hands, which have somehow become tightly wrapped around the arms of the chair. We have signals. Up, I raise my thumb. Thumbs up, for more gas.

People still call nitrous oxide the laughing gas. I don't get the giggles like some people do, but I make some very funny jokes—profound, meaningful jokes with a subtle poignancy and the hint of tragedy that brings classic humor to life. I never forget that I've taken a drug, but somehow the idea that my funny jokes, the funniest jokes I've ever made, are not really very funny and are entirely the product of chemistry, makes them funnier still. There is some vast and deeper humor here, a whistling past the graveyard that lightens the burden of my fear.

Dr. Johnston has been my dentist for a long time. We've gotten to know each other over the years and have a friendly relationship. One day, as I am fading in and out of the room, she suggests that we take care of a filling at the same time she works on the crown. "Get it over with," she says.

"Yeah," I smile. Long pause. "Why don't you do a pelvic while you're at it and cover all the bases?" I think this is very funny and start chuckling.

She just thinks *I'm* funny right now, and rolls with it. "I'm afraid I'd get arrested for that," she says.

"Oh, we should just get married, we love each other so much," I say, apropos of who knows what.

"That's illegal, too," she answers, and after a few more laughs, I go back to the clouds, and she goes back to work.

I'M SITTING IN the park on a sunny day, reading my book and eating a bagel. And crack. A *bagel*. A bit of my tooth falls into my hand. And here I go again; I know what's next. I know the whole story, each chapter, and the long arcs of tension and release to come.

I come in to have the impression made for another crown. Dr. Johnston is gone, and this is my first appointment with Dr. Bennett. Dr. Johnston is brisk and practical. Dr. B is padded and cheerful, and seems willing to wait as long as necessary for me to get comfortable. I'm nervous today—I'm always nervous, but she's a stranger to me, and so I tell Dr. B about Grandpa Doc.

Large sections of my childhood reel off in my head like a film noir starring Gloria Grahame—all sharp shadows and lurching camera moves. Grandpa Doc wasn't really my grandfather. My grandfather, the rumor goes, killed himself, but no one ever talked about it. To this day I'm not sure what really happened; there's no one left to ask. Doc was my grandmother's third husband—a tall, thin, bald dentist who loved to fish and hunt. I saw him in my parents' living room, holding a highball and laughing, and I saw him in his office. He didn't like children much, but as a favor he did our dental work for free on the weekends, when his office was closed.

Childhood trips to the dentist are one of the dream sequences in my dark B movie, full of quick cuts and freeze frames: cold, dim office; echoing voices; white walls; bright metal trays. I'm alone in a high, high chair. The images are vague but immediate, lingering the way dreams do. I am six years old, under fluorescent light, and looming over me is a tall, thin, bald man in a high-collared white coat. He is not smiling.

I asked my brother recently what he remembered of these visits, and he answered with the same bleak smile I bring to the chair today. "I had the pleasure of that office many times," he said. "My youthful oral hygiene was more like lowgiene."

"Were you scared of Grandpa Doc?" I asked. My brother is a little older than I; we were partners as children, friends to each other along the way. He is the only person I can ask about things like this.

"I don't remember being afraid of *him*," he said. "Just of the upcoming procedures. The needle, the awful taste of the novocaine that trickled out, the sound, and of course the swell stench of ground enamel."

When I think about Grandpa Doc, I don't remember the drill. I don't remember shots. I don't even remember pain. Everything is much more fragmented than that. The tile floor, a long way down—the big cold vinyl arms of the chair—the bald man bending way down, face close to mine—that's what I remember. What I remember is dread.

Dr. B says, "Did your mother really send you there *alone*?" She did—she was sitting out in the waiting room with my brother and sister, waiting their turns.

"He was my *grandpa*!" I say. "You're supposed to like your grandpa." I want to defend my mother, who did the best she could. "Besides," I add, "I don't think I ever told her I was scared."

There were a lot of things I never told my mother.

Those first visits to Grandpa Doc became visits to a nice young dentist in a sunny office up the street from our house, and in time led to my steadfast refusal to see a dentist at all. Do I have a post-traumatic stress disorder, as one helpful friend suggested? No, as long as I'm not actually at the dentist, there's no problem. Am I phobic? Phobias are usually a bit more occult, and this isn't as hard to explain as a fear of ants or peanut butter. I think this is as simple as it sounds: a lonesome and somewhat secretive child made to do something hard and never telling how hard it was and holding on until she was old enough to say, no more. Telling it to Dr. B in all the pink light, I feel a little silly. But when I get the stupid nose mask on and take a deep breath, all I feel is relief.

I GO FOR a new kind of porcelain crown, because this time the tooth I've broken is in the front. It costs about the same, and this new kind of crown is supposed to be easier; it requires only one appointment instead of two. Dr. Johnston doesn't do this procedure, so that means seeing another new dentist, Dr. Fischl, a slim young blond who looks about twenty-one years old. Like all of the dentists, at first she doesn't understand why I need nitrous for such a benign procedure.

"There's hardly any drilling at all!" she exclaims.

I reach for the mask.

I watch the light above me, the bright color in the sky. I know where I am, and what's happening. "I'm going to numb you now," she says, and I feel the weird push of the shot into my gum, the slowly spreading fog that blanks out cheek, lip, tongue, my lower eyelid. But she goes for the 20 percent, and except for a few brief moments, I never have enough nitrous. I strain for it, as though in chains. Then I find out that this easy new kind of crown involves a slow, vibrating drill that rattles the inside of my skull like a hammer and makes me shiver from scalp to toes, and that the one appointment is a very long one.

When everything is done but the last fitting on my new porcelain crown, I can finally relax a little bit, knowing we're almost finished. But Dr. Fischl doesn't know me. She turns off the nitrous and switches to oxygen, without telling me—before the crown is polished. After all, this is when they typically turn off the nitrous for everyone else. It hasn't been enough, but a lot more than nothing. I don't know what's going on; I only know that I'm coming back while the work goes on—polishing and grinding, tugging and pushing, the buzzing and the *smells,* and I've shrunk into a shell and the minutes stretch very slowly out and on and on as I twist and flinch inside like a cat stuffed into a small box.

When I'm finally able to make a sensible complaint, the assistant tells me, "But the work is just on the crown, not the tooth!"

"Look," I say. "Look. You can't turn it down. You can't, not until we're done, not for any kind of drilling or polishing or *anything.*"

"But it's not on your tooth, it's on the crown," she says again.

"*No,*" I answer. "No—no vibration, the sound, the smell, I don't know, I *can't.*"

She looks at me for a moment, and I guess she sees something in my face, because she just nods. "Okay," she says. "Okay. I'll make a note."

ONE DAY, ONE of the dentists told me not to exhale through my mouth. I had thought I should do just that, in order not to inhale my own carbon dioxide. (My sneaky hope being, of course, that I could get a bigger dose of nitrous that way; I thought I might be getting away with something.) "The nitrous off-gases when you breathe," she said. "Breathe through your nose, so we don't get any of the nitrous ourselves." Then she paused. "Not that it isn't fun."

I work part-time as an oncology nurse; part of my job is to cause pain, and a bigger part is to treat it, which means to witness it, ask about it, talk about it, listen to all the things people want to say about it. It means acknowledging the almost infinite number of ways we shame ourselves. A lot of people are ashamed of their pain, and most are a little ashamed that they want it to go away.

Somehow, and this is a story for another day, people come to believe that they should feel pain, that they deserve it or must accept it. I completely agree in principle: we harm ourselves in endless ways with avoidance and denial, by resisting the facts of the life before us. I think life is best lived head on, leaning forward into what comes: into loss, gain, change. Facing things squarely— this is the straightest way through, the way of least suffering, and most joy. But I don't extend this to physical pain that can be treated. There is enough waiting for us that can't be helped.

I have a friend who says he looks forward to going to the dentist because it's a challenge—he likes to find out if all his careful flossing has worked. Okay—there's a bit of the Boy Scout in that, but I question his motivation. I know two people who don't use lidocaine. One has an allergy. Another—well, she believes that life is suffering, and that we should feel it, that we shouldn't flinch, that resistance is futile. I agree, up to a point; but when the shot is there and a few billion people would be grateful for it, not resisting may be the irrational choice. And I think she has some twisted idea of what it means to be strong; she wants others to watch her feel it and be impressed by her power to handle the pain, which is at least a little insane, I think. But so am I, on the other side of things. Like most counselors, I need my own advice; in the dentist's chair, I am like a flinching boxer past his prime, dancing around the ring with the young contender. I try to face it squarely, but what I face is how to make it through the fear at all.

I want the dentists to reassure me, tell me that my cowardice is understandable, or at least not that uncommon. But I know I am way out on one end of this continuum. I know the pain can be treated, but the existential terror of pain known from the past becomes a new pain today. I am curious about almost everything in the world, but I am not curious about dentistry, about the battlefield of my mouth. Curiosity requires the willingness to engage, to know. I actually conquered a fear of flying; I talked myself out of it by learning and rational discussion and a few judicious doses of Xanax and Inderal. I can't do that in the dentist's chair; I can't begin to engage. This is the plain fact: I'm not as afraid of being afraid, or of being ashamed of being afraid, as I am afraid of the dentist.

A long time ago, I worked in an outpatient surgical clinic. We sometimes used nitrous on our patients. At the end of a long day, one of the doctors, another nurse, and I were sitting around the back room. We were all feeling the stress of too many patients, too many hours. The doctor reached out and grabbed the mask on the nitrous cylinder, spun the knob, and took a couple of whiffs. He smiled and handed it to me. Straight from his hand to mine, like a prescription; I took the mask and a few quick breaths and felt a little light-headed and then guilty. My drug reference lists "euphoria" as an "adverse effect" of narcotics because feeling good is not the intended purpose of narcotics. When I took that single whiff of nitrous oxide, I felt as if I were cheating in some big way—cheating because I didn't "need" it, because I wasn't sick, because it felt good. Because it was fun. I never cease to wonder at the vast injury we have done ourselves this way—that we fear feeling pleasure means not paying for our sins.

THERE HAS BEEN the one root canal. I dreaded root canals the way other people dread public speaking or cancer. I go for a consultation first. Just to talk. The endodontist has a large binder of helpful full-color drawings telling me exactly what he is going to do down in my tooth root with his gutta-percha and drill and strange tools. He looks at my X-rays and says, pointing, "I think you'll need a root canal on this other tooth, as well." He pauses. "We've got time, we can do it right now."

The tears start rolling down my face. The whole world has shrunk to the size of a root canal, or the root of my tooth is the size of the world, I can no longer tell. I look at him and see that he is embarrassed. A little annoyed with me, with my babyish tears.

Even now, I'm surprised at the lack of sympathy. I am periodically reminded by my patients that what is normal to me (the sounds, the smells) is a strange and frightening world to them. I'm not the typical dental patient, and I have to remind them of that. This is very far from normal to me. I don't like the looks of the tools; I quite hate the sounds coming from the next cubicle, and I'm not in what would be called the proper frame of mind for learning. I had asked the receptionist about sedation as soon as I arrived—real sedation, a drug called Versed that causes amnesia. It's used for painful procedures like colonoscopies and bronchoscopies, and I've seen time and again how easily patients get through difficult hours this way.

"It costs $500," she tells me; and so that's that. It's lidocaine and nitrous, or nothing.

When I finally arrive for the procedure, a few weeks later, I find out that one of the assistants is the woman who was my best friend for a while in high school, when we prowled the streets of our small town in a plague of dissatisfaction and restless urges. She makes cheerful small talk while I take the chair, the stress vibrating through me. She gets me started on the mask, chatting about my siblings and the weather and her apartment and her boyfriend and her car and who cares and I don't care and I watch the cloud passing across the window and after a while stop answering and after a while she leaves, and I think to myself that no one's feelings will be hurt because we can blame it on the nitrous. On nitrous, all is forgiven.

The root canal didn't hurt more than a filling or a crown. Pain—the physical pain is covered. The numbness required was deep and extensive, spreading through my eyeballs, far up into my nostrils and scalp, into the canals of my ears, and it lingered for many hours. The procedure was long, so long, on and on. And I am cursed with imagination, and wish I'd never seen the binder with its color pictures. It filled my dreams.

TIME TO HAVE another permanent crown cemented on, a gold one on a back tooth. This is a procedure many people do without lidocaine. In the days before an appointment, I might go through a rainbow of experience: stress and anger, an undirected vague resentment, self-pity, more impotent anger. As it approaches, anxiety begins to crowd out everything else, anxiety felt in the palms and stomach. The morning of the appointment, the secretary calls and warns me there is something wrong with the nitrous setup and it won't be available today. My tooth is hurting, I'm sick of it all, I want to be done. This one tooth has probably been worked on eight times or more in my life. I hang up and a small, bleak terror envelops me, and I'm crying, lying on my bed in the dark. *I can't I can't I can't I can't.* And I don't; I make another appointment.

When I get there a few days later, I try to explain to Dr. B. It has been so long since I've had dental work without nitrous. "I kind of fell apart," I say. "I really am a strong person," I say. "I'm not scared of many things. Really, I'm pretty good in most places. Really."

I imagine my pioneer ancestors facing the pliers with only a bottle of whiskey. I imagine the sidewalk dentists in India. None of that helps; gratitude is a crappy antidote for terror.

I look up and back at Dr. B, where she sits behind me, and say, "You're my mommy now." She smiles, but doesn't laugh. We're all five years old inside. I've told patients this a thousand times, and I tell myself the same: we are all children, we are all vulnerable, we are all helpless in each other's hands.

She hands me the mask. The pink walls turn orange, the light expands, a tingling, cottony sensation surrounds me. I turn up the music, and David Byrne is crooning to me: "Hold tight / We're in for nasty weather." Pinching. Pushing and pulling, clamping and scraping. Empty skylight. No cloud.

I realize that I am alone. There is no one near me. Perhaps they have forgotten me. Perhaps they went to lunch, or home for the weekend. I feel a rush of self-pity. *I'm just going to sit here, all alone*, I think. My pity slowly drifts across the skylight with everything else, finally, like everything else, fading away.

Antioch Review, Spring 2008

I'm still going to the same dentist's office. They know me there. I am sure there are special code words all over my chart. Everyone smiles patiently and takes their time and pats me on the shoulder.

The Sutra of Maggots
and Blowflies

THE GREAT ENTOMOLOGIST JEAN-HENRI FABRE COV-
ered his desk with the carcasses of birds and snakes, opened the
window, and waited.

He didn't have to wait long.

FROM THE TIME I was quite young, I loved cold-blooded creatures. I had to be taught not to pick things up in the woods: to me
it was all good, all worth examination, from beetles to mushrooms
to toads. I was stealthy, and in the thistle-ridden fields near my
house, I caught many blue-belly lizards to keep as pets. My father
built a cage for them, a wonderful wood-and-screen contraption
that smelled of pine and grass and reptile. I kept garter snakes
and frogs and chameleons too. Once, someone gave me a baby
alligator. I had several praying mantises, and built them elaborate
branch houses in the cage, and fed them crickets. I don't know
where this came from, my appetite for the alien; it feels like an old
question, long and mysterious.

My study of living things, part inquiry and part the urge to
possess, became inevitably a study of predation and decay. I had to
feed my pets, and most preferred live food. Mantises always died,
their seasons short. The chameleons died, too delicate for my care.
The alligator died. I tried to embalm it, with limited success—just
good enough for an excellent presentation at show-and-tell. When
one of my turtles died, my brother and I buried it in my mother's
rose bed to see if we could get an empty turtle shell, which would

be quite a good thing to have. When we dug it up a few weeks later, there was almost nothing left—an outcome I had not anticipated, and one that left me with a strange, disturbed feeling. The earth was more fierce than I had guessed.

In time I became specifically interested in human bodies, how they worked and how they got sick and what they looked like when they died. This did not pacify my mother, who worried aloud about my ghoulish preoccupations. I did enjoy the distress I could cause by something as simple as bringing an embalmed baby alligator to school in a jar. But I was also—and for a long time I could not have explained why it was of a piece with my impassioned studies—exquisitely sensitive to the world's harsh rules. I regretted each cricket. An animal dead by the side of the road could bring me to tears, and I cried for each dead lizard, each mantis. A triad, each leg bearing weight: sensitivity, love, and logic. The weight on each leg shifts over time. Now, a penetrating awareness of the cruelty seemingly built into the world's bones. Now, a colder logic, an awareness of the forces that balance systems at the cost of individuals. At times, in brief pure blinks of my mind's eye, a love painful in its intensity, an unalloyed love. I love the tender, pale blossoms opening now on the cherry tree in my yard, the sudden pound of lush raindrops from the empty sky: each thing I see is a luminous form in a sparkling world. Such love is a kind of grace; enshrined in it, all is right with the world. It is a little touch of madness, this kind of love—raw and driving.

Some years ago, I began to study the small things in the forest that I didn't understand, moving from the lovely and lethal amanita mushrooms to the stony, invincible lichens to the water skippers coasting lightly across the little creeks. I began to study insects especially and then flies in particular.

Flies are so present and innumerable that it is hard to see their presence clearly, hard to believe in their measure. There are around 120,000 species of flies, depending on who's counting, and they have many names: bee flies, cactus flies, papaya flies, warble flies, brine flies, nimble flies, biting midges, green midges, gall midges, mountain midges, dixid midges, solitary midges, net-winged midges, phantom midges—so called because the larvae are transparent and seem to disappear in water. Studying flies, my head begins to spin with suborders and divisions, tribes and clades, and the wild implications of the Latin names: Psychodidae and Sarcophagidae and *Calliphora vomitoria*.

The order Diptera is old, as are most insects; it was well established by the Jurassic Era, 210 million years ago.[1] (Unlike all other insects, flies do not have four wings. Diptera comes from the word *di* for two and *ptera* for wings.) Fly biology is a vast and changing field. New species and subspecies of flies are always being discovered. Familiar species are found in new locations; variants between species are analyzed in new or subtler ways, and so the taxonomic distinctions between flies are always being revised. But in the general term, flies are defined by their single set of wings, legless larvae, and mouthparts designed for biting, sucking, or lapping.

Inside these templates, there is stupefying variation. They are divided into families, genera, and species by the varied location of veins in the wings, their color, body size, type of mouthpart, the number of stages of larval development, the type and separation of eyes, antennal structure, the arrangement and number of bristles on the body, the length of the legs, and habitat—differences controversial and infinitesimally detailed.

We often know them as the most common and familiar things, as single things: individual flies rescued or swatted, struggling in webs, crawling dizzily across cold windowpanes on a milky October day. One finds flies in odd places, but so often they are

1 We are one kingdom with flies: Animali, and then we diverge. (You can remember the taxonomic series of kingdom, phylum, class, order, family, genera, species with an appropriate mnemonic: Keep Pots Clean; Our Food Gets Spoiled.) Flies are found in the phylum Arthropoda: exoskeletons, jointed legs, and segmented bodies, a group that includes crabs, centipedes, and spiders as well. The flies are in the subphylum Mandibulata, which means mandibles on the second segment past the mouth opening, and just imagine that. We are not in Kansas anymore. Class Insecta means a body is divided into head, abdomen, and thorax. The insects from here on out—beetles, fleas, ants, scorpions, walking sticks, and many other types—are entirely separate orders.

not a surprise even in surprising locations—in the laundry basket or buzzing inside the medicine cabinet, or caught unawares in the wash water. Almost every fly you catch in your house will be a housefly, one of the family Muscidae, chubby and vigilant flies that can birth a dozen generations every summer. (Houseflies are found in virtually every place on earth save for Antarctica and a few isolated islets.)

Sometimes we know them as plagues: I've been battered by biting flies in forests, near mangrove, and in sand, flies the size of pinheads in clouds so thick I couldn't walk twenty feet without getting a crop of angry red bites on every inch of exposed skin. These are the ones we call punkies or gnats or no-see-ums, the fly family known as Ceratopogonidae. There are more than four thousand species of them—tiny, almost invisible flies with stinging bites, inexplicable dots of pain.

The *Encyclopædia Britannica* says simply, "It is not possible to discuss all dipteran habitats." Flies live in the air and the soil and under water and inside the stems and leaves of plants. They live high in the mountains, in sand and snow, tide pools and lakes, sulfur springs and salt lagoons. The brine fly lives in the thermal springs of Yellowstone at temperatures up to 43 degrees Celsius. There are flies in the volcanic hot springs of Iceland and New Zealand living at even higher temperatures. Certain flies handle extreme cold easily too, blessed with a kind of antifreeze and other strange gifts. The wingless snow fly lives underground in burrows and wanders across the white fields during the day—wee black spots walking briskly along in the afternoon. The Himalayan glacier midge prefers temperatures around the freezing point but has been seen active at minus 16 degrees Celsius. (When placed in a hand, it becomes agitated and then faints from heat.) One carnivorous fly lays its eggs in pools of seeping petroleum, where the larvae live until maturity. One wingless fly lives inside spiders. Certain flies can live in vinegar. There are flies munching contently on spoiled vegetables. When we eat them by accident, they just ride the peristaltic wave on through, exiting in our feces and moving along.

The single pair of wings that is crucial to the identity of flies may be very small or startlingly large or vestigial, may lie open or closed, look scaly, milky, beribboned with black veins, smoky or transparent. Instead of a second set of wings, flies have small bony structures called halteres. They are mobile gyroscopes for flight, beating in time but out of sync with the wings, twisting with every change of direction to keep the fly from tumbling. Most are astonishing flyers, able to move in three dimensions at speeds hard to measure. Some can hover motionless and fly backward or forward or sideways like helicopters. (Flower flies, which look alarmingly like wasps but are harmless, will hover in front of your face, appearing to gaze directly into your eyes.) Midges beat their wings more than a thousand times per second; this is too fast for nerve impulses and instead involves a mysterious muscular trigger effect. A fruit fly can stay aloft for an entire afternoon, burning 10 percent of its body weight every hour. There are clumsy flies: the march fly travels laboriously only a few feet off the ground, and so is continuous fodder for car radiators; march flies are often seen banging into people and bushes, and even the walls of buildings. Soldier flies can fly, but don't very often; they sit for long periods of time on leaves or flowers. Other species prefer to walk or run, sometimes on the surface of water; the louse fly, often wingless, walks sideways, like a crab.

John Clare wrote of flies that "they look like things of mind or fairies." There are flies so small they can barely be seen by human eyes; others are as wide and long as a man's hand. Their bodies may be lime green or shiny blue, glowing black, metallic or dull yellow, pearly white, leathery, variegated in browns, matted with dust. A few are flecked with iridescent gold and silver. They are squat or slender or wasp-waisted. Their legs may be very long and fine or stubby, delicate as a web or stout and strong. Fly genitalia, one text notes, are "extremely polymorphous." Some flies have beards or even furry coats made of bristles; others seem hairless. The hover flies mimic bees and wasps, growing yellow-brown bristly hair like the fur of a bumblebee; they are sometimes striped like yellow jackets. The tangle-veined fly, which is parasitic on grasshoppers, has a loud, bee-like buzz. A fly's antennae may be akin to knobs or threads or whips or feathers or pencilline brushes. Insects do not breathe exactly; they perform gas exchange in a different way from mammals, through tubes called spiracles. Their larvae breathe in many ways, through gills and snorkels, or by taking up the oxygen stored in plant roots and stems. Spiracles show up just about anywhere: beside the head, in the belly, in a maggot's anus.

What great variety they have! When Augustine argued that the fly is also made by God, he spoke of "such towering magnitude in this tininess." The family Nycteribiidae, the bat ticks, are true flies but look like spiders without heads. They live only in the fur of bats, sucking bat blood, hanging on with claws. Exposed, the stunted bugs run rapidly across the bat's fur before disappearing underneath. But the family Tipulidae, the crane flies, fill your palm. They look like giant tapered mosquitoes, with very long, slender, spiderlike legs, three eyes, and big veiny wings that may span three inches. They do not bite. These are the ballerinas of the flies, delicate and graceful. Male crane flies form mating swarms that dance above treetops at sundown, or flow over pastures in a cloud, pushed by the breeze.

So one fly seeks light and heat; another avoids both. One is a vegetarian—another a terror. They flit like tiny shadows in the night skies, crawl across the windowpane and out of the drain and into the garbage and into our eyes. Sometimes flies migrate out to sea far from anything human, flitting across the white-capped waves of the ever-moving sea for miles, for days. The fly is grotesque and frail and lovely and vigorous, quivering, shivering, lapping, flitting, jerking, sucking, panting: theirs is an exotic genius, a design of brilliant simplicity and bewildering complexity at once.

I study flies; I am stunned by them. I love them, with a fleeting love—with the triad: love, logic, sensitivity. Did you notice how calmly I noted that there is a fly that lives inside spiders? Another that is parasitic on grasshoppers? This is a humming, buzzing world; we live in the midst of the ceaseless murmur of lives, a world of strange things whispering the poems of old Buddhas. The world's constant rustling is like the rubbing of velvet between distracted fingers; it can drive one mad. Beside the cherry tree, under that bright sky, lives the sheep bot fly. It enters a sheep's nostrils, where it gives birth to live young. The maggots crawl up the nasal passages into the sinuses, where they feed until they are grown— a process that lasts nearly a year. The sheep's nose runs with pus; it shakes its head at this odd itch, shakes and rubs its nose into the ground, grits its teeth, jumps about, growing ever weaker. The condition is sometimes called the blind staggers. One day the sheep gives a great sneeze, and out shoot mature sheep bot flies. They are ready to mate and make more babies.

It is right here with flies that I face a direct and potent challenge: What do I really believe? What do I believe about beauty and the ultimate goodness of this world?

Jean-Henri Fabre lays out his corpses by the open window. A few days later, he writes, "Let us overcome our repugnance and give a glance inside." Then he lifts the bodies, counting the flies that have come, the eggs they lay, the larvae that form "a surging mass of swarming sterns and pointed heads, which emerge, wriggle, and dive in again. It suggests a seething billow." He adds, as an aside, "It turns one's stomach." He examines and measures and counts, and then gently places a few hundred eggs in a test tube with a piece of meat squeezed dry. A few days later, he pours off the liquescent remnants of the once-hard flesh, which "flows in every direction like an icicle placed before the fire." He measures it, and keeps careful notes.

"It is horrible," he adds, "most horrible."

I have been a Buddhist for more than twenty-five years, since I was a young woman. My avid urge to understand bodies didn't stop at the bodies themselves; I sought for a way to think about the fact of life, the deepest query. Buddhism in its heart is an answer to our questions about suffering and loss, a response to the inexplicable; it is a way to live with life. Its explanations, its particular vocabulary and shorthand, its gentle pressures—they have been with me throughout my adult life; they are part of my language, my thought, my view. Buddhism saved my life and controlled it; it has been liberation and censure at once.

Buddhism is blunt about suffering, its causes and its cures. The Buddha taught that nothing is permanent. He taught this in a great many ways, but most of what he said comes down to this: things change. Change hurts; change cannot be avoided. "All compounded things are subject to dissolution"—this formula is basic Buddhist doctrine, it is pounded into us by the canon, by the masters, by our daily lives. It means all things are compounded and will dissolve, which means I am compounded and I will dissolve. This is not something I readily accept, and yet I am continually bombarded with the evidence. I longed to know this, this fact of life, this answer—that we are put together from other things and will be taken apart and those other things and those things we become will in turn be taken apart and built anew—that there is nothing known that escapes this fate. When one of his disciples struggled with lust or felt pride in his youth or strength, the Buddha recommended that the follower go to the charnel ground and meditate on a corpse—on its blossoming into something new.

We feel pain because things change. We feel joy for the same reason. But suffering is not simply pain: it is our peculiar punishment that we know things change and we want this to be otherwise. We want to hang on to what is going away, keep our conditions as they are, people as they are, ourselves as we are. In Buddhist terms this is variously called thirst or desire or attachment or clinging. It means that we hold on to the hope that something will remain, even as it all slides away like sand in running water, like water from our hands. Knowing the answer does not stop the question from being asked.

Desire is not always about holding something close; it has a shadow, the urge to push things away. Buddhists usually call this aversion—the desire for the extinction of something, for separation from it. The original Pali word for aversion, *dosa*, is various and shaded, translated sometimes as anger or hatred, sometimes as denial, as projection, aggression, repulsion, and now and then as disgust or revulsion or distortion. Aversion has as much force and fascination as the positive desires we know. It may be simply a reflexive flinch, a ducking for cover; it may be much stronger. Like desire, aversion is a many-colored thing, flavored by circumstances. It is a kind of clinging—clinging to the hope of *something other than this*.

When I began to study flies, I couldn't seem to stop. Fabre wrote, "To know their habits long haunted my mind." I think of the violence with which we describe such prurient obsessions—we say we cannot tear our eyes away. My eyes are glued to flies and it is as though they are stitched open against my will. I feel revulsion, I flinch, I turn away, I duck for cover. I get squeamish, which is a rare feeling for me. But I also feel curiosity and admiration and a kind of awe. The buzz of a fly's blurred wings is one of the myriad ways the world speaks to us; it is one of the ways speech is freed from our ideas. I feel that if I could listen, if I could just listen without reacting, without judgment or preference or opinion—without reaching for a dream of how things might be otherwise—there is something I would understand that I have yet to know.

Compassion in all its flavors is woven through the enormous canon of Buddhist thought. Its root meaning is *to suffer with*. We are able to feel compassion toward those beings who look like us and those who are most familiar. (These are not the same thing; dissimilar creatures can be deeply familiar, as we know from our time spent with dogs, with horses—even with lizards.) At what point do we extend this circle past what is known, past what looks like us? At what point do we suffer with what is completely strange? And how far must that circle extend before it includes the sheep bot fly?

This mix of push and pull I feel when I look at insects is akin to the way the tongue longs for an acquired taste. The first time one tastes certain complex flavors they are unpleasant, even offensive. But in time it is that very flavor, its complexity—the bitterness or acidity mingling with other layers—that brings you back. Whether it is wine or chili powder or *natto*—a Japanese delicacy of soybeans bound into a sticky, cobwebbed mold—one returns in part because of the difficulty. We are sharply, pleasantly excited by the nearness of rejection, by skirting along the edge of things, the dank and sour things that instinct reads as dangerous. These shadings of flavor ever so briefly evoke poison and rot—the urine scent of beer, the lingering oily bitterness of coffee, the rank tang of certain cheeses (and I will return to cheese; it factors here). There is a brief shrinking away, perhaps very brief, minuscule, but there nonetheless.

This is a little bit of what I feel toward flies. Let us give a glance inside—a glance, a gasp, a shiver, the briefest reactivity: and then another look, a bit sideways though it may be, and then another. Then there follows the need to look: interest turning into inquiry into passion; the desire to know, to see, and something more, something crucial—the need to bear it, to be able to bear it, to be able to look as closely and thoroughly as I can.

FLIES HAVE LONG been considered the shells and familiars of gods, witches, and demons. They are associated with reincarnation, immortality, and sorcery. They are so unutterably strange, all swarming and speed and single-mindedness, and they cannot be avoided. I really mean that; we eat flies every day.[2] The FDA per-

---

2   Consider the cheese skipper, a kind of black fly found all over the world. They are so called in part because they skip, or leap, when disturbed; they curl up, grabbing the tail with the hooked mouth, tense, and then let go—springing like a coil, fast and hard. Cheese skippers are attracted to meat, cheese, and corpses, which develop a cheesy smell at a certain stage when butyric acid is present. Their family name, *Piophilia*, means milk-loving. The larvae can be eaten accidentally, and may survive ingestion and burrow into the gut. One imagines the little thing shrugging its nonexistent shoulders and changing course. When the larvae infest a hard cheese like pecorino, they decompose the fats until the cheese turns creamy and pink, at which point the Italians call it casu marzu, "rotten cheese." Gourmets like it, and will blend casu marzu into a paste to spread on bread. Most people try to remove the maggots first. Selling this cheese is illegal in Italy because even shredded maggot parts are dangerous—all those hooks. But not everyone does this. Some consider the maggots part of the delicacy—an aphrodisiac, or a peculiarly nutritious food.

mits thirty-five fruit fly eggs in every eight ounces of golden raisins, up to twenty maggots "of any size" in a hundred grams of canned mushrooms, and a fair number of both eggs and maggots in tomato products. Last night's mushroom pizza? A womb of flies. Flies sense the world in every way, its faintest textures: minuscule currents of shifting air, the vibration of a bird's approaching wings, the scent of decaying flowers or a mouse's corpse a half mile away. Some flies have a complex and unique ear, a flexible tympanal membrane in a structure behind the neck. A few parasitic flies listen for the distinct sound of their selected prey; one imagines a head carefully cocked.

They taste and smell in ways far more subtle than ours. There is no profound difference between the two senses anyway; both are a way of identifying chemicals, defining them, discriminating. They sense the sex pheromones released so hopefully by their prey, and follow; they smell the prey's feces, its breath, or the small damage done by other hunting insects. Biting flies are sensitive to stress chemicals, including the higher levels of carbon dioxide emitted when mammals exert themselves. The black flies respond directly to the scent of human sweat. Many flies have taste and smell receptors on their complex mouthparts, their antennae, their delicate legs, and their fine-clawed feet. Walking, they sample the coming meal; instantly, the proboscis unwinds. Flies are sensitive to minute differences in the world's chemistry, and its surprising similarities: One of the parasitic *Lucilia* flies is attracted, according to one text, to "wild parsnips and fresh meat." One molecule attracts the male to the female; another causes the male's ritual courtship flight; a third causes the female to relax and hold still. Their world is a superdimensional pheromonal architecture, a mingled and vaporous mist multiplied by sight and sound and space.

Consider the compound eye, common to all insects, variously evolved in flies. A fly's eyes may be huge: the eyes of horse flies are bulging black caps filling the face. Other flies may have tiny eyes, and some flies have no eyes at all. (The pyrgotid flies have strangely shaped heads that protrude in *front* of their eyes, an evolutionary development hard to comprehend.) The eye may be flat or bulging, round or triangular in shape, shining like jewels. A deer fly's eyes are brightly colored, green or gold with patterns and zig-zags. Tachinid flies have reddish eyes; dance flies have orange ones. Each facet of a compound eye is held at a unique angle, independent of all the others. They are capable of differentiating between the wavelengths of light and can distinguish the angle at which sunlight falls, allowing them to navigate off the surface of water. A fly has a thousand eyes, four thousand eyes, side by side without gap. The fly cannot focus on a single form, but sees each form from many angles at once. Each single thing is multiplied, the object broken like a mirror into shocks of light, and remade like water into a single lake, a prism, a drop of dew.

Flies eat blood and meat and feces and other insects and each other, but also pollen, nectar, algae, decaying seaweed, and fungi. Bulb fly maggots are tiny dilettantes, seeking only the inner tissue of hyacinth, tulip, narcissus, and lily bulbs. Fruit fly maggots are picky: one species eats walnut husks, another eats cherries. Pomace flies live on rotting fruit, but they don't eat the fruit; they eat the yeast that grows on rotting fruit. (This is a brief world indeed; a new generation is born every ten days or so.)

Flies bite, suck, slice, lap. Bee lice live in the mouths of bees, eating nectar. Stiletto fly larvae sometimes live in wool blankets and decaying wood. Among the black flies, which plague cattle, each species specializes in a cow part—one sucks blood from cows' bellies, one from cows' ears, and so on. The flat-footed flies, which run in a zigzag pattern across plants, include a variety called smoke flies; they are attracted to fires and eat the burned wood afterward. Eye gnats are drawn to tears, sweat flies to sweat, face flies to eyes and noses.

Flies hurt us, but only in passing; sleeping sickness, malaria, yellow fever, river blindness: mere accidents. The sheep bot fly can live in many places, including human eyes if eyes are more convenient than the sheep—but it prefers the sheep. We are simply more food, more warm and meaty beings among endless beings. But what food!—palaces of muscle and blood, rich and fertile fields.

I read otherwise sober and mechanical descriptions of flies and trip over the anthropomorphic complaint. Both Pliny and Plutarch complained that flies were impossible to train and domesticate. Among modern thinkers, one fly is "good" and the other is "bad," one is a "pest" and another a "bane" and another a "benefit." The tachinid flies are parasitic on destructive caterpillars, and snipe flies eat aphids, so they are described with kind words. Their predation does us good, but all predation does something good and not just the predator. Predation makes way. It makes room.

Even entomologists hate flies, on principle. Edwin Way Teale, who wrote of the natural world his entire life with reverence and cheer, hated the housefly. He obsessed over the number and variety of bacteria, fungi, viruses, and parasites they carried from place to place, and finally seems to have simply flung his hands into the air and given up, declaring the housefly "an insect villain with hardly a drop of redeeming virtue." Leland Howard, a USDA entomologist, wrote an encyclopedic account of insects in 1904 that is still quoted today. He called the harmless saltwater flies "sordid little flies," and the wingless bird tick "apparently too lazy to fly." Of the bluebottle, which sometimes has parasitic mites, he wrote, "It is comforting to think that the house-fly has these parasites which torment him so. Such retribution is just."

Humans are a nightmare; we tear the earth apart. We trepan mountains and pour them into rivers, take the soil apart down to its atoms, sully the sea, shred our world like giants rutting after truffles. We poison our nest and each other and ourselves. We eat everything, simply everything, but we turn away from flies.

The circles of compassion can suddenly expand. Federico Garcia Lorca wrote that he rescued flies caught at a window; they reminded him of "people / in chains." And of course I've done the same. I often do—catch flies and crickets and spiders and let them go, careful of their frailty. This brief moment of the widening circle; it is easily challenged by the maggot, by the swarm. The larvae of the fungus gnat sometimes travel in great masses, for reasons no one can guess—huge groups called worm snakes piled several deep, squirming along about an inch a minute. I know why Beelzebub is Lord of the Flies; is there any other god who would slouch so towards Bethlehem?

I long sometimes for a compound eye. It is a tenet of my religious practice, an ever-present thorn, to remember that my point of view, that any point of view, is merely a point. My eyes cannot see a landscape, let alone a world. But how we judge things has everything to do with where we stand. Can I learn to see a form from many angles at once? Can I see other beings, this moment, my mistakes, my words, like this? Can I know multiplicity as a single thing?

So many flies: Mydas flies, sewage flies, robust bot flies, gout flies, scavenger flies, snipe flies. Big-headed flies, thick-headed flies, picture-winged flies, stilt-legged flies, spear-winged flies, banana-stalk flies, flower-loving flies, stalk-eyed flies, flat-footed flies, pointed-winged flies, hump-backed flies.

THE LITERATURE OF Zen Buddhism is thick with nature—nature images, metaphors, puzzles, and questions, but mostly the calm and serene inhuman world of clouds, seeds, spring shoots, meadow grasses, and ponds, the moon and the mountain and the wave and the plum blossom. (Kobayashi Issa, an eighteenth-century Buddhist haiku master, wrote: "Where there are humans / there are flies / and Buddhas." But he is talking, I think, rather more about humans than flies.) Such images are used as metaphors for all kinds of Buddhist concepts, but they are partly an effort to convey how Zen Buddhism describes reality itself, the world. Hongzhi, a great Zen master of China, described it as "sky and water merging in autumn"—a vast, shifting, unbounded world.

Central to Zen Buddhism is a belief in *bussho*, usually translated from the Japanese as Buddha Nature. (In English we like to capitalize words like *buddha* and *nature*, to distinguish subtly different ideas with the same sound. Today, glancing inside the seething billow of life, it seems to me an impotent fist shaking at the greatness of what we try to say with the words. But I will follow the rule.)

Bussho is shorthand for something that requires quite a few words to explain—or it is already one too many words for what can't be explained in words. Buddhism is founded on the idea that all things are impermanent, that nothing has a fixed self-nature that passes through time unchanged. Change is not an aspect of the matrix but the matrix itself. It is because no one thing is permanent that we are not separated from anything—not bounded, not contained. All beings are constantly appearing, constantly springing into existence, hurtling out of themselves, of what they were, what preceded. Buddha Nature is—what? Original nature. Perfect nature—the substrate or source of all things. But it is not God, it is not ether, it is not simply a womb that gives birth. It is all things; it is that which manifests as things—as the world—as people, rocks, stars, dewdrops, flies—all beings, all forms, all existent things. All existence.

What do I know about Buddha Nature, anyway? I can't even tell you what it is—and Buddha Nature isn't an *it* and it isn't really an *is* either; not a quality attached to anything or a state of being or a space in which things exist; Buddha Nature as I understand it—there's that *it* again—is this, this, this, here, this minuscule and gargantuan and muscular relational and organic now, the luminosity of the sparkling world, the vast inevitability of loss, and not that exactly either. I use that phrase, Buddha Nature, even as it fills my mouth with ash, to mean all those things and more—relation, aspects, moments, qualities, acts, aeons, and bodies—and I use it in a positive way, with pleasure, with outright joy, to mean that all of us—those of us who think we are something unique and those who never think about it, and all those creatures who don't do what I might call thinking but are yet alive, and all those things we bang up against and assume aren't alive at all—are in some way kin, in some way both source and effect, eternally and continually and without hesitation, spontaneously and instantaneously and infinitely giving birth to ourselves, spilling out of nothing into nothing, with great vigor—leaping, sliding, appearing, disappearing into and out of a lack of solidity, into and out of the nonexistence of permanent nature, and that because this is the law—the muscle, the hinge—of reality—it's good. It's all right. Everything is all right.

Everything is all right. The female horsefly favors large warm-blooded animals. They see quite well and will fly around their prey just out of reach, finally biting one's back or leg. (As is true with many other biting flies, including mosquitoes, only the females bite. The males live on plant pollen and juices. It so happens as well that the males live brief lives while the females live the whole long, hot summer. The story is told that the Declaration of Independence was signed on July 4 because the horseflies in Philadelphia were intolerable that year, and the delegates called for an early vote so they could get out of town.) The *Phlebotomus* insects, as they are called, have anticoagulant in their saliva; after a bite, the blood continues to run, sometimes dangerously so. (To be precise, the horsefly slices rather than bites; its mouthparts are like tiny knives.) In their turn, horseflies are eaten by robber flies, who capture them on the wing and then find a convenient twig to rest on while sucking them dry. Robber flies are sometimes called bee killers; they prize honeybees and will watch them from the shadows while the bees gather pollen, then suddenly dart out and seize one from behind so it can't sting. They drain the bee dry and drop its empty shell; below a familiar perch, the bodies slowly pile up.

The cluster fly lays its children inside an earthworm. If you crush a cluster fly, it smells like honey.

The female thick-headed fly hangs around flowers, drinking nectar, like a bully at a bar. She waits for a bee or wasp, and when one comes close, she grabs it. The bee seems not to care, does not resist, while she deposits an egg before letting go. The bee flies away, the larva hatches, and burrows within. The larva eats the bee slowly until it dies, then falls to the ground within the bee's body and burrows underground to pupate. Flies are holometabolous, meaning the young undergoes a complete metamorphosis into the adult form, into a completely different form. The pupa is the quiescent phase between, and may last days or weeks or even longer. The pupae of flies are not protected by cocoons like those of butterflies; they simply harden, or build a shell from soil or spit. Some flies make a puparium from their own skin. Eat the bee, crawl underground, sleep the winter through, and emerge as a fly, seeking bees. That is the cycle, the great web of its life, round and round.

Pyrgotid flies do the same thing to May beetles, except that instead of burrowing into the ground, they live in the empty beetle shell over the winter. Flesh flies live under the skin of a turtle or in the stomach of a frog. The sheep bot fly—I have described this creature already. But there is also a bot fly that infests rabbits, and a bot fly that lives in horses' throats, a bot fly that favors horses' noses, and another bot fly that prefers horses' tongues. There are bot flies specific to kangaroos, camels, warthogs, zebras, and elephants. The human bot fly, transmitted by mosquitoes, is cosmopolitan in its tastes; besides people, it infects dogs, cats, rabbits, horses, cattle, and sheep.

One of the drawbacks of a long Buddhist practice is that one sometimes has the urge to present one's self as more composed than one actually is. (Let's be clear here; I mean me.) Emotional equanimity is a Buddhist virtue, a reflection of one's ability to accept reality and a sign that one is not contributing to the heat of suffering in the world by resisting that reality. That this equanimity is a real thing to me, a true tranquility found through steady practice, is beside the point. My tranquility may be real but it is not immune to conditions; it is no more permanent or unchanging than my skin. At times there is a loud voice inside me, complaining indignantly: *Explain this!*

Someone please explain this.

In my dreams, I could not make *Apocephalus pergandei*. It is named after Theodore Pergande, a renowned entomologist of the latter nineteenth century who was particularly interested in aphids and ants. He was observing carpenter ants one day when he saw the heads of the ants begin to fall off one at a time. When he investigated, he found what has become known colloquially as the ant-decapitating fly. The mature fly lays eggs on an ant's neck. The larvae hatch, and then bore into the ant's head, eating it from the inside. Eating, the larva grows, slowly killing the ant, which apparently expires just as its head pops off. But as many of us wish we could do, it does not leave its childhood home behind. Instead, the little vermin remains inside for a while, and if you look closely that is what you will see: ants' heads, walking around, filled with the children of flies.

A Buddhist practice requires rigorous self-disclosure— mostly to one's own self—and a kind of undefended willingness to be present in one's own crappy life as it is. This means noticing how often we tell lies about ourselves. I lie about many things, to myself and others. I lie about the way that triad on which I balance tilts: sensitivity, logic, love. It limps at times, or I find myself one-legged, just plain falling down. I am not always at home in this world, not always relaxed, not always in love with this great big Buddha-Nature-ridden place.

The *Tachinidae* is one of the largest, most selective, and successful fly families. "Ingenious," says one entomologist, for how they have solved the problems of their peculiar niche— "respiration in particular," since it is tricky to breathe inside things. Tachinid larvae are pure parasites, infesting virtually every kind of insect. One type lays its eggs on the leaves preferred by a certain caterpillar; the caterpillar eats the eggs, and the larvae hatch inside—born, as it were, at the buffet table. Another chooses crickets and katydids. The female fly can hear the precise frequency of the cricket chirp. (She can also hear, though the calls are many times higher, the ultrasound calls of the insectivorous bats she wants to avoid.) She follows the chirp carefully through a mechanism. When she locates the host, she lays her live babies beside or on them. They burrow in and eat selectively to keep the host alive as long as possible.

Caught in a certain light, tachinid flies glow, their wings like violet veils, ovaline eyes the burnt orange of sunset. I sit in the dark summer night, pleasantly melancholy, listening to crickets and contemplating *bussho* in a pulsing world.

I can pretend to have this settled. I can pretend to not mind. Certain midges are parasitic on themselves: the larvae hatch inside the mother and eat her from the inside out. I am appalled, even as I recognize the marvelous efficiency. Then I turn away from my own appalled thoughts. I am practicing acceptance. I bow. I tell myself it is a kind of compassion. It is sacrifice. (As though I understand *that* in some way.)

The horsefly bites a horse, and the blood runs, and before the wound even closes the face fly creeps in and settles down to stay. The bot fly captures a bloodsucker, such as a mosquito, and lays eggs on its body—just enough that the mosquito can still move freely. Then the mosquito finds a host and lands. The heat of the host causes the bot fly larvae to hatch; they slide off to the host's skin, down a follicle of hair, and in, another accidental gift. The larvae live just under the skin. They form a breathing hole with their hooks, keeping it open by digging constantly. This is called myiasis, flies developing in living flesh. (Many fly families indulge; the human bot fly is just one.) The maggots live under the skin until they are about an inch long. One observer of the condition wrote that myiasis causes "intense discomfort or pain," which is not a surprise. But the maggots are never still; he adds that people also complain of "the disquieting feeling of never being alone."

A person with myiasis must be patient; it is damaging to try to remove tiny larvae. One treatment is suffocation: coating the openings with paraffin or nail polish or turpentine, or lathering on chloroform dissolved in vegetable oil. One of the most effective methods for removing them is to lay slices of raw bacon across the wound; the larvae come running. Squirming, rather, in their roiling, systaltic wave.

Oh, well—parasitism is routine in the insect world. Can we call it cruel, this life governed by instinct? Consider this: two flies glued down by their wings to a table, for convenience. A drop of paraffin is carefully poured on their backs and then scooped out into a crater. Each fly's thorax is opened into the crater with a tiny scalpel, exposing the muscle. Saline is dropped into the craters for moisture. The flies are then rotated and joined, back to back, the paraffin gently sealed with a hot needle to form a double fly. This new kind of fly can walk, sort of, each taking a turn riding the other piggyback—or it can be neatly glued to a stick. For convenience. Now the scientist has a wonderful thing, a little monster with which to study many things: metabolism, hunger, dehydration, decay.

Explain that.

The larva grows, then settles into pupation. After time, after a mountain of time, the maggot disappears, the cask opens, and a fly emerges. It is fully mature; it will grow no more. The larvae of black flies are aquatic; the matured fly secretes a bubble of air and rises in it like an astronaut to its new life in the air, bursting out of the bubble at the surface. One observer said that a sudden hatching of black flies leaves the water "in great numbers with such force and velocity" that it seemed as though they were being "shot out of a gun." In contrast, the net-winged midge makes a submarine, a stiff case that floats to the surface, where it bursts open; the adults rise from their boats as delicate as mist. At first it is a wrinkled and empty fly bag, without color or strength. The new being takes a great gulp of air and expands, incalculably vast and whole, the actualization of fly.

So many flies: tabanid flies, green bottle flies, bronze dump flies, stilt-legged flies, bush flies, stable flies, louse flies, fruit flies, dung flies, rust flies, elk flies, seaweed flies, rust flies, scavenger flies, gadflies, skipper flies, soldier flies, Hessian flies, Richard flies, light flies, stone flies, sand flies, grass flies, eye gnats, wood gnats. A myriad mosquitoes.

There is something so simple and clear about the speech of flies; if I knew fly words, what would be clarified in my own? I study how flies use the world—how they make something of it that wasn't there before. They liquefy the dead, they slurp up the world, inhaling the bodies of others. They shoot out of lakes and the ground and out of bodies, joyous, filled with air. If I believe—and today, I think I do—that every being is Buddha Nature, that there is no place Buddhas cannot or will not go, then I must give a glance inside.

I don't know what a Buddha is.

ONE FLY, ITS passing hum, this we know—but they mob up, don't they, into masses of flies, into rivers and mountains of life, crawling and skipping and vibrating without rest, working at disintegration and change. Phantom midges form such enormous swarms they have been mistaken for smoke plumes, humming with such force that, in the words of one observer, they sound "like a distant waterfall."

Many fly swarms are birth explosions, others are orgies. Male dance flies join in huge mating swarms, graceful ellipses that flow up and down across meadows and gardens. They make frothy structures called nuptial balloons to carry on their abdomens for attracting females. Some species put seeds or algae in their balloons; others go straight for dead bugs—the bigger, the better, as far as the female is concerned. (Female dance flies routinely eat during sex—maybe from the nuptial balloon they have accepted as part of the bargain, but often, they eat another fly.) One type of dance fly uses only saliva and air, creating a lather of emptiness; as they dance, the empty bubbles glitter like lights.

Long-legged flies do their mating dance in slow motion, their rhythms complex and mysterious; they wave black and white leg scales back and forth in front of the female like a vaudeville stripper waves her fans. Pomace flies have tufts of dark hair on their legs called sex combs, with which they hold the female still during mating. The male penetrates from behind, the female spasmodically jerking in response. Already mated females are unreceptive; they curl their abdomens under, fly away, or kick at males.

The impregnated female seeks a nest. A few flies give live birth, and a few incubate their young. The tsetse fly, keds, and bat flies all hatch within their mother and are fed with something akin to a milk gland until they are ready to pupate, at which point they are finally expelled. But most flies lay eggs—a single egg, or hundreds, or thousands. She has a telescoping ovipositor, fine and small, which emerges from her abdomen and gropes its way inside—into the soft spaces, in the dark. Flies lay their eggs in the roots and stems of plants, in fruit, in the algae of a still pond, in shit, in hair and hide, in the bodies of other insects, in the stomachs of cows, in the dirty hunks of wool around the anus of sheep, in the pus of an infected wound. (The preference of many carnivorous species is the corpse.) Blowflies deposit eggs in the eyes, ears, nostrils, mouth, vagina, and anus. Female flies are choosy; many have taste buds on the ovipositor to help them pick the best location—each fly to its own place. Insistent and shy, the ovipositor worms its way down: into garbage and wounds, into the rotten flecks of meat on the floor of a slaughterhouse, into stagnant water, between the membranous layers of a corpse, between fibers of living muscle, on the umbilical cord of newborn fawns—into "any convenient cavity," says the *Britannica*—and deposits tiny eggs shimmery and damp, masses of them. She is careful not to crowd them, filling first one newly made womb, and then another and another. A day later, she dies.

Horrible. Most horrible.

Larvae are the unfinished fly; they are like letters not yet making a word. Maggots are the simplest of larvae; they are the ur-fly, the refined essence of the fly, the marvelously simplified fly—its template, a profoundly primitive thing. Many kinds of maggot have no head, consisting only of a body and a mouth filled with hooks. They move by wavelets of muscular contraction and relaxation, grasping with the mouth hooks and other hooks along their sides. They can roll and spring and slide.

After they hatch, they eat and grow. This process may be slow or fast. The chironomid midge larva in West Africa grows in spurts, drying out and reviving through extreme temperature variations and waves of drought and rain. When it is almost completely desiccated, it enters into a condition called cryptobiosis—still alive but with no signs of metabolism. Sprinkled with water, it wakes up, takes a meal, and starts growing again until the next dry spell. Blue bottleflies require an almost totally humid atmosphere—

something a corpse can easily provide in most cases—and in good conditions hatch almost as soon as they are laid. They begin to eat, and never stop. I am being literal: they never stop. (Trashmen call maggots "disco rice" for the way they wiggle through the waste.) If undisturbed, a maggot will eat without ceasing until it is grown. There is a distinct advantage to maggots having anal spiracles; there is no need to stop eating in order to breathe.

Aristotle, like many others for most of history, believed that some flies "are not derived from living parentage, but are generated spontaneously … in decaying mud or dung; others in timber." They simply appear all at once from manure and corpses, with no sign of having been born. How else to explain this locomotion, this primordial fecundity?

Maggots can reduce the weight of a human body by 50 percent in a few weeks. In the decomposing of a body, there are several waves of insects, each colonizing in its turn in a strict sequence. The first wave is blowflies and houseflies of a certain species; they begin to arrive within minutes of death. Their bodies are beautiful, glass-like in shimmering greens and blues, their eyes a deep, warm red. They glisten, tremble, and the larvae hatch and eat. They are ingenious little maggots—so much that the body seems to move of its own accord from their motion. The sound of all this movement, all this life, writes one entomologist, is "reminiscent of gently frying fat."

In time, other species of blowflies and houseflies arrive. The corpse begins to blacken, soften. (Corpses at this stage are called "wet carrion" by biologists.) The meat on which the maggots feed begins to liquefy and runs like melting butter. This is the fluid Fabre contemplated in quiet shock. "We here witness the transfusion of one animal into another," he wrote. If the maggots fail to move in time, they drown in the broth of the corpse they are eating.

By the time these larvae have fallen off into the soil to pupate, a third wave of flies arrives—fruit flies and drone flies and others, flies that prefer the liquids. Toward the end, the cheese skipper appears, drawn to the smell, and carefully cleans the bones of the remnants of tendons and connective tissue.

I contemplate my ordinary, imperfect, beloved body. I contemplate the bodies of my beloveds: individual, singular, unique, irreplaceable people, their skin and eyes and mouths and hands. I consider their skin riddled and bristling with that seething billow, I consider the digestion of their eyes and the liquefaction of those hands, my hands, my eyes—the evolution of the person into the thing, into wet carrion and eventually into a puddle, into soil, into earth, and flies. And it will come, whether I turn away or not.

We are nothing more than a collection of parts, and each part a collection of smaller parts, and smaller, the things we love and all we cherish conglomerates of tiny blocks. The blocks are built up; they will be taken apart the same way; we are nothing more. (And yet we are something more; this is one of the mysteries, I know. I cannot point to it, hold it, name it, except in the limited and awkward ways I have already tried. But there is something more, and it is the totality of this *nothing more*.)

Flies are wholehearted things, leading wholehearted lives. They understand dissolution, and by understanding I mean they live it. The parts are separated, they become something new. Pouring one's life into compoundedness without resistance, living by means of compoundedness and its subsequent falling apart—this is the wisdom of the creatures of the earth, the ones beside us, the ones who don't fight it. Because the human heart is devoted to compounded things and tries to hold them still, our hearts break. (One more thing to dissolve.) How can we know their lives? How can we understand the spongy proboscis, softly padded, with its small rasping teeth?

What better vision of the fullness of birth and the fullness of death than the maggot and the fly? A legless, headless, gill-breathing vermiform, giving way to the complete stillness of the pupa, and emerging as a land-based flyer—each stage utterly unlike the others, with nothing remaining of what was before. In their turn, maggots and flies help us along in our own fullness of birth and death, until what we were is completely changed. Decomposed, recomposed, compounded, dissolved, disappearing, reappearing—a piece from here and a fleck from there, a taste of this karma, a speck of that memory, this carbon atom, that bit of water, a little protein, a pinch of pain: until a new body and a new life are made from pieces of the past. The wee bit they claim, can you begrudge it? Dissolved, our flesh is their water, and they lap us up.

"Placed in her crucibles, animals and men, beggars and kings are one and all alike," wrote Fabre. "There you have true equality, the only equality in this world of ours: equality in the presence of the maggot." What lucky flies smelled the flowery scent of the Buddha's death, and came—flowing through the air like a river in the sky, a river of flies! What lucky maggots were born in his body, in the moist heat of the afternoon while the disciples still mourned! The maggots and blowflies are the words of the old Buddhas, singing of the vast texture of things, a lullaby of birth and death. They came and turned him into juice and soil, the Buddha flowing gloriously like cream into the ground.

AFTER A NIGHT of more routinely menacing scenes—an insecurely locked door, a strange man in a wig—I woke in the early morning from a brief, vivid dream. There had been a series of burning rooms, and finally a room completely engulfed in flames. I saw several people walking calmly through the room, untouched, smiling. I woke as one turned and looked at me and said, "I can't tell you how safe I feel in this house."

One of the most famous parables of Buddhism is that of the burning house. The story is told by the Buddha in the Lotus Sutra. A man's children are trapped in a burning house and won't leave when he calls them. In order to get them out, safe and free, he promises carts full of treasure, great treasure. Finally, tempted, they come out, and are saved. Fire is change, loss, the impossibility of holding on; fire is also the burning, ceaseless desire we feel to hold on to that which can't be held. The house is burning, and we stupidly stand there, refusing to leave—until we are tempted by the promise of treasure—the precious jewels of the Dharma, the practice, the Buddha himself.

RIGHT HERE, WHAT do I believe? I do believe in perfection, right here—and not just perfection existing in the midst of decay, but decay as a kind of perfection. I believe in beauty, especially in the moments when one least seeks it—not just the dewdrop, the grass, but beauty in the shuffling of papers on the desk in the little cubicle thick with the snuffles of the sweaty man a few inches away. Beauty in the rattle of the bus sliding halfway into the crosswalk right beside you. Beauty in the liquid aswim with maggots. In everything, in anything. I can believe this, without in any way really understanding. Even after I have my answer, the question is always being asked.

When I begin to truly accept myself as a flit, a bubble, a pile of blocks tilting over, my precious me as a passing sigh in the oceanic cosmos of change—when I accept this moment passing completely away into the next without recourse—when I begin to accept that its very fragility and perishing nature is the beauty in life, then I begin to find safety inside a burning house. I don't need to escape if I know how to live inside it. Not needing to escape, I no longer feel tempted, no longer need promises or rewards. I just walk through it, aware of fire.

The north woods in summer smell like blackberry jam, and in the pockets of sun the tiny midges dance in the heat-sweetened air. They are drunk with it, galloping round and round as their lives leak quickly away. They are points of light in the light.

Conjunctions, Fall 2008

I have been practicing Soto Zen Buddhism for more than thirty years. One of the great masters of Soto Zen is a medieval Japanese teacher named Dōgen, and one of his most famous essays is called "The Sutra of Mountains and Waters." Like most of Dōgen's work, it is elliptical, imagistic, and dense; one understands it in an arational way, through experience. One day I was walking through the woods, watching summer flies, and thought I could write about them in the same way—celebrating their lives, their perfection and wholeness. Very quickly the essay grew into a meditation on the way life, in Dōgen's words, "flashes out of emptiness." And returns to it.

Falling

MY BROTHER, BRUCE, STILL CALLS ME "SIS" AND SOME-times "baby sister," but we don't see much of each other. For a long time we've been gradually drifting—if not apart, then into an accommodation of being apart.

We are both a bit skittish, abrupt, a little profane. Some-times our conversations feel like the wrestling matches we used to have—fun, but a little painful. I call him, but he isn't good on the telephone. His voice rises and falls, the phone in his hand half-forgotten as he throws a ball for his dog or tells my nephew to go do his homework. He comes back to me all at once, demanding, "What?" In the photos I've managed to snap over the years, he is almost always frowning at the camera or making a face.

When he has to come to the hated city and renew a few of his many licenses, he stays with me. He limps up the steps and throws open the heavy front door. "Sis!" he shouts, dropping his small suitcase and slapping my shoulder hard.

We open a bottle of wine and he props his tattered right knee on a pillow. Broad and strong and fighting his weight like everyone in our family, he fills a room.

"Totaled the Beemer on Christmas Eve." He is breezy. "James and me, we spun out on black ice going up the mountain. Thirty-five years I've been driving that road, never hit ice like that. But the Beemer did what it was supposed to—nobody hurt."

Now wait one damned minute here. That BMW was one of his most prized possessions. He totaled it? With James, my twelve-year-old nephew? On the *mountain*, in ice? Not to mention that he hasn't had steady work for a couple of years and had to let all the insurance lapse.

"My big regret, I just filled the gas tank. Now *that's* gone."

We drink for a while.

I ask him about the knee, about the next operation, put off with the insurance.

"I mostly drag my right leg around behind me," he says.

"Does it hurt when you ski?" I ask, watching him lounge on my couch like a king, head back on a pile of quilted pillows. He glances at me, like it's a stupid question. And of course it is; I can see the scars from across the room.

"It hurts right now, sitting here," he says.

For a long time, as most people do, I've nurtured a seed of doubt about my place in others' hearts. In all other hearts. Sometimes I find myself being careful around Bruce, afraid to upset him, because I can't take him for granted. His most abbreviated comments echo and sing to me; a single name or phrase evokes a world. But between siblings, there are no vows, no contracts. No promises. It is so goddamned dangerous to love somebody.

Bruce worked more than twenty-five years as a skier of one kind and another. The walls of his house are covered with pictures of him upside down in space, skis akimbo, flipping off lethal cornices over canyons of snow. Bruce can read snow—layer by layer, its crystal language. He knows when a cornice wants to fall, when a side of the mountain is turning to avalanche. He is trained to handle explosives; for years, it was his job to stand at the edge of a crevasse on skis and toss dynamite into a few hanging tons of ice. He is trained in emergency medicine and rope rescue and can fix a ski lift. He's won several gold medals in the Ski Patrol Olympics. For a while, his job title was mountain manager.

Summers were for construction jobs and river trips. He can run whitewater, so there are photos of him in the rapids too, in boats tossed like autumn leaves. He can handle Zodiacs and portage rafts along a cliff. He has a Coast Guard Master Marine license, so he can run bigger boats in open water. He loves fishing and rivers, but his life was about snow. Then the knee went, and the other knee, and it was the end of all that. He still works a little on ski patrol, keeping his hand in, but the legs aren't up for more than that. Mostly he gets by as a part-time fishing guide in Alaska, scraping through the winters the way he used to scrape through summer.

We drink some more, and he tells me a few stories I've never heard before—harrowing accidents, close calls. Some are old stories, from our stupid kid years. Finally I have enough of listening. I pull up my pants leg and show him a little scar I'd gotten from being banged on some rocks in the surf. He answers with a long jagged line on his calf, and then we are both pulling up our shirtsleeves and yanking down our pants, bending over to point at the marks left behind.

I WAKE UP in a room blurry with dawn. Strange light. The room is fogged and soft, and I know it is snowing. The whole world is falling in snow, the kind of snow that is without beginning—without end. I barely move, coy under the blankets with all the time in the world. And then I jump out into the cold room and fling up the blinds and holler for my brother.

Later Bruce and I make angels in the dry, sibilant snow. Our padded limbs swish in rhythm, whispering. The shattered sky falls like ash, covering me in tiny scraps of white. I can hear the puffs of impact all around me. It covers me, it covers my brother an arm's length away, a new world covering the broken world, leaving us safe and clean and cold.

We grow up in a small town in a high, dry valley braced by mountains. He is two years older, but we look so much alike that we pass for twins, spend that much time together. Summer is clear and hot, and we live outside as much as in—soaring hours spent in fields and vacant lots, clambering over boulders and climbing into the great cups of maple trees. Winter is clear and cold. We do everything in the snow but ski—skiing is pricey beyond words. So we slide down the hills on battered silver discs and patched-up inner tubes, shooting recklessly through the trees. We build snow forts and snow caves and snow houses. We stuff snow down our little sister's shirt so she cries and goes home and can't tell Mom we're going into the culvert where we aren't allowed.

Our mother teaches fifth grade at the elementary school and our father teaches industrial arts at the high school. He fixes televisions and radios on the side, in a cluttered shop behind our house, where the tools hang on pegboards in careful wax-pencil outlines. Dad is a volunteer fireman; all the able-bodied men in town are expected to volunteer. He drinks, more and more with each year, but he takes to driving the trucks, training other men. We grow up around policemen and firemen and ranchers—people who can fix things and build things, people who aren't afraid of weather or work. People who run into burning buildings without looking back.

At two, at four, at eight years of age, I stare at the Polaroid camera my mother holds. I look at her as though she is under a microscope. Bruce, beside me, a little taller, grins stiffly. He is the oldest, he is the only boy, so he is getting the lessons I can't have—how to use tools, build things, fix things. My father is an unsparing man, and he teaches with sudden slaps upside the head. Bruce is learning fast.

My grandparents own a small cabin on a big river, and sometimes we go up for days with boxes of groceries and books. We spend our days on the water, with little supervision. I like to swim across the wide, steady river to the sandy shelf under the cliff— swim with the unflagging, graceless stroke of a strong child, the slow current tugging against me, pushing back. I can feel the cold pull of the deeper, darker water beneath. Sometimes Dad drives us a few miles up the river in the back of the pickup and drops us off with our inner tubes to float back.

One day, when Bruce is almost twelve and I am just nine, we keep going past the cabin, around the blind curve of canyon wall where we are not allowed to go. We dip through a few shallow whorls and rocky turns, and then suddenly we're caught in a narrow slot of white water, real rapids. I still remember only froth and foam, the power of it, falling, and then a hazy view back up a small waterfall we had somehow ridden down. I sit huddled on the rock where Bruce has dropped me after pulling me up from the bottom of the pool by my hair, the way he'd been taught in his junior lifesaving course.

I've lost my shoes. We walk back on the road, its sharp gravel biting my feet. Water runs in trickles down my thighs. We walk through thirsty sunlight, the breathless air suddenly cool under the pines. We walk in silence down the dusty road, carrying our secrets together. Then: "Don't tell Mom," he says. And I nod. Telling Dad never occurs to either of us.

TELLING THE TRUTH is a lot like telling lies, in the end. It is all just stories; like snow falling, they cover everything up. Family, for most of us, includes lifelong agreements about what is not said. Certainly the heart of my family is a maze of agreements, the main one being not to speak of things. At ten years, at twelve, at fourteen, I meet the camera with a mocking half smile, with scorn. Bruce gazes toward the horizon like Captain America. The fear of humiliation and the need for self-reliance is strong in us both, driving us differently. He wants to be perfect; he is taking lessons in it. I want the lessons too, but not the grades—not the snicking of the leather belt as our father pulls it off his waist and wraps it twice around his meaty hands.

I discover books and theater and politics and trouble, and he finds football and gymnastics. I can't fight fires or use a table saw, so I do more dangerous things. I ride motorcycles with men I meet in the park. I talk back at the dinner table. Bruce wins his varsity letter, and I start writing manifestos to my English teachers. *Truth* is what I insist on telling. I call it *speaking up*—words flying from my young mouth, flying up, filling the sky.

Right after graduation, Bruce leaves on a gymnastics scholarship to the Air Force Academy in Colorado Springs, eight thousand feet high in the Rockies. He shaves his head, learns to handle a rifle, marches for hours. He goes skiing for the first time. He never takes a lesson—just pushes off and flies.

While Bruce spit-polishes his shoes, his very short romance with the military already over, I am getting kicked out of English class. When I am sixteen I quit high school before they can fire me, and somehow talk myself into early admission at the college one state border and a world away from home. After a year, Bruce quits the academy and joins me. There is a little of Captain Kirk now, a nerd with cool depths. He lets his hair grow and falls in with a gang of ski bums who cut classes and head up the mountain whenever they can cadge enough gas money together. My father tears the Air Force Academy bumper sticker off his truck and won't speak to him.

When I leave college to test my ideas about truth and beauty in a commune, Bruce finds his way to the Rockies and begins to study snow in earnest. Each morning, he wakes up to the cold, bright Colorado sky, and skis straight from his apartment steps to the slopes. He skis his last run to the door of the restaurant where he washes dishes and chops vegetables each evening. Late at night, he skis home, under sulfurous streetlights. In the cones of light, snowflakes swirl, blinking in and out like shadows, extinguished when they touch the earth.

THE WRITER PETER Stark describes how winter saved him: how, at a time when his life was out of control, he was able to use its canvas to "spread out the chaos that was once my life and assemble something that I hope approaches grace." We learn to walk by falling; we learn to relax into gravity until we dance with it. Skiing is just another way to fall, and dance. In the inhuman snows of the high mountains, there is not much more one can do; surrender is your only choice.

A few years ago, Bruce came to the city to receive an award for some outrageously complicated rescue involving ropes and winches and a whole night in the snow, and we went to a banquet room and ate bad chicken at big round tables with police and firemen and people who run toward what most people flee.

I'm comfortable underwater, in hospitals, in strange cities where I don't speak the language. But I can barely swing a hammer. I don't like being cold, and I'm scared of heights. People like my brother, my father, the men and women who speak this language of physical skill and risk sometimes seem like creatures from another time, made for battle and repair. Listening to their laconic, tech-laden slang, I can be stung by remorse, by that old, familiar wish—that I had become someone else. That I had done things differently all along.

There is something painfully obvious about it all, this overcompensation, this hoarding of skill. We've both done it; we've collected our gold stars, become experts in our fields, worked as professional helpers—that group a therapist might say has issues. Some lessons I never seem to learn. I sent a copy of each of my books to my father. He never mentioned them, and when I finally asked, he told me he didn't have time to read.

One day, Bruce takes me up to the top of his mountain. He leads me away from the lift and the runs, to a line of closure ropes at the top of the steepest bowl. He skis without poles, moves like a dancer. Directly below us is a glaciated cirque, a smooth plane dropping far away, an ocean of white.

"No way!" I say—almost shouting.

Bruce laughs, then gets a look at my face and stops smiling. "If you start to slide, turn your feet downhill," he says. "Dig your elbows in and keep your head down." Then he grins and throws his arms wide, taking in the slope, the trees, the whole damned mountain. "Hey, Sis! You just have to ask yourself—what could *possibly* go wrong?"

OUR MOTHER IS dead for many years when Dad dies, a few days before Christmas in the middle of a snowstorm. The day of his funeral is calm and clear, and many of the town's firemen come in dress uniform. One stands in each corner of the room during the service, holding bells, and at the end, they ring the signal for firemen returning to the station. Then the big red ladder truck leads the hearse to the cemetery.

We are left with four houses, two workshops, a garage, and

the debris of many whiskey-laden years. Three of the houses are rentals in various states of repair, and the house where we were raised is reduced to narrow pathways through mazes of piled-up newspapers, books, clothes, laundry, and box after unlabeled box. Our sister lives in town and is the executor of the estate; she finds missing stock certificates, lost photographs, and a few hefty, long-expired checks in the detritus. But months later, Bruce and I decide it's really our turn, and make a date to tackle the garage, the final piece.

I drive alone down the interstate on a beautiful September day, listening to NPR for hours. I stop at gas stations and minimarts, and everywhere there are people gathered around small televisions hanging from the ceiling, over the pepperoni sticks and Slurpee machines. No one says much. I reach Bruce's peaceful ranch house in a little town off the old highway, and we hug and sit silently in front of the television for a few more hours, watching the towers in their strange, slow, eternal fall, and we are both thinking about the firemen and neither of us says a word.

The next day we sort through boxes. The silence is broken only now and then—"Oh, look at this!" holding up a yearbook or a battered balsa-wood airplane. We find brass knuckles, a box of Super 8 porn flicks, a bottle of mercury, ancient calipers. "Remember this?" we say. We work all day.

Then we stand in the driveway between the house where we grew up and the little rental bungalow next door. It looks much the same, a tidy white house with a dark-green square of lawn. Behind Bruce, where we grew up, is a bed of thirsty old roses, a leaning fence, dead grass—the work of decades let go. And the crumbling chimney of our fireplace, the one he scrabbled up, screaming, when Dad chased him with the belt.

He tells me a story.

He was in his thirties, married, rearing three children, and living near the mountain where he was head of the ski patrol. He came down to town to help Dad paint the rental house. They prepped for a week and were ready to paint. Just as they opened the cans, the fire alarm went off. Dad dashed for his pickup and was gone without a word, the same way he had disappeared at the sound of the siren our entire lives. Bruce kept working.

"And, by God, I did it myself. I painted the whole damned house by myself that day. And I cleaned up too. It was done when he got home."

What are the words for how we stand here in the midst of things? On the top of the mountain, I had lifted my borrowed goggles, and the ocher world flipped into black and white: every shade of ash and pearl and dove, a floury, glaucous place with shadows dappled and milky. Snow without beginning, without end. The whole world was glistening and silky, like a fall of tinsel lay across the land. I felt, perhaps for the first time, his vast gladness of winter. What are the words for this kind of snow, snow that is always falling, has always been falling, snow that fills our hearts and turns us into angels?

"When he got home, he didn't say anything. He just walked around the whole house without saying anything. He looked at every bit of it and the paint cans and the brushes. And finally he said, 'Good job.' And that was it."

Standing on this broken asphalt in a driveway I know rut by rut, I look at him. He stands up straight, holds his head back. Captain America.

"It was the first time he ever told me I did a good job."

We are all riding down our lives, a few hidden rapids around the bend. Hang on tight. Sometimes we walk back home again, together.

Conjunctions, Fall 2011

I have been writing about, and around, and to my brother for many years. This particular essay is a response to the word kin, a themed issue of Conjunctions. *I've told some of these stories in other ways and have many more stories to tell. He's up in Alaska as I write this, with a bad shoulder and sore knees, catching big fish.*

Here Be Monsters

DAN, THE YOUNG DIVEMASTER, SET US UP WITH WEIGHTS
and tanks for the required checkout dive, running through the park
rules as he worked. The checkout dive was one of the rules. Taking coral or spearfishing outside permitted areas was against the
rules; feeding fish was most definitely against the rules.

"Some idiot started feeding the moray eels hot dogs," he said,
swinging a tank to me. I pretended not to stumble when I caught
it. "Some *idiot*." He was half my age and naked except for a pair
of ratty swim shorts. "They're myopic, the eels," he added. "They
can't tell the difference between your finger and an octopus tentacle and a hot dog. A woman had half her finger bitten off last year."
He paused. "Don't be *stuuupppid*."

I learned to dive in chill, dim Puget Sound and promptly
gave up on cold water. I had never dived in warm water or been to
a subtropical island, except for Hawaii, where I went snorkeling
for the first time and was seized with the need to go below, to stay
down there. And Bonaire was a fever dream of a desert island, a
tilting tabletop barely out of the sea. In the north, the narrow interior is scrub and cactus and tikitiki trees pointing to the southwest with the eternal wind. The arid land is filled with birds, wild
donkeys, goats, and iguanas six feet long. The small towns in the
center are sun scorched and still; the people are mostly African
by descent, with Arawak and Spanish and Dutch and Portuguese
mixed in. The south is salt flats, towering white cones lining the
road beside giant loaders and pink evaporation ponds; twinkling

crystalline drifts of salt powder float across the highway like low fog. A row of tiny slave huts is protected as a memorial, the size of dog houses and hot as saunas. A large flock of pink flamingos lives in the south. They step daintily through the shallows on silly delicate legs, turning their big heads completely upside down to feed on tiny shrimp. The birds chatter constantly, *cho-go-go, go-go*, the sound mixing with the wind, *cho-go-go! go-go, cho-go*, like gossip or the mild chronic complaints of old aunts. Sometimes they fly to Venezuela, fifty miles away—the flock rising at twilight all at once like a vapor flashing flame in the last light.

Sand and scraped sky above the waves; below, an immense work of eons. The naturalist William Beebe said of the coral reef, "No opium dream can compare." The reef looks like the rumpled ruins of a great city, slumped boulders and bushes and pillars and branches cascading down and down, an architecture that is truly stone—the skeletons of tiny animals piled one atop another. I was a novice diver and a complete tyro on the reef. After a few days of barely coherent dives, I began to learn names: tilefish, wrasse, moon jelly, lugworm, overgrowing mat tunicate, southern sennet, whitespotted toadfish, honeycomb cowfish, porgy, the tiny scrawled filefish hiding in a gorgonian like a shivering leaf. I learned the names of things, but that is not the same as knowing the things one can name.

On the second day, I saw my first eel. Dan pointed to a rough rock near an overhang and I paddled over in stupefied and clumsy strokes. The big head, the jaws working—a green moray, all muscle and velvet.

FAMILY *MURAENIDAE* IN the order *Anguilliformes*. Hundreds of species of moray eels all created on the fifth day, if Genesis is to be believed. They are brown, green, ivory, gray, yellow, orange, black, and neon blue, and all these in combination: speckled, spotted, polka-dotted, striped, tessellated, piebald, brindle. A couple of the species are two-toned like saddle shoes. Morays live in every tropical and temperate sea, mostly in shallow water. They make dens in caves and crevices and holes in rocks; some live in hollowed-out burrows in the sand, mixing mucus and grains of sand into cement. They live alone, wolves sharing out the territory. The redface eel in the Atlantic and Indian Oceans is eight inches long at maturity; the slender giant moray in the Indian and the Pacific can reach twelve feet. A study in Hawaii found that up to 46 percent of the carnivorous biomass on the reef was moray.

They are fish but don't look like fish; they have no pectoral fins, no fishiness. Instead the dorsal fin runs the entire length of the body, fimbriated and smooth from the aerodynamic head shaped like a jet cockpit to the tapering tail. Morays are covered in mucus. The green moray is really blue. Or is it brown? Or gray? Or a funereal black? I'm not sure; sources vary. The mucus is green, or perhaps yellow; the mucus is poisonous. Or not; sources vary. These are no long-distance swimmers; they are immensely strong but slothful, like high-school boys on a Sunday afternoon. Morays are mostly nocturnal, shy, and spend much of the time curled in their dens, often with just their heads peeping out. Morays don't see well, but they have a great sense of smell, and mostly wait for prey to wander by—lobster, octopus, fish of all kinds. Divers and snorkelers are most likely to see only the wavering head, the long sinuous body curled out of sight in a den. (Often, if you look carefully, you can see that snaky body wound round and round the rocks and coral like loose rope.) Most morays stay in exactly the same place for years—the same part of the reef, the same den. Divers recognize specific eels and tend to name the big ones.

Sources always vary in this world. Morays are dangerous, I read in a fish guide. They are ugly, fearful beasts. Such adjectives recur again and again, in science as well as stories. My beloved Britannica says, "they can be quite vicious," an oddly subjective entry in that careful publication. My well-worn *Peterson Field Guide* warns, "Before sticking your hand into a crevice, look into it carefully. A dreaded moray eel may be hiding there."

The mouth—that's what scares people. The big, wide mouth and all those pointy teeth, gaping at you. Morays have small gills;

breathing requires them to open and close their mouths continuously to force water through. They look contemplative, like a man working off the novocaine. Fish have a second set of teeth in pharyngeal jaws in the throat, to clench onto captured prey and pull it quickly down into the gut. Pharyngeal jaws seem odd, but they are common. Human embryos have extra jaws that fade into the skull early in development. The moray, however, is unique. They catch prey with the long, needle-sharp front teeth and then the pharyngeal jaws shoot out of the throat like a questing blind skull and bite again. The front jaws let go and the pharyngeal jaws retract, and the prey ratchets down, gone in a second or two.

There are many videos on the internet purporting to show moray attacks. Like *dreaded* or *vicious*, like *ugly*, the word *attack* is one colored by imagination. In many of the videos, divers are making faces and showing off, darting out of reach with a scared giggle, egging each other on. One of the most well-known shows a moray biting a diver's thumb off with a crisp pop. (If a moray bites your finger, the pharyngeal jaws won't let go—do we think they would reconsider if they could? Do we imagine an eel listening— *Let go, you shouldn't eat that?*) If the eel gets a finger, it simply bites the finger off. If the eel gets hold of something bigger—an arm, a thigh—well, there's not much to be done. The diver gets out of the water with the eel attached until someone can smash its head in and cut the jaws off. In the case of the thumb—in every case I've heard of in twenty years of diving—the divers were petting eels or teasing eels or trying to coax the eel out of its den to take pictures. These are big ones, eels with names, the reliable local celebrities that tourists want to see. They are conditioned to come out of their dens to be fed. Conditioned, but not domesticated. Mostly, the divers were feeding the eels hot dogs, which look, even to my human eyes, a lot like fingers.

ONE CAN LET go of a surprising number of concerns underwater, drifting slowly down into the blue like a pebble in honey. After the first startled moment, the inside-out reorienting of the world that comes with sinking underwater, I'm at ease; at times, I'm so relaxed I can almost nap. Since that first dive off Bonaire, I've seen many morays: spotted and goldentail morays, dwarf and zebra morays, and once a chestnut moray, a trick to find. Off Glover's Atoll in Belize, I drifted down a huge boulder to a little sandy plain like a courtyard, falling without hurry through water clear as air. When I reached the sand, I looked casually to the right and saw a green moray several feet long resting under a ledge with his eye on me: *Gymnothorax funebris*. Green morays can reach eight feet in length and weigh up to sixty-five pounds. *Gymno* is bare or naked, and the word *funebris* means funeral, for the dark color, perhaps. Or for the fear.

Later that day, in a cavern, my dive partner, Carol, kept gesturing vaguely at me, and when I shrugged at her—*I don't understand, what are you trying to tell me?*—she grinned and shook her head. Back on the boat, I asked her what she'd meant. "A moray," she said. "Right behind you in his den, the whole time."

In Roatán, off the coast of Honduras, the sand is smooth as white silk, and the foam flows along at the edge with a snake's hiss. The little village of West End is scattered with wanderers from around the world, many sporting cherry-red sunburns. I dove one afternoon with Sergio, a six-foot-tall Spaniard twenty years younger than me. Such pairings are the stuff of diving. We took a little skiff out to the reef wall at the end of the lagoon. Everyone on the island was in siesta, it seemed; there was no one in sight, no current, just the two of us buzzing on glassine water under a hazy sky. We hooked to a mooring and slid in, to drift slowly along the coral wall with barely a kick. The tumbled stone wall was interlaced with the lilac vases and greenish lettuce leaves of sponges, the twisted pipe cleaners of wire coral, and the wavering Christmas ribbons of soft corals called knobby candelabrum and dead man's fingers. Two huge crabs shuffled back and forth like gunfighters at high noon. A small, tight band of black margate formed a square wall to one side, turning in unison as we passed.

I was floating in the kind of sensuous abandon that drives time out of one's mind altogether, hearing only my own exhala-

tion, when something slipped into my peripheral vision. I turned
to see a great green moray right beside me, glorious and iridescent. He matched my speed, watching me with a thoughtful eye.
Sergio was ahead, hovering, absorbed by some small creature.
His tan, lean body hung horizontally beside the wall. The moray,
with what seemed a meaningful glance in my direction, slid sideways toward Sergio and parked just above him, inches behind his
head, like a semi heading smoothly into a truck stop. Morays smell
through two small tubes like snorkels jutting out from the snout;
the eel seemed to be inhaling the scent of Sergio's shampoo. Its
huge, undulant body was as long as the man.

I slowly sidled over, trying to get in front of Sergio, wanting
to catch his attention in a quiet way. I could feel myself grimacing a
little. Finally he looked up and I gestured, Come here, with just my
fingertips—nothing dramatic or abrupt. He must have noticed my
darting eyes, because he turned around and then leaped away. He
stopped beside me and there we hung; we watched the eel and he
watched us and this just went on and on for a long while. The eel
was an elephantine leaf, a scarf, a nymph, a dragon. A sea monster,
a dream. I longed to touch it.

Morays are hermaphrodites, sometimes transmutating
male to female, sometimes fully both genders at once—screwing
willy-nilly with whatever moray or Spaniard comes along. They
court when the water is warm (who doesn't?) and they really gawp
then—breathing hard, wrapping around and around each other's
long, slippery bodies like tangling fringe, like braids, like DNA.
Eggs and sperm are released together, and the eels return to their
anchorite dens. When the eggs hatch, endless uncountable larvae
called leptocephali dissipate, a million shreds of wide ribbon—
tiny fish heads on long, flat bodies. The larvae float for nearly a year.
(The ocean is always a bath of barely visible infants; one swims in
a snow of newborns.) The survivors of that perilous year absorb
their pectoral fins and grow into elvers, which is what juvenile eels
are really called, and in time each finds an empty spot and makes a

den and lives for decades. They have few enemies: a couple of the biggest fishes. Bigger morays. You.

The Roman aristocracy loved morays; they farmed them as livestock and kept them as pets in elaborate ponds. Now and then, a master fed his less obedient slaves to the eels, presumably in pieces; human blood was thought to fatten a moray nicely. Delicious or not, it's always a bad idea to eat an alpha predator. A bit like unprotected sex—when you eat the top of the food chain, you eat every link. A wee dinoflagellate (*Gambierdiscus toxicus*, a microalga that feeds on dead coral) produces a neurotoxin called cinguatoxin, becoming more concentrated in each successive species. It's possible to get ciguatera from herbivorous fish, and little guys like snapper, but the alpha predators bank it like gold. The toxin is a nasty one—almost everyone who eats a fish with cinguatoxin will get sick. Victims vomit and suffer diarrhea; their lips and fingers go numb; cold sensations switch with hot; they feel profound weakness and pain in the teeth and pain on urinating and arrhythmias and respiratory failure. The symptoms last for months and you can pass the toxin to others through sexual activity and pregnancy. King Henry I of England may have died of ciguatera; he collapsed after gorging on eels. At one Filipino banquet featuring a large yellow margin moray, fifty-seven people got sick; ten went into comas; two died.

WEEKS OF WIND and rain lashing the sea kept us land bound on Cat Island. Carol made hats out of sticks and wrack. I restlessly walked the same path several times a day. One morning I found a perfect set of frog legs lying on the path. They had been nipped off at the waist. An hour later, they were boiling with brown ants. By afternoon, the ants had dug a hole beside the path, and tugged the legs halfway in; they were bowed, as though swimming into the earth. By morning, there was only skeleton; long, slender toe bones pointed to the angry sky.

The world is a strange place, for all of us—strange to me, strange to frogs, to ants, to eels. Strangely full of all those others, who are utterly unlike us, who look and act insensibly. If they are thoughtful, these are thoughts that have nothing to do with me; if the glance is meaningful, there is no way for me to know the meaning. But we do insist that we know what it is, that it is familiar in some crucial way.

Everyone wants the familiar. (Yes, people often say the opposite, that they crave the new and long for adventure and novelty. They really don't. What we call adventure is the process of meeting the new and turning it into the known as fast as possible. We want to name the unnamed and touch the untouched so that they are no longer unnamed and untouched. No longer strange. Then we can go tell people all about what we've found.) Perhaps it is always most difficult with the sea, to which so many are drawn as though by a piper, and where none of us belong. No shared fundament in the sea; coral and sponge and fish are a wonder to me, but there is nothing of me there.

Ah, we long for commonality. The idea that an animal is simply out of reach, forever opaque, is not to be tolerated. The unknown makes sociopaths of us all, turning animals into objects to meet our needs, affirm us, *befriend* us. So one imparts motive, emotion, even morals to an animal. And one sees what one expects to see. Perhaps a vicious sea monster. Perhaps a puppy who takes a biscuit from your hand. In both cases, one will be wrong.

Since that first trip to Bonaire, I've seen a lot of fish feeding. The point is a good photograph, an exciting moment—a good tip at the end of the dive. Hot dogs are used because they don't fall apart; frozen peas sink nicely in the sunny water. Cheez Whiz is quite popular—people find it amusing to squirt a can of Cheez Whiz underwater and stir a school of damselfish into frenzy. As a species, we are easily amused. Besides the nice tip, fish feeding gives us control. It bounds the boundless. We've *interacted*, we've *made a connection*. Whether the damselfish or stingray or moray eel feels the same way is not at issue here (though people are remarkably quick to ascribe motives like pleasure or play or, God knows, *affection* to the behavior of a carnivore chasing a sausage).

The last thing we want to admit is that they may be indifferent to us. We tiny, fragile mammals, stunned by the danger of the world; we press our fear against the vast, improbable gestalt of the sea.

I like to dive at night; the reef is wide awake, softened and kinetic with a million little bodies. Slipping into black water is always a little spooky, a reminder: my legs dangling out of sight above the primeval deep. At night I carry only a little light and cover a smaller territory, so I can focus on one thing at a time. The stalk eye of a conch slowly turns as it hauls its great shell across the sand. Coral polyps dance like hands hauling in a net. Carol's fairy light bobs in the distance. A red snapping shrimp rises up to a boxer's stance when my light passes by. A basket star unfurls itself into a burnt-orange tumbleweed. And at the edge of my little circle of light, a moray slides across the ivory sand and is gone into the dark.

On one night dive, with a group too big for me, too much the herd, the divemaster led us to a moray's den, the young green eel's head caught in a dozen headlamps like a startled deer. It turned from side to side, trying to watch all of us at once. A German man with a big video camera kept darting in, trying to get a good close-up of the eel's face; finally, he took the camera and started bashing the eel on the head. I felt myself retract far deeper than the eel could go, retreat all the way out of the human species. *Bite him*, I thought. *What are you waiting for?* He had fingers to spare. But I also knew it would likely be the death of the eel. Finally the divemaster pulled the man away, and we ascended to a rocking sea. The sky was close and thick with stars; there was sheet lightning all across the horizon, silent, huge. In that moment I wanted never to speak to a person again.

Some time later, I was back on Roatán. Carol and I dove through a splendid set of winding, narrow coral canyons separated by rivers of sand. The day was bright and wide beams of sunlight shone down on the reef. We flew through the wonderland, this solid chunk of long time. We finned slowly up one canyon, around, and down the next, back and forth, watching the abundant schools of blue tang and sergeant majors like flocks of butterflies.

I stopped to watch a glorious queen triggerfish hovering shyly in the distance. Then I turned around and saw a huge green moray hanging there, a single poised muscle a few feet away.

We hung eye to eye. He was more than five feet long, a dusky, piney green that seemed to shimmer in the light. For a half hour the eel stayed near us: flowing straight along the reef an inch off the coral, matching every curve; sliding over low ridges like, well, water; slipping sideways in and out of thin breaks and reappearing around a turn as though waiting. I felt blessed—not by some imagined connection, not by recognition or a meeting of minds, but by the strange that will remain forever strange and by its strangeness tell me who I am. We found ourselves fifty feet down at the base of a straight ridge, Carol and me and the big green eel, and then it spun around and swam straight up the coral mountain toward the bright sky and was gone.

Conjunctions, Fall 2013

Conjunctions did a themed issue on animals, and I found myself thinking about how easily we anthropomorphize other species. Perhaps it's a trait of the human animal to think other animals share human traits. I'm drawn to alpha predators and to strangeness, and morays are certainly both. People endlessly try to make them more familiar; I like them as they are, inexplicable and outside my ken.

The Indigo City

ON THE WALLS OF THE LITTLE HOUSE WHERE I GREW UP hung three images. Above the television in pride of place, a nocturnal cityscape in wavering shimmers of blue and green and purple, prone to a slight jiggle if you bumped it. On the wall above the dining table, an amateur watercolor of a pioneer cabin painted by my grandmother. On the wall of my parents' cramped bedroom, a studio portrait of my brother and sister and me in Sunday clothes, with wide, false smiles.

I grew up in a small logging and ranching town in the mountains of northern California, a Gold Rush town of three thousand people surrounded by rolling hills. I was used to wide streets, small stores, big trucks, bigger skies. One movie screen, one library, one small history museum. One elementary school, where my mother taught, and one high school, where my father taught. We all rose at the same time to get ready for school, and I hitched a ride with a parent or walked with friends along the same blocks, past the same houses, every day. We ate dinner at six each evening, around the big white Formica table: canned peas and dry roast beef and slices of Wonder bread. The only radio station we could reliably get in the valley played country and western music, though my parents' record collection was dominated by Percy Faith and Don Ho. More often, we ate to the rhythm of the television news. Then Dad fell asleep on the couch, Mom did the dishes, and the kids watched *The Wonderful World of Disney* or *Lost in Space*.

My mother was the first person in her family to get a college degree—five years of normal school and an elementary education certificate. I didn't know she had taken a minor degree in Spanish until I found her textbooks after she died; I never heard her speak a word of it. I sometimes wondered, in the brutal way children consider their parents, why she had settled for so little—teaching fifth grade, cooking and dishes and laundry, evenings with a novel and a cigarette. Her own mother had been a farm girl and then a truck driver and then a truck driver's wife. But instead of our spare walls, my grandmother's house was a paint-by-numbers gallery—mostly rural and bucolic scenes of hayricks and carriages, dogs trotting alongside. She spent a year on the Famous Writers correspondence course and had the certificate to prove it. I didn't belong with these people; I was an exile—misunderstood but destined, like falsely adopted royalty. I thought precocity was a kind of ticket, a promise of something; I had little enough patience for the long wait of childhood and its endless ordinary days.

My mother's novels were what she bought with her long days of work; she was a great reader, and I became one, too, as soon as letters formed shapes I could recognize. Our yearning (and did she yearn? I only imagine so; she never complained) was spent in the elsewhere of books. I leafed for hours through her mysterious library, the dense novels and works of history with no pictures, each with her name inside in careful penmanship. A salesman knocked on the door once, trailing a suitcase of *World Book Encyclopedias*; I wanted them like food, and to my shock, she bought a complete set. My father built a bookcase, and they displayed it like treasure in the living room, beneath the indigo city—volume after volume of slick pages, photographs, charts, maps, and a fascinating overlay of human anatomy: bones, muscles, nerves, and genitals. The hallway was lined with Reader's Digest Condensed Books, which came every month in a plain brown package, like secrets. I loved books dense with print, their unambiguous intent to take me away. In my half-reveries, working my way through the sentences of *Marjorie Morningstar* and *The Durable Fire*, flipping the overlay back and forth, I always had one eye on the watery, rippled city above the television and its opaque buildings reflected in a dreamy dark river. How she decided on that particular piece of hotel decor, I do not know. I suspect it came from Silverman's Furniture and went with the new drapes.

Art was a man's name at our house. My mother taught the lower-grade music classes. I started lessons at eight, plinking away at the upright she'd bought secondhand and inexplicably painted light blue. I made lanyards and pine-needle baskets at Girl Scout camp, crayon scratch drawings and clay ashtrays in school. I was intrigued by paint-by-number, the possibilities; even better was the sedative painting instructor on television, his voice like pudding as he magically produced sunny skies, trees, twilit mountain peaks in just half an hour.

I talked my mother into sending me to a private class. The studio was on Miner Street, an avenue of tall, narrow, pioneer-era buildings, up a dim flight of stairs above Don's Sporting Goods. The big room had soft wooden floors a century old, a dozen easels in a half-circle. The teacher was a big, dark man with a brooding, gentle manner; he would point us at the inevitable vase and bowl of fruit and walk quietly behind us for a few hours, leaning in to make suggestions. I took to it all at once, the dusty floor and the smells of linseed oil and fixative, the romance of belonging. I loved the rustling silence of the class at work—a few housewives, a couple of teenagers, and this oddly confident ten-year-old throwing herself into the lessons. We drew boxes and apples and flowers, graduating over several weeks from pencil to charcoal to chalk and paint.

At the end of every class, the teacher would stand up abruptly, clap his hands once, and say, "All right! Now spend the rest of your time doing whatever you want!" I always grabbed for the tubes of cobalt blue and olive green and smeared them about on the canvas, trying to make my own magic city in the mist.

Usually I walked home from art class. I did not think my mother was sophisticated enough to be in the studio, with her red lipstick and sad purse and old-lady scarf tied below her chin. But sometimes she picked me up and stayed to chat a little, teacher to teacher, while I wandered around the studio, running my finger along the backs of the cheap plastic chairs on which we perched. I liked to examine the day's uncertain drawings on hunks of torn butcher paper taped up casually on the easels, and the proudly displayed paintings of bouquets and mountain scenes hung on the walls. How did he get there, my dark art teacher, to that little town in the mountains? I have no idea. But I knew I wasn't the only refugee stranded there.

"I know she likes it here," I heard him say one day. "But. Well, you know." Mom murmured something. "Well, she is determined," he answered.

"What did he say?" I asked her on the way home. She cleared her throat. My mother was often reluctant to answer my questions, many of them stimulated by advertisements in the back of magazines she never thought I would read, but she always told me the truth.

"Well," she said. "Well, he thought that maybe I, maybe we, should think about something else. Maybe we should save the money for the class. Do you know what I mean?"

I swallowed something that day, a loss without words; I never went back to class. Instead I decided to focus on my study of piano, as I was wont to describe it even at the age of ten—if my rote lessons could be called a study, with a large, laconic German man who wore bow ties and walked to our house with the slow dignity of the educated tramp. Another refugee. I could do no more than read the notes to the tick of the metronome, but I constantly asked him to give me harder pieces to play. I'd discovered Satie and his deceptive simplicity, a fateful error for the amateur pianist.

I read my way through three shelves of *Reader's Digest* Condensed Books and then whatever I could find at the Carnegie Library, from a biography of Carl Sandburg and an encyclopedia of historical costume to Pierre Boulle's *Planet of the Apes*. With Sandburg, I started reading adult poetry instead of the insipid anthologies at school (Robert Louis Stevenson: "A birdie with a yellow bill / Hopped upon my window sill, / Cocked his shining eye and said:

/ 'Ain't you 'shamed, you sleepy-head!'"—awful stuff). I began to copy lines in my own quote book—the special wisdom of Robert Frost and Richard Brautigan, guru advice.

I was dreaming of dark cities and university and basement cafes where I would read my poetry ("it is day / beloved listen / I hear the singers / coming winging / on the cobblestones coming singing"). I felt pressure forcing me up from this house, this town, up and out; it had to be art—the siren call of talent waiting to surface. One summer I took a photography class. We spent hours over fine plates of Steichen and Weston and Arbus, talking about contrast and shadow and unexpected detail. But my own photographs were dull and predictable. If I accidentally captured any effect, like graininess or a portrait with half the face cut off, I would print them immediately. When the class ended and I ran out of film, I put the camera away, vowing to save money for a better one.

To no one's surprise, I joined drama club as soon as I got to high school. I was cast as the Maid, the Bystander, the Pedestrian, and finally the assistant stage manager, but I was undeterred. I entered the Shakespeare competition, choosing Lady Macbeth's monologue—"Come to my woman's breasts, and take my milk for gall, you murdering ministers ... " I recited this in a growl, my face pinched with something like angst, or a bad oyster. I loved saying the word *breasts* out loud and always leaned hardest on that great word *gall*, which said so much about the world's vexations. By the age of fourteen, I had a lot of sympathy for Lady Macbeth.

My own native iconoclasm, my ceaseless overreaching, made any direct route to success impossible; I shot myself off course like a North Korean rocket. I dropped the sad German piano teacher one day, never bought more film, didn't take the art elective, and spent a lot of hours sitting in the park with unemployed men who rode motorcycles. I read what I wanted, studied what I wanted, went to class when I couldn't find a way out of it, and wrote manifestos explaining why I would not be turning in the assignments I found insulting and small. I got through two years of high school with only two arrests and several court-mandated visits to a psychologist. Then I walked away, walked clean out, and with the psychologist's help, talked myself into the little college over the snowy mountain pass.

College—a state college, a football school, but to me the height of culture. I was finally with my people. I didn't take art classes. I took philosophy, semantics, bacteriology, sailing, religious studies, and one class of art history—the golden mean and *Un Chien Andalou* and what exactly was the difference between Impressionism and Expressionism. This was *fine art*, and I was glad my mother had spurned the dusty studio after all. What could he have known, upstairs from the sporting-goods store? I loved Seurat; I was drawn to pointillism the way I was drawn to Erik Satie. Seurat's dots of light, the wild splatters of Pollock, and the easy crayon colors of Klee: such art, mere spots and lines, seemed possible. This, I thought, this I could do—if I wanted to try. (I never tried.) Instead I had obsessive infatuations and read like crazy: Kurt Vonnegut and T. S. Eliot and Sigrid Unset, Dorothy Parker and Tolstoy and Kant and Edna St. Vincent Millay, and Wallace Stevens, who thought that "… to have put there / A few sounds of meaning, a momentary end / To the complication, is good, is a good." I copied that, and many other lines, not always with understanding. I pored over the slick reproductions in library books I couldn't afford, *Modern Art in America* and *Picture History of World Art*. Now and then I wandered across fragments of the shimmering city and all it implied. "Above all else, do not mistake me for someone else," wrote Nietzsche—or so I wrote in my book of quotes.

What happens with disappointment is the way it digs in like a splinter; the pain is small, precise, unavoidable; it wears on you. I had the soul of a painter and the heart of a musician and the spirit of an actress—"I will crawl with the shellfish through puffs of waterdust, sideways claw by claw," I wrote, "I hang with one clutching hand above the black rabbit's hole"—and so it felt as though I had been promised that life, promised the right to be in that world. The right to be better than I was. I secretly bought books on how to draw and tricks with acrylics and I played on a pottery wheel and bought another camera. I played Chopin—the simplest nocturnes—and Pachelbel's *Canon in D* and, of course, the *Gymnopédies*. Again and again, I could almost feel the movement, trace the curve, the necessary line, but I could not; it was as though the drawing of the necessary line was trapped in my hand, locked away out of my reach. I couldn't act, could barely play music, and worst, could not paint. Sometimes this felt like amputation or a birth defect, this is *not*. My lack was no matter of draftsmanship or tools, but something far deeper, existential, molecular. I made collages.

By the age of eighteen I was jittery as an ant heap prodded by sticks. I'd already had two years of college, and I couldn't wait through another—wait for what, I still don't know. One mild spring day, I went to the college bookstore and sold my textbooks—I was moving on to something else, somewhere else, anywhere else. On to whatever I was expecting. That day I went to the remainder table as I always did and picked up a book called *Michelangelo and His Art*, mainly for the cover—a carved marble man's head, small horns jutting out of his curly marble hair. The book cost me all I had just earned.

I moved into a communal house a few hundred miles away. In time, a poster of the Delphic Sybil hung on one wall, a poster of Rousseau's *The Sleeping Gypsy* on another. I had a copy of Klee's *Fish Magic* in the kitchen and a murky miniature of *Water Lilies* in the bathroom. I spent hours with Michelangelo, reading about the *David* and the tombs and the ceiling. I memorized entire sections of text, loose bits of context and criticism woven around dull photographs of rough captives and muscular women. I realized that I loved with passion works of art so common that they were sold as key chains and coasters. But I held these dissonant truths without concern: that I knew nothing of art or literature or culture or history, and understood them all with a discerning skill. Gradually I turned toward the church of politics and spent my time at co-ops and free clinics and in long, wordy committee meetings. One day, I sold my piano and bought a typewriter.

The rent would be paid somehow—how? At nineteen, I went back east to interview at a couple of universities, trailing my fragments of education like a vestigial fin. I found myself in New York City for the first time. I had a few days, a few dollars, so I went to the Museum of Modern Art. What this meant, I did not really know; I had never been to an art museum before. I had never really thought to find the real paintings in the books I read until someone said to me, "Of course, you're going to MoMA!" But of course. Suddenly I was dream-walking—right before me, Klee's strange fishes and Weston's *Nude on Sand* and Rousseau's gypsy. I found a small room with two Seurat paintings and several of his small charcoal drawings. There was *Guernica* and Steichen's portrait of Garbo and in its own big dim room, *Water Lilies* in all its quiet, outsized glory.

I was alone and broke and at sea, and I spun through the rooms in a strange chaos of feeling. Giacometti. Miró. Brancusi. Brancusi! I sat for a while near Matisse's *Dance (I)*, with a punch-drunk global citizenry slumped together on the padded benches. I saw what faint clones I'd come to love—fraying posters and book covers speckled with cooking oil—and I saw that everything I'd thought about this art was wrong. There was nothing haphazard or easy here; all the chaos was deliberate. The casual curve I had traced was a meticulously planned and unrepeatable single stroke at once. These were objects, not pictures; I could trace layers of paint, note the bare edge of canvas, the scratch of a chisel, rough strokes so dismissively confident they left me fearful and breathless. Those points of color, those drops of paint were more than beyond me—what had seemed simple turned out to be instead transcendent, to be born of the true simplicity that has passed through complexity into knowledge, into knowing exactly which drop, where. What a wash of feelings broke over me, evoked by those drops. By the knowledge that I would never. Never. Never be able to do this.

Later, almost too tired to go on, I turned a corner and saw *Starry Night* and started to cry. A guard watched me, concerned. I was crying in a strange mix of gratitude and envy and greed. *Starry*

Night was real after all; it was raw, disturbing, confusing, and it was there in front of me. I could stand there as long as I wanted. For the first time, I knew why people steal art, knew what it means to love the image and its real insertion into the world so much that one wants to consume it like cake or heroin, like water slaking a long thirst.

A few years later, I walked to the Metropolitan along Fifth Avenue through Central Park in the snow, and felt that I was in one of the novels my mother used to dream over in our little mountain town. Back to MoMA, where I discovered Boccioni's *The City Rises* and its frenzy of men and horses so fraught with life and fantastic optimism and power. I found Picasso's fine *Woman in a Flowered Hat* and Klimt's enthralling *Park*. I discovered more than one indigo city, more than one dark river. I went to the Tate Gallery and then the National Gallery in London, walking through each with the kind of private thrill one feels upon hearing important news for the first time. You know you will remember and you know you will soon enough ask someone where they were when they heard, if only so you can say where you were when you heard. Eventually I read Robert Hughes's *The Shock of the New*—a great opening of doors; I was shocked by it all and everything was new. Once I had stepped irrevocably down another path, I could see the almost infinite size of this world where many people live their entire lives. How much more there was, always so much more: Vermeer, Daubigny, Holbein the Younger, Courbet, Daumier. The annoyance of Pissarro, the challenge of Kandinsky, the frustration of David Hockney. Richard Dadd's *The Fairy Feller's Master-Stroke*, stopping me in midstep. Looking at great art was, for years, an extended single moment of waking up from a dream in which I'd thought I was already awake.

So much more. Millet. Rembrandt. Willem Kalf. The Masters, what a shock of the new. The portraits of Amsterdam smell of supper breath and faint sweat. Heda's *Still Life with a Gilt Goblet* brought me to a standstill, an intensely tactile scene. (I heard an Englishman behind me say, "Can't see the point, quite.") The extraordinary

Kitchen Maid—rather small, vibrant, glowing—leaped across the room with its light. If something left me cold—Pop Art stymied me for years—I returned to it a few years later with fresh eyes. I was promiscuous, hungry, indiscriminate, as infatuated by genres and periods and artists as I'd been with Lisa or Keith. (And really, hasn't that been true all along, this dilemma of the generalist, the appetitive, drawn to so much breadth that depth is sacrificed?) Alone, I finally found the Frick—how did I not know? I went to Los Angeles, Philadelphia, the Whitney, the de Young. I watched a woman in line at the Rijksmuseum suddenly start pushing people out of her way, shoving to the front; people stared at her in bemusement as the guard smoothly stepped in and cut her off before she reached the doors. "I don't understand what he is saying!" she complained loudly to the rest of us, when the guard pointed her back. "I have a plane to catch and I have to see *The Night Watch!*" Tokyo. Miami. Pittsburgh! How much more. How much I didn't know.

I got to Florence, at last, on someone else's dime because I did not have enough dimes of my own. In my years poring over the graying plates of the *Pietá* and the sibyls and Moses, I had imagined Florence as a medieval gallery. How strange the real Florence looked, peopled and busy, but I warmed to it: brocade and origami, marbled paper and tiny glass candies, the casual arrogance in all things Florentine. I went after Michelangelo until I had seen everything of his in that whole bustling town—his house and the tombs and the crucifixes and every sculpture and painting. One always struggles to know the difference between love and need; love is so often acquisitive and demanding. To see the desired, to be allowed only to see—this is not enough. One wants to consume it, to make the thing part of oneself. The sculpture or the painting that is so undeniably and enduringly there is as elusive as water because it can't be saved; the object itself is a memory, ephemeral, disappearing in the irreplaceable moment of sight.

I stood in the tomb, surrounded by marble in every shade, by *Night* and *Day* and *Dawn* and *Dusk*, and felt a capacious, almost infinite joy, eternal and brief and pure. More than once I walked down the long hall lined with the unfinished slaves to warmth and daylight and David. I watched for hours as people slowly paced down that dim hall, as though they were afraid they would die before they got to the end; I watched people emerge under the skylight, break into laughter and sometimes tears, take photographs, chatter to each other, and reach up toward the cool calves without a word. I left knowing that all the key chains and coasters in the world can't take away the thing itself.

Melancholy seeped in. Ambition is, if not actively corrupting, corroding. To simply be happy is not enough; to bake a really good pie or play Monopoly with the kids, go out for a game of tennis with a friend—not enough. The wanting corrodes. I thought I was a prodigy until I met a few. I reached for the brush, the light, eventually for the words, and perfection evaded me—even a shadow of what I could see in my mind evaded me until something simply broke, or rather grew: a membrane that sealed me to the past, away from the glassy world. I suppose genius is no picnic, but to be moderately talented is a chronic wound. "Human speech is like a cracked kettle on which we tap crude rhythms for bears to dance to, while we long to make music that will melt the stars." How do we adjust to that, what kind of answer is there to such disappointment? To not being able to make what seems so possible to make, play what seems so easy for others to play? To knowing that Flaubert, who occupies another planet from me, felt himself to be a dullard? To be stuck with kettles. Sometimes I teach writing workshops. Sometimes midway through a workshop, I want to take one of my earnest students aside, the woman who quit her accountancy job to write travel books, the retired plumber who has the outline of a novel in his hand, and say, "Save your money." I know you like it here. I know you are trying. But. You know.

Thirty-some years after I saw *Starry Night* for the first time, I tiptoed into the Van Gogh Museum in Amsterdam. He took no classes, began painting in service to God—later, with more of an eye to profit. His magnificent triptych of orchards in bloom was meant to sell—"motifs which everyone enjoys"—but he couldn't help himself, he always went too far. So much work, such hurried work—such a frenzied eye. Those wild strokes like the scuffing of thoughtless heels in the dirt, those slaps and smears of paint tossed off almost in irritation, skidding off the edge—blossoms and twigs hanging in space without anchor. Somehow in a few flowering sprigs of almond van Gogh trapped the instant of change—beauty fading even in its beauty; the death to come in all bright gay life. He got genius, and that's all he got. Art is about being broken, I think; I suspect that great artists are reaching out of a totally shattered place, and it is nothing to envy. (But I envy it still.) He believed he'd done nothing new, nothing truly good; he shot himself.

I found my way to Rome—to one of the dark cities on a river, to the rest of Michelangelo. On a fine morning, I was one of the first people into the Vatican Museums, and while everyone else lined up to get headphones for the audio tour, I walked quickly through a series of galleries opening one into the next like Russian nesting dolls, lined with tapestries and murals and maps and Etruscan bowls and vestments and medals, the ceilings wrought with *trompe l'oeil* and the floor a turmoil of *pietra dura*. The rooms were splendid and deranged, and as I walked they piled layer upon layer until I floated just above the floor in a fever dream. I got lost and finally went backward down an up staircase past warning signs, past *If you wish to avoid the embarrassment of alarm signals, refrain entirely from touching any work of art* signs and finally pushed open a door that I think was not supposed to be open and found myself in the Sistine Chapel. The empty, silent Sistine Chapel. Michelangelo left years of his life in here, most of them spent lying on his back in lamplight with flakes of plaster watering his eyes until he couldn't see what he painted. Toward the back, behind the choir screen, straight up, I found the Delphic Sibyl. Serious, extraordinarily strong, she turned from her concentrated study, turned completely. She had endured the long thin line of time that brought me to her at last. I wonder if this love I feel, tainted always by hunger, by infinite shades of hunger, is in fact what love always is. If wishing is a necessary part of love.

I find my way up a back street near the Coliseum to the little San Pietro di Vincoli church, the ancient church of St. Peter in Chains, the old links kept as relics in a bronze tabernacle under the altar. To the right in the small dim room is a large white statue; it costs fifty cents to turn on the lights, and I don't have the change. I beg without shame until a gracious Frenchwoman near me puts in the coins and the lights click on. Moses is just beginning to turn his head. His face is angry and severe; he thrusts out a leg as though about to rise. How sad he is (I see this at last), what a piercing sadness, fierce and disillusioned. I am grateful to be free of my younger obsessions, I think. But I wonder at times what happened. Once I thought all of life was lifting me toward something like a great wave. When did the wave break and slide along the shore and drop me in the foam?

Stevens again: "I wonder, have I lived a skeleton's life?"

Conjunctions, August 12, 2014

I've been writing this essay for more than twenty years. I never forgot that moment when I turned a corner in MoMA and saw Starry Night. *Right then I learned lessons about intimacy and beauty and hunger that I have never forgotten. What was acutely painful for years is now simply wistful, but the hunger never seems to completely disappear. Frank O'Hara wrote a wonderful poem called "Oranges" about how we are driven to create in particular ways, whether we like it or not. Go read it.*

So Long As
I Am With Others

ONE YEAR WHEN I WAS IN MY EARLY TWENTIES, THE WORLD came to weigh upon me without reason. I was often afraid or crying for the want of something nameless and large. I went to see a woman, a beautiful woman with thick honey hair, who looked at the palms of my hands and asked me several odd questions: *Did I dream of robbers? Did I sweat when I ate? Were there times when one foot was cold and the other was hot?* She gently took my wrist and felt my pulse for a long time. Then she prescribed: herbs, a homeopathic remedy, and herself. I was to spend a few hours each week looking into her eyes. They were terrifying, those hours, but so was everything else and I had nothing more to lose. I shivered with embarrassment, the simple weirdness of it: the two of us in a sunny room, knees touching, hands together, looking at each other without a word. I don't know if it was the medicine or her amber gaze, but I got better. The world lost an ounce at a time and one day I could hold it by myself.

Socrates said that one should simply be as one wishes to appear. But one self implies another, *makes* another; without two, how can there be one? "*Up to a point* we can choose how to appear to others," wrote Hannah Arendt, who knew a thing or two about choices. "Living things *make their appearance* like actors on a stage." In hundreds of photographs, Arendt stares at the camera, ironic or solemn; she doesn't smile. She is alert to self-display, its possibilities. Its sorrows. Be as one wishes to appear—an absurd idea. I don't know what I wish for, and I don't seem able to control the being part, either. I am alive and so I present myself to others.

I align with Arendt—up to a point, I choose. Trouble is I am often past that point; by existing, I have crossed it.

Light falls across objects like oil, spilling everywhere. It sticks to things, beading up, bouncing back—reflection. I realized somewhere in the nineties that everyone was recording everything, the jam of cameras and camcorders spreading; now the smallest event doesn't happen until its capture. A passing fad, I thought, these big, expensive toys—and then it was smaller cameras and tablets and cheaper everything and more of them so that now even the click is an application. Click. Click. Everything. Pictures of everything. The world, if it cared, can see photos of my street, my house, my lawn, the broken lawn chair on my faded deck, the weeds beneath my chimney. But why would the world care?

At some point I just stopped taking photographs, even when I know I'll wish for one later—vacations, weddings—I forget to record what I'm doing in the midst of doing it. Another of my modern failures. I have a lot of photographs of my first child, the earliest when he was crowning, damp black hair emerging from my strained vagina into the shadowed dimness of my bedroom. At first I took a lot of photographs of my second child and my third child, too. But as they grew, I took fewer pictures, for lack of time and because more than half the time they seemed to scowl; they didn't care to be seen—not by me. Their friends, that was a different story and still is; the peer group reflects; this is where they emerge. With me, once the source of everything, they turn aside.

I FLINCH AT photos now. Friends cheerfully send me pictures of my hand blocking the lens, trying to turn away; I get pictures of my feet, my buttocks, my graying hair bent over a book, unaware. Up to a point, I think, I can choose how I appear to myself. But most of us glance at ourselves and glance away, unsure. One wants to own oneself, *be* oneself, but how? *This is how I look.* I present myself to myself, and what a disappointment. On certain days, the mirror shows me a conjoined twin I've come to hate and can't escape. My face is like a sinner dangling in purgatory, strung between enemy and friend. The sagging eyelids, the coarsened skin, the false smile. At least I'm dressed. A friend is diagnosed with a small lesion and all her skin must be examined, inch by inch. All her skin must be photographed, several times: armpits, belly, between her toes, her breasts, inside her labia. She stands naked, arms spread, legs apart, staring into the future. Every inch of her skin. On the one hand, she could die. On the other, she might as well.

I would hide from Diogenes's lamp; my secret fear is that this is it, this is as real as I get, this false and slippery face like a funhouse mirror, attenuated, swollen, halved. I am mirrored inside and out, stuck in this meaty machine and not always happy about that, and stuck also in this consternation. I am split: observing, observed. Observing the observer, aware of being observed. Helplessly distant. "So long as I am together with others, barely conscious of myself," (Arendt again; I always think of her as the old woman, weary, a bit gnomish) "I am as I appear to others." *Barely* conscious?

One of the most radical inventions surely must be the Renaissance self-portrait: Europe is lined with tired faces, burdened by velvet and lace in darkened rooms, one after the other with sorrowful eyes, vaguely aghast. The damp brush is stayed for a moment in slow surprise. The young Rembrandt, still recovering from what he's seen, covers his own face with shadow; he looks away, not meeting the eyes.

FOR A BOOK tour, I need photographs. I have long resisted, but finally I submit. I hire a model to teach me what to do. She brings a makeup kit—I usually wear none at all—and she *tsk-tsks* over my wispy eyebrows, painting new ones on, rubbing in foundation, sprinkling powder, color, balm.

"You should get settled, then look down, away from the camera," she tells me. "Think of a secret, and then look up."

"A secret," I say. "What kind of secret?"

"Something no one else knows," she says. "Something very private." She grins, and then demonstrates: she crouches, bent, eyes closed and hair falling forward—a still and pensive body, without a face—and then she looks up and the room is alight, her eyes bright and a tiny smile, the barest part of a smile, a smile that makes you want more, that makes you want to say something, anything, to make her smile a little more. To discover her. And then she turns to me and says, "See?"

Until the first century of the Common Era, there were no full-length mirrors, no way to see one's entire body. People saw only parts of themselves. Imagine that first time: at last the whole, no longer rippling and shadowed in a pond but *there*, upright, lit, still. Complete, or seeming so. At last an answer to the burning question: *How do I look?* And not so very much later, an entire gallery of Versailles was mirrored, so that all the diamonds in Louis XIV's crown could reflect upon themselves. He walked down the hall, and one Louis after another turned to see—to see himself, itself, each Louis admiring the Louis who walked; each Louis leading to this one in particular, so multiplied that he had no end. How much ignorance of the world would I need to be that sure of myself? To believe that nothing else is as precious as me? I long to be so blessed.

The model's advice works. It takes me a while; I am aware of her watching, of the blank black eye of the camera, the stiffness of my pose. But I am also full of secrets. I review a sexual fantasy, eyes cast down, and then look up, my crotch warm with memory. "That's good!" she says. "Keep going." I think of sex for a while. Then I think of crimes. Wishes. I think of running away and changing my name. I think of being famous and rich. I am full of contempt and pride, and pleasure in my contempt, comfort in my pride. I glance up, see the camera, and think, *you don't know anything about me.* And the photos are good and in a few I have a tiny smile full of promise.

A BELOVED FRIEND tells me that I *hold myself apart*, and it feels like a death sentence. It doesn't matter that she's right. I do. At a staff meeting with its invariable chatter of phone messages and weather and *where did you get those shoes*, I sit in a corner, doodling daisies on the agenda. I sit in a circle of friends and listen halfheartedly to another's confession, my thoughts on my own. Really, you don't know anything about me. My head hums with a countering stream of comments, ironic and amusing. I rehearse arguments—I always win. I dream of disasters, myself the hero, romances where I am the prize. While others speak. While others think I am listening. *This* appearance is unwelcome, this reflection a distortion, surely this can't be the truth. Smooth mirrors reflect sharper images, more precise imitations. "Reflection at rough, or irregular, boundaries is diffuse," I read, and this is what I seem to be—a rough boundary, diffusing any image close to true.

I seem to have lost years of my life when I wasn't looking. Rilke prayed: "Fling the emptiness out of your arms / into the spaces we breathe." Pay attention. My selves flash out of emptiness; they jostle like a crowd at the fair, giving way, pushing back. I am less concerned with the place from which they appear—with whether it is a nothing or a something, with whether knowing would be a comfort or a nauseating vastness outside my reach— then with the *becoming*. Who wins today? The self who displays (who preens, poses, curries favor) or the self who watches (wonders at, pities)? The judge? The one who flees the very sight? Selves multiply like layers of paint, and in the crowd it seems impossible to wholly become one, to completely *become*, anything, even for a moment. Impossible to be complete. Rilke, who wrote a great deal about the struggle of being and appearing, spent his life creating a veneer; he was his own brand, the brand *Rilke*, a narcissist and philanderer; Rilke was a bit of a creep.

Who is it—what is it?—that knows the difference between itself and another? That knows itself to be a self, this face to be its face? What knows its own hiddenness, its self-deception? I am me because *I know myself* to be me, but how? Here I am; I am me partly and confusingly because of what I know myself not to be; what I feel as difference. I am me because I am not you. You are the other, forever *an* other, irrevocably *not-me*. And thank god for that. I am irrevocably *not other*—and yet I seem always to be the tiniest fraction removed from being *this*. (What would it be like to be you? Instead of this? To be her? Him? To be, for just one damned second, *not me*.)

And Socrates be damned, most of the time we are not trying to be as we wish ourselves to appear, but the opposite: ever more expert at acting. Did he think it was such a simple matter? Pick from the grab bag of possibility, like buttons from a box? The urge to claim a space for the self collides and colludes with the urge to construct a self to fit the space. We are not entirely in charge here; habits long lost to memory are driving the bus; we wake up in the midst of action. And the actor is only the self, of course; how could it be otherwise? There is nothing this wormy ego does that isn't mine. All of it—growth and loss like a rash; endless rebirths of a self beyond boring, refusing to die. The mask, the play, the rehearsed grin, the ritual gasp, the parsing of threats—the certainty of not wholly belonging to any other, of being never wholly *with*. All mine.

Grieve—*I* grieve, you should, too—for the inability to be true, that one is never authentic. One is only, in Arendt's words again, "an appearance among appearances"; nothing and everything is false, authentic, whole, broken. More or less. "Our modern identity crisis could be resolved only by never being alone and never trying to think." We're working on that. She believed, or claimed to, that we are all the same in some buried place, that a kind of psychic fundament exists, a ceaseless biology of mind—a sameness of selves as our cells are the same. (They are not, though, our cells: not exactly the same, any more than a blade of grass in a meadow is like another.)

We claim to want this place where *we are the same*—claim that we would run to meet each other there. Finding that space is the purpose of our lives, we say, glibly taking each other's hands and swaying in affirmation. *Kumbaya.* Perhaps we mean it. I think I do. I think I don't; I am not certain about this. Where we are the same is, for now, just mine; this space remains mine alone. I may not want to share. I look at my sister, my son, faces known all their lives—so familiar, even with all the thoughts behind the face opaque as snow—and a buried lonesomeness flies up, stinging.

In the midst of washing my breakfast plate I am dizzied by a great gulf of difference; I have no idea who they are, what they want, what they need.

Facing those others who believe themselves to know me, I smile and say hello. How nice to see you. A *me* speaks, a *you* listens—at least with half an ear—to words upon which we might in part agree. What is intimacy but having a few more words in our shared vocabulary than we have with the others to whom we turn in longing?—though the meaning of each word is always a matter of debate, and one we no longer have the heart to carry on because of the risk we will find there is no agreement after all. The words hunker down like ticks, digging in, thick with cliché, the giant delicacy of the social sphere. You are so far away, your desires so different and vague, and language is little more than the demilitarized zone in which we try to negotiate some unstable peace. Never mind that these are old concerns, that they are solipsistic and infinitely regressive, that many good minds have followed them into tiny corners from which they seem unable to escape. *Communication* is the second self, or third, always false; the first one cowers or cries out, depending.

I say to a friend, *I want to be done with the witness*, and he turns away, hissing, *I want to obliterate it*. He would like to die as a self aware of itself, in order to be seen as a self at all. We can be exactly as we long to be, appear exactly as we are, only by not knowing we have appeared—and what a thought of heaven *that* is. Our struggle to be at peace with ourselves would be gone; we would no longer be trying to *be* ourselves at all. Awareness without reflection—animal life. Or perhaps more the the heliotropic plant, quivering toward the light. Responding, but never having to act. The dream of extinction while still blessedly alive.

Walking on a summer evening. Just walking. The power of the stride. Leg swinging foot, shadowed trees, cloth sliding on skin. Barely conscious. Almost barely conscious. And then conscious again. So rarely felt. Look at them now: my children's past lives, their rebirths, their many deaths. How can we know, how can we *be known,* when all this knowing and striving to be known is done by fragile beings in the midst of arriving and departing, too barely conscious to be quite here? For the briefest of seconds, we meet, and then are lost again. The immutable opacity of *relationship* is as rippled and broken as the pond into which our ancestors gazed. This shrill striving for proximity that we seem to trade only for the echoing hall of solitude—how to bear it?

I have friends; I have family; I love; I am loved. But what mystery, this solitude in the midst of these specific people. For a long time I thought love meant not feeling alone. I thought love would cure the bounded self. In moments, so it seems: transparent collapse into the space of another, the rainbow oil of the bubble's skin splitting without breaking until two are one and still two. How elusive, that Venn diagram of the wounded psyche; most of me still outside, a fraction shared, and we call this trust.

I AM IN Kampala, on my way out to a rural village for a stay of weeks, when I realize that I have forgotten to pack a mirror. I spend a day looking—and a day shopping in Kampala is a long day—without luck. The dim little shops selling thongs, hair gel, liquor, and dish soap do not have mirrors. But neither do I find mirrors in the bigger stores, not even the supermarkets white with fluorescent where you can fill your cart with groceries, cosmetics, lawn furniture, DVDs, and Christmas tree lights. Finally I give up in a kind of existential panic. I cannot see myself at all. Now when everything, everything is recorded, presented, reflected, preserved, when all image is manipulated and no photograph is real: now, I do not know how I look.

So I give up and go, and for some time I share a cool room with several Ugandan women I know. They deflect compliments even as they invite the eye, each one beautiful and perfectly groomed; their warm brown skin clear, smoothly lotioned, with careful makeup. Their hair is done in elaborate braids; they seem to have no luggage but wear different clothes every day, all mysteriously pressed where there is no electricity. They love to talk, they are always together, laughing, shushing each other, lightly teasing, touching on the forearm, the neck, lying in the bunks together, murmuring under the mosquito nets. "So long as I am together with others, barely conscious of myself, I am as I appear to others." Beside this unfettered beauty, I curl up alone in my bed. I hold myself apart. I wonder, *how do I look?* but I don't really want to know.

We are never visible to others exactly, nor is the world wholly visible to us; the shell is always there in between. I look out through a fogged window. So I accept that mine is a partial view, the product of untold errors and limits; I accept that I can't see all of a thing because I can't see everything. I accept that no *one* can be seen, and so I believe that no one will ever wholly see me—and what relief, at once, to know this. So I will call myself planetary, cosmic; my darkness hidden in the darkness, in the far side. (I do not, of course, really accept this. I am being as I long to appear. I will pretend this is some kind of consolation, that this is the point, that it is due to our largeness, the very size of our selves, that we are each larger than each other's views.)

Perhaps we are not reflections at all. Do I have it completely wrong? Are we instead completely brightness, completely light? Such light that it casts no shadows? For weeks in Uganda I am surrounded by their warm darkness, the laughter, the damp perfume of clean skin. Either they are radiating bodies themselves, or they are perfect mirrors, each reflecting the other. What closeness. *How do I look?* one says, tilting her head. The others say, *Yes.* They say, *You look fine.*

Unpublished

Over the years, the themes of family, time, memory, body, and expression have begun to meld into a theme I think of as presentation. How do we appear in the world—to others, to ourselves? How much of the self is merely reflection? These are the questions that I carry into my writing now.

Publication notes

"Orphans" was first published in *Zyzzyva*, Winter 1986–87.

"Fetus Dreams" was originally published as "We Do Abortions Here" in *Harper's*, October 1987.

"The Only Harmless Great Thing" was first published in the *New Yorker*, January 23, 1989.

"Burning for Daddy" was originally published as "Bound Upon a Wheel of Fire" in *Harper's*, January 1990.

"Gentleman Caller" was first published in *Zyzzyva*, Fall 1991.

"The Weight" was first published in *Harper's*, March 1993.

"The Happiest Place on Earth" was first published in Linny Stovall, ed., *Kids' Stuff*, Left Bank #6, Blue Heron, 1993.

"Meat" was first published in *Antioch Review*, Summer 1994.

"The Basement" was first published in Sharon Sloan Fiffer and Steve Fiffer, eds., *Home: American Writers Remember Rooms of Their Own* (New York: Pantheon, 1995).

"The World Made Whole and Full of Flesh" was first published in Linny Stovall, ed., *Secrets*, Left Bank #9, Blue Heron, 1996.

"Big Ideas" was first published in *Antioch Review*, Summer 1997.

"The Hounds of Spring" was first published in *Salon*, July 1, 1997.

"Temporary God" was first published in *Salon*, September 16, 1997.

"Crossing to Safety" was first published in *Salon*, August 7, 1998.

"Recording" was first published in *Threepenny Review*, Fall 2002.

"Violation" was first published in *Tin House*, Summer 2001.

"Second Chair" was first published in *Antioch Review*, Fall 2002.

"The Birth" was first published in *Portland Magazine*, Spring 2003.

"Scars" was first published in *Portland Magazine*, Winter 2003.

"On Being Text" was first published in *Creative Nonfiction #22*, 2004.

"Balls" was first published in *Seattle Review*, Summer 2007.

"Chemo World" was first published in *Harper's*, June 2007.

"Twitchy" was first published in *Antioch Review*, Spring 2008.

"The Sutra of Maggots and Blowflies" was first published in *Conjunctions*, Fall 2008.

"Falling" was first published in *Conjunctions*, Fall 2011.

"Here Be Monsters" was first published in *Conjunctions*, Fall 2013.

"The Indigo City" was first published in *Conjunctions*, August 12, 2014.